AF655174

DR. MANMOHAN SINGH
Architect of India's Economic Renaissance

About the Author

Dr. U.P. Sinha has devoted more than 45 years of his career serving prominent organizations and universities of India and delivered the best of his capabilities fulfilling the need of the organizations and meeting their standard to take its pride and honour to the next level. In the span of 45 years, he has authored 24 books and more than 100 research papers from various international and national publications and journals. As a belonging of economics, he has served the economics department of several institutions and successfully delivered more than 55 PhDs under his supervision. Professor Sinha also served as a Vice-Chancellor of Central University of Haryana; and additionally as Executive Council too, Expert members of Different Committees of UGC, Chairman and members of NAAC committee of various colleges/universities comes under Indian government, Expert of Economics at CSTT (Commission for Scientific and Technical Terminology), Government of India.

DR. MANMOHAN SINGH
Architect of India's Economic Renaissance

U.P. Sinha

CONCEPT PUBLISHING COMPANY PVT. LTD.
NEW DELHI - 110 059

© Author

All rights reserved. No part of this work may be reproduced, stored, adapted, or transmitted in any form or by any means, electronic, mechanical, photocopying, micro-filming recording or otherwise, or translated in any language, without the prior written permission of the copyright owner and the publisher. The book is sold subject to the condition that it shall not, by way of trade or otherwise, be lent, resold, hired out, or otherwise circulated without the prior publisher's written consent in any form of binding or cover other than that in which it is published.

The views and opinions expressed in this book are editor/author(s) own and the facts reported by them have been verified to the extent possible, and the publishers are not in any way liable for the same.

ISBN: 978-93-6344-457-7

First Published 2025

Published and Printed by

Concept
Since 1974

Concept Publishing Company Pvt. Ltd.
A/15-16, Commercial Block, Mohan Garden
New Delhi-110059 (India)
T: +91-11-41101460
E: publishing@conceptpub.com, *W*: www.conceptpub.com

Cataloging in Publication--Courtesy: D.K. Agencies (P) Ltd. <docinfo@dkagencies.com>

Sinha, Udai Prakash, 1956- **author.**
Dr. Manmohan Singh : architect of India's economic renaissance / U.P. Sinha.
pages cm
Includes index.
ISBN 9789363444577

1. Manmohan Singh, 1932- 2. Prime ministers--India--Biography. 3. Economists--India--Biography. 4. India--Economic policy--1991-2016. 5. India--Politics and government--21st century. I. Title.

LCC DS481.M3537S56 2025 | DDC 954.052092 23

Preface

India's journey toward becoming a global economic power is one of the most compelling stories of our time. At the heart of this transformation lies the remarkable vision and steadfast determination of one man—Dr. Manmohan Singh. Renowned as the architect of India's economic renaissance, Dr. Singh's life and legacy embody the power of intellect, integrity, and quiet leadership in shaping the destiny of a nation. This book, "*Dr. Manmohan Singh: Architect of India's Economic Renaissance*", seeks to unravel the extraordinary contributions of an economist-turned-statesman whose policies and reforms redefined the contours of India's economic landscape. From the tumultuous crisis of 1991 to the era of globalization and beyond, Dr. Singh played a pivotal role in crafting a modern, resilient, and globally competitive Indian economy. As a scholar, policymaker, and prime minister, Dr. Singh left an indelible mark on India's economic and social fabric. His vision of liberalization, coupled with a commitment to inclusive growth, empowered millions, lifted barriers to entrepreneurship, and set the stage for India's rapid rise in global prominence. Yet, his legacy extends beyond economic reforms; it is a testament to the values of humility, ethical governance, and the relentless pursuit of progress. In writing this book, my aim is to provide a comprehensive narrative that goes beyond the headlines and policy papers, delving into the man behind the reforms, the economist behind the numbers, and the leader behind the vision. It is an exploration of his early influences, the philosophical underpinnings of his policies, and the challenges he faced in navigating the complex intersection of economics and politics. This book is not merely a biography or a historical account; it is also a reflection on the lessons and inspirations that Dr. Singh's life offers to policymakers, economists, and leaders worldwide. As we grapple with the challenges of the twenty-first century, from economic inequality to climate change, his approach to reform and resilience remains a guiding light. I invite readers to join me on this journey of discovery—to understand the legacy of a quiet reformer whose ideas and actions continue to shape India's future.

U.P. Sinha

Contents

Introduction

Dr. Manmohan Singh, widely "regarded as the architect of India's economic renaissance", stands as a towering figure in the nation's modern history. His legacy, spanning decades of dedicated service, academic brilliance, and visionary leadership, transformed India from an economically fragile state into a global powerhouse. Born in a modest household and rising through the ranks of academia and public service, Dr. Singh's journey is a testament to the power of intellect, integrity, and determination. His contributions to India's economic framework, particularly during its most turbulent times, remain unparalleled and have earned him recognition as one of the most influential policymakers in the world. Before the 1990s, India grappled with deep economic challenges. Decades of a closed economy governed by the License Raj, coupled with stagnant industrial growth and insufficient foreign reserves, had brought the country to the brink of economic collapse.

The post-Independence economic model of self-reliance, though well-intentioned, created inefficiencies and stifled entrepreneurial growth. A balance of payments crisis in 1991 exposed the fragility of the Indian economy and highlighted the urgent need for bold reforms. It was during this time of despair that Dr. Singh, as the finance minister under the leadership of Prime Minister P. V. Narasimha Rao, emerged as a beacon of hope, implementing transformative policies that would lay the foundation for India's journey toward liberalization and globalization. Dr. Singh's background as an economist played a crucial role in shaping his approach to policymaking. Armed with a doctorate in economics from Oxford University and extensive experience in academia and international institutions such as the International Monetary Fund (IMF) and the World Bank, he possessed a rare blend of theoretical knowledge and practical understanding of global economic systems.

This unique combination enabled him to craft policies that balanced fiscal prudence with the imperative of growth, while also addressing the socio-economic realities of a diverse and populous country like India. The economic reforms spearheaded by Dr. Singh in 1991 marked a radical departure from the past. By dismantling the License Raj, liberalizing foreign trade, and encouraging foreign investment, he unlocked the untapped potential of India's economy. These reforms not only stabilized the immediate crisis but also catalyzed a period of sustained economic growth, lifting millions out of poverty and enabling India to emerge as a significant player on the global stage. His policies reshaped industries, encouraged entrepreneurship, and opened up new opportunities for millions of Indians.

The success of these reforms, however, was not without challenges, as they faced criticism from various political quarters and resistance from those sceptical of globalization's impact on India's self-reliance. Nevertheless, Dr. Singh's unwavering commitment to the long-term vision of a prosperous and globally integrated India helped steer the country through these turbulent times. Beyond the economic reforms of the 1990s, Dr. Singh's legacy extends to his tenure as prime minister, where he oversaw landmark initiatives aimed at inclusive development. Programmes such as the Mahatma Gandhi National Rural Employment Guarantee Act (MNREGA), the Right to Information Act, and rural infrastructure development schemes were instrumental in addressing the needs of India's marginalized populations. His emphasis on inclusive growth demonstrated a deep understanding of the socio-economic disparities that characterized Indian society.

Dr. Singh recognized that economic progress would be incomplete without addressing poverty, illiteracy, and inequality. Under his leadership, the government made significant investments in infrastructure, education, and health care, laying the groundwork for a more equitable society. Dr. Singh's contributions to India's global standing are equally noteworthy. As an advocate of multilateralism and international cooperation, he played a pivotal role in strengthening India's relationships with major global powers and regional partners. His participation in forums like the G20, BRICS, and WTO negotiations showcased India as a responsible and emerging global economic leader. Dr. Singh's quiet yet firm diplomacy enhanced India's credibility on the world stage and positioned the country as a key player in global decision-making processes.

His vision extended beyond economic policy to encompass a holistic understanding of India's role in the global community, emphasizing collaboration and mutual growth. One of the most remarkable aspects of Dr. Singh's leadership was his ability to combine technical expertise with humility and integrity. Known for his soft-spoken demeanour and non-confrontational style, he navigated the complexities of Indian politics while staying true to his economic vision. Despite operating in a coalition government that often required compromises, Dr. Singh maintained a focus on long-term goals rather than short-term populism. His leadership was defined by a commitment to evidence-based policymaking and an unwavering belief in the transformative power of economic reforms. His reputation as an honest and dedicated leader further bolstered his ability to inspire trust, both domestically and internationally.

However, Dr. Singh's tenure as prime minister was not without challenges. The later years of his leadership were marred by allegations of corruption and policy paralysis, which tarnished the image of his government. Critics questioned his ability to assert authority in a politically volatile environment. Yet, even amid these controversies, his personal integrity and his legacy as a reformer remained intact. Dr. Singh's contributions to India's economic foundation and his role in steering the country through some of its most challenging periods continue to be acknowledged and celebrated. Dr. Manmohan Singh's legacy as the architect of India's economic renaissance is a story of transformation, resilience, and vision. His reforms not only rescued India from economic collapse but also redefined its trajectory, paving the way for decades of growth and progress.

The impact of his policies can be seen in the thriving IT sector, the expanding middle class, and the increasing global recognition of India as an economic powerhouse. Dr. Singh's vision transcended numbers and statistics; it was about creating an India that could stand tall on the global stage while ensuring that its growth story included all its citizens. In the contemporary context, Dr. Singh's ideas and policies remain profoundly relevant. As India grapples with the challenges of balancing growth with sustainability, addressing inequality, and navigating a rapidly changing global economic landscape, his emphasis on inclusive growth and prudent policymaking serves as a guiding light. Dr. Singh's contributions remind us that true leadership lies in the ability to inspire change, uphold integrity, and leave behind a legacy that shapes the future for generations to come. His role as the architect of India's economic renaissance is not just a chapter in history but a cornerstone of the nation's journey toward realizing its full potential.

■ Overview of India's Economic State before the 1990s

India's economic state before the 1990s was marked by a mix of state-led development, protectionism, and the pursuit of self-sufficiency. The country, emerging from British colonial rule in 1947, adopted policies that aimed at transforming its agrarian economy into an industrialized and self-reliant one. These policies were rooted in the vision of leaders like Jawaharlal Nehru, who, influenced by socialist ideas, believed that the state should play a dominant role in economic planning and development. At the heart of this vision was a focus on import substitution industrialization (ISI), which sought to reduce India's dependence on foreign goods by fostering domestic industries.

The government implemented high tariffs, import restrictions, and encouraged local production of goods that were traditionally imported. In this economic framework, public sector enterprises played a crucial role, with the state taking charge of industries such as steel, energy, and transportation. However, the outcomes of this economic strategy were mixed. While some sectors, particularly heavy industries like steel and power, showed progress, the overall economic growth remained sluggish. The economic structure was marked by inefficiency, low productivity, and slow innovation, as the state-controlled model limited the scope for competition and entrepreneurship. In the absence of competition, industries were often protected by high tariffs and regulatory controls, which, instead of promoting efficiency, led to the proliferation of inefficient public sector enterprises.

These enterprises, shielded from market forces, often became bloated and inefficient. Bureaucratic delays and the License Raj, a system where businesses had to seek government approval for investment, expansion, and new ventures, further exacerbated inefficiencies. The state's role in economic activity was seen as central, and this created a system that was resistant to change. At the same time, the agricultural sector, which employed a majority of the population, remained largely stagnant. The early years of India's Independence saw some success with the Green Revolution, particularly in the 1960s, when new high-yielding varieties of seeds, fertilizers, and irrigation techniques were introduced in key regions like Punjab. These innovations resulted in a boost in food production, especially in wheat and rice. However, the agricultural sector's growth was uneven. While some regions benefitted from the Green Revolution, large parts of rural India remained untouched by these changes.

Productivity growth in agriculture remained slow, and farmers were burdened by a lack of modern techniques, insufficient irrigation, and an over-reliance on the monsoon. This agricultural stagnation was compounded by issues like low investment, inadequate credit facilities, and insufficient rural infrastructure. India's economic development was also constrained by a lack of infrastructure, which impeded growth in both industry and agriculture. Despite attempts to modernize transport systems, the country struggled with poor roads, inadequate railways, unreliable electricity, and insufficient telecommunication networks. These infrastructure deficits created bottlenecks in the economy, limiting the potential for industries to scale and hindering the movement of goods and services across the country. Inadequate infrastructure also affected rural areas, where lack of access to basic services like electricity, roads, and water further hindered development. The fiscal situation of the country was another challenge.

The Indian government's heavy involvement in economic planning and public sector enterprises led to a steady rise in fiscal deficits, which were financed by borrowing. The government's spending on public enterprises and subsidies resulted in growing debt, and by the 1980s, India faced mounting fiscal problems. The country's current account deficit was also a persistent issue, leading to a reliance on external borrowing and aid. The balance of payments crisis became a reality, and India was often forced to borrow from international institutions like the World Bank and the IMF to meet its financing needs. These loans came with stringent conditions that further exacerbated the country's dependence on external agencies. India's dependence on foreign aid and loans further limited its economic sovereignty.

The country received substantial economic assistance from both bilateral and multilateral sources, especially from the United States, the Soviet Union, and international organizations. However, the aid came with strings attached, often forcing India to align its policies with the interests of the donor countries or institutions. This dependence on foreign assistance not only restricted India's policy flexibility but also led to a sense of vulnerability, as the country was unable to assert full control over its economic future. At the international level, India's economic performance and policies were influenced by its non-aligned foreign policy, which sought to maintain neutrality during the Cold War. India chose not to align with either the United States or the Soviet Union, and its policies were aimed at balancing relationships with both powers while asserting its independence. While India's relationship with the Soviet Union was strong, especially in terms of defence and economic cooperation, the country was cautious in its relations with the West.

India's economic isolationism during this period meant that it did not fully participate in the global economic boom of the post-Second World War era, especially as the capitalist world underwent rapid industrialization and integration into global markets. The Cold War era had a significant impact on global trade and economic relations. While countries in the Western Bloc, particularly the United States and Western Europe, were opening up their markets, India was largely inward-looking, focusing on building its domestic economy. This economic isolation meant that India was not able to fully integrate into global supply chains or benefit from the wave of technological and economic advancements that were sweeping across the world. By the 1980s, as the global economy became increasingly interconnected, India's insular economic policies began to appear outdated and limiting.

In summary, India's economic state before the 1990s was marked by a combination of protectionist policies, state-led industrialization, and limited progress in key sectors like agriculture and infrastructure. While the country made strides in industrial development and self-sufficiency, its overall economic growth was slow, and inefficiencies within the state-controlled system hampered its potential. The agricultural sector struggled with stagnation, and infrastructure deficits hindered growth. Fiscal challenges and reliance on foreign aid further constrained India's economic prospects, and the country's non-aligned foreign policy kept it somewhat isolated from the broader global economic trends of the time. As India entered the 1990s, it was clear that the existing economic model had reached its limits, setting the stage for the sweeping reforms that would soon follow.

▪ Introduction to Dr. Manmohan Singh and His Academic, Professional, and Political Background

Dr. Manmohan Singh is widely regarded as one of India's most prominent economists and statesmen, with a career that has spanned academia, international finance, and politics. His contributions to India's economic transformation, particularly through the reforms of the 1990s, have left an indelible mark on the country's economic landscape. Dr. Singh's life story is one of intellectual rigour, technical expertise, and a commitment to national service, which culminated in his tenure as India's thirteenth prime minister from 2004 to 2014. Born on 26 September 1932, in the village of Gah, now in Pakistan, Dr. Singh was raised in a modest Sikh family. His early education took place in Punjab, where he was exposed to a range of subjects and developed a strong foundation in the sciences and humanities. However, his intellectual curiosity and passion for economics would eventually define his future path.

He pursued his undergraduate studies at Panjab University in Chandigarh, where he earned a degree in economics. His academic journey was marked by an eagerness to delve deeper into the complexities of economic theory, a trait that would guide his career in the years to come. Dr. Singh's desire to understand economic systems on a global scale led him to pursue higher education abroad. He first attended Cambridge University in the United Kingdom, where he earned a degree in economics. It was during his time at Cambridge that Dr. Singh was exposed to the ideas of Keynesian economics, which emphasized the role of government intervention in stimulating economic growth, especially during times of economic downturn. This perspective would later influence his policies as an economist and policymaker.

His time in Cambridge also provided him with valuable exposure to the intellectual currents of post-war economics, which were shaping economic policy in the West at the time. Dr. Singh's academic credentials were further strengthened by his doctoral studies at Oxford University, where he completed his PhD in economics. His thesis, focused on the economics of trade and development, was an exploration of how developing nations could benefit from international trade and the challenges they faced in competing with industrialized countries. His work laid the foundation for his future contributions to India's economic policies, especially in terms of how the country could navigate the complexities of globalization and international trade. In addition to his formal education, Dr. Singh's academic journey was profoundly shaped by his mentors and intellectual influences. He was inspired by global thinkers and economists, particularly those advocating for a more market-oriented approach to economic development.

His exposure to these ideas during his time in the West helped him develop a deep understanding of economic theory and policy that would be crucial in his later professional and political career. Upon completing his education, Dr. Singh's professional career began in India, where he initially taught at prestigious institutions like Delhi School of Economics and Panjab University. He quickly gained recognition for his expertise in economic theory and development, and his academic work became influential in shaping India's economic thinking during the post-Independence period. His time in academia also exposed him to the economic challenges facing India and the limitations of the country's existing economic policies, which would later inform his approach to policymaking.

Dr. Singh's early career took a significant turn when he joined international financial institutions, where he gained valuable exposure to global economic issues and policymaking. He worked with organizations like the United Nations Conference on Trade and Development (UNCTAD), IMF, and the World Bank, where he contributed to global economic discussions and developed a reputation as an economist with a deep understanding of both the theoretical and practical aspects of development economics. His role in these organizations allowed him to interact with world leaders and policymakers, further shaping his vision for India's economic future. Dr. Singh's return to India in the early 1980s marked a shift in his career as he transitioned from academia and international finance to the realm of policymaking. He took on key roles within the Indian government, and his economic expertise was soon recognized by political leaders across party lines.

In 1982, Dr. Singh was appointed as the Chief Economic Advisor to the Government of India, where he played an instrumental role in formulating economic policies. His tenure saw the introduction of important reforms that set the stage for India's economic liberalization in the 1990s. In 1991, Dr. Singh was appointed as the Finance Minister of India, a position that marked the beginning of his most influential phase in Indian politics. At the time, India was grappling with a severe balance of payments crisis and an economic slowdown. Dr. Singh's pragmatic approach and deep understanding of economic theory allowed him to spearhead a series of bold economic reforms, including liberalization, privatization, and globalization. These reforms sought to open up the Indian economy, reduce state control, and attract foreign investment.

Dr. Singh's role in these reforms, often in collaboration with then-Prime Minister P.V. Narasimha Rao, is widely regarded as a turning point in India's economic history. Dr. Singh's contributions to India's economic transformation were not confined to his role as finance minister. His reputation as an economist and a statesman grew, and in 2004, he became India's prime minister, a position he held for two consecutive terms. As prime minister, Dr. Singh continued to push for economic reforms, focusing on inclusive growth, poverty alleviation, and improving infrastructure. His tenure saw significant advancements in India's information technology (IT) sector, foreign investment, and economic diplomacy. Dr. Singh's leadership style was characterized by humility, integrity, and a commitment to long-term goals. He was known for his quiet, methodical approach to governance, preferring to work behind the scenes rather than engaging in political drama.

Despite facing criticism from various quarters, particularly in the later years of his tenure as prime minister, Dr. Singh's economic vision and policies had a profound impact on India's economic trajectory. In addition to his domestic achievements, Dr. Singh played an influential role in shaping India's position in the global economy. He represented India in various international forums, including the WTO, the G20, and the BRICS summit. His vision for a more integrated global economy, while balancing national interests, shaped India's approach to economic diplomacy in the twenty-first century. Throughout his career, Dr. Singh's academic background, professional experiences, and political leadership combined to create a unique blend of intellectual rigour, economic pragmatism, and political foresight. His legacy as a key architect of India's economic liberalization and his contributions to global economic leadership make him one of the most influential figures in modern Indian history.

Dr. Singh's academic, professional, and political journey reflects a commitment to the idea of India's economic rise, driven by a belief in the power of market-oriented reforms, the importance of inclusive development, and the need for prudent, long-term policymaking.

1

Early Life and Academic Journey

▪ Introduction

Dr. Manmohan Singh's early life and academic journey are pivotal in understanding the intellectual foundation and philosophical outlook that shaped his later achievements as an economist and a statesman. Born in a modest Sikh family in the village of Gah in undivided Punjab (now in Pakistan) on 26 September 1932, Dr. Singh's childhood was marked by the trauma of Partition, which displaced his family and forced them to flee to India. Despite these early challenges, his parents, particularly his mother, instilled in him a strong sense of discipline, integrity, and the importance of education. These values would go on to play a significant role in Dr. Singh's remarkable career in academia and public service. Dr. Singh's academic journey was characterized by a deep commitment to learning and a relentless pursuit of knowledge.

His early education took place in India, where he excelled in his studies. He was known for his sharp intellect and academic rigour, attributes that earned him a place at some of the most prestigious educational institutions in the world. After completing his undergraduate degree in economics from Panjab University, he moved to the University of Cambridge in the United Kingdom for his postgraduate studies, where he earned his degree in economics. The intellectual environment at Cambridge, known for its liberal and progressive approach to economics, exposed Dr. Singh to the economic theories of prominent economists such as John Maynard Keynes, whose ideas would profoundly influence his own economic thinking. Following his time at Cambridge, Dr. Singh continued his academic journey at Oxford University, where he pursued a DPhil (Doctor of Philosophy) in economics.

His doctoral thesis focused on international trade and development, specifically examining the trade policies of developing countries. It was during this phase that Dr. Singh developed an acute understanding of the economic challenges faced by emerging economies and began formulating ideas that would later form the basis of his policy decisions as an economist and political leader. Dr. Singh's academic achievements, underpinned by his intellectual curiosity and deep understanding of economic principles, set the stage for his entry into the world of economics and public policy. His time at Cambridge and Oxford not only honed his analytical skills but also shaped his world view, which emphasized the importance of integrating global economic practices with the needs and challenges of developing countries.

The knowledge he gained from his academic journey would later contribute significantly to his role in transforming India's economic landscape, particularly in the realms of economic liberalization and global economic integration. Thus, Dr. Singh's early life and academic journey were fundamental to the development of the intellectual frameworks and values that guided his leadership in the decades to come.

Roots in Punjab

Dr. Manmohan Singh's roots trace back to his early life in Punjab, a region in northern India known for its rich cultural heritage, agricultural economy, and a history of resilience and transformation. He was born in Gah, a small village in what is now Pakistan. His early years were shaped by the backdrop of the Partition of India in 1947, which had a profound impact on his family. Following the Partition, Dr. Singh's family, like millions of others, migrated to India, settling in the State of Punjab. This traumatic event left an indelible mark on his early life and his perspective on India's socio-political landscape. Dr. Singh's early education took place in Punjab, where he was introduced to formal schooling in the village schools. Growing up in a post-Independence India, his exposure to the ideals of freedom, nation-building, and economic development during his formative years played a critical role in shaping his world view. Punjab, at the time, was a predominantly agrarian society, with agriculture being the backbone of its economy.

This rural environment instilled in Dr. Singh an appreciation for the importance of agricultural growth and rural development, themes that would later resonate in his policymaking. The cultural influences on Dr. Singh during this period were also significant. Punjab has a deep-rooted history of Sikhism, Punjabi language, and traditional arts, and the values of hard work, humility, and social service were an integral part of the cultural fabric of the region. Sikhism, with its emphasis on equality, justice, and community service, had a profound impact on Dr. Singh's character and philosophy. These values are reflected in his calm demeanour, his belief in inclusive development, and his focus on societal welfare throughout his political career. In terms of academic influences, Dr. Singh's exposure to education in Punjab also led to his early interest in the sciences and economics. His parents placed a high value on education, which provided the foundation for his future academic success. This period in Punjab allowed him to nurture an intellectual curiosity that would later take him to the West for further education.

Moreover, Dr. Singh's early years in Punjab introduced him to the economic challenges faced by rural India. The region, though economically vibrant in some areas, was also dealing with issues such as poverty, poor infrastructure, and limited access to educational opportunities for the masses. These formative experiences helped shape his later emphasis on poverty alleviation and rural development, which were central to his policy priorities as an economist and policymaker. In sum, Dr. Singh's roots in Punjab provided him with a strong sense of community, cultural values, and an appreciation for the challenges faced by India's agrarian society. These early influences laid the groundwork for his deep commitment to inclusive growth and economic reform, values that would later guide his career as one of India's most influential policymakers. The blend of academic curiosity, cultural heritage, and personal experiences in his early life helped shape the character and vision of the man who would go on to be a key architect of India's economic transformation.

Early Education and Cultural Influences

Dr. Manmohan Singh's early education took place in the agrarian heartland of Punjab, a region known for its educational institutions as well as its deep cultural and historical significance. Born into a Sikh family in Gah, a village now located in Pakistan, Dr. Singh's family moved to India following the Partition in 1947. They settled in the Punjab region of India, which played a crucial role in shaping his intellectual growth and academic aspirations. In the early years of his education, Dr. Singh attended local schools, where he received a solid grounding in the fundamentals of education. The schools he attended were located in the rural and semi-urban areas of Punjab, where access to quality education, although improving, was still not as widespread as in larger cities.

Despite the challenges posed by the limited educational infrastructure, Dr. Singh's innate intellectual curiosity and academic discipline stood out. His parents, particularly his father, were great advocates of education and made significant efforts to provide their children with the best opportunities despite the financial constraints they faced as a refugee family. This commitment to education played a pivotal role in Dr. Singh's early development as a scholar. He showed a keen aptitude for mathematics and science during his schooling years, subjects that would lay the groundwork for his later interests in economics. However, it was his exposure to a more formal and structured curriculum in these schools that helped him cultivate the skills of critical thinking, reasoning, and problem-solving that would become fundamental to his academic journey later in life.

In addition to his academic pursuits, the cultural environment of Punjab also had a significant impact on Dr. Singh's early education. He was exposed to a range of intellectual and cultural ideas, often blending traditional Sikh teachings with the modern scientific and academic values he encountered at school. This balanced perspective would influence his later academic philosophy, especially his approach to inclusive development and rational policymaking. Through his education, he learned not only the importance of individual achievement but also the value of contributing to the greater good, which became central to his future work in public service.

Cultural Influences in Punjab

Punjab, with its rich history and unique cultural identity, played a significant role in shaping Dr. Manmohan Singh's personality and world view. The region is deeply rooted in the Sikh religion, which has historically emphasized values such as equality, justice, community service, and humility. These values, imbibed through Dr. Singh's upbringing, profoundly shaped his approach to governance and policymaking throughout his life. Growing up in a Sikh family, Dr. Singh was instilled with the values of selfless service and a commitment to the well-being of others, which are cornerstones of Sikh philosophy. The emphasis on equality before God and the need for social justice had a deep impact on his later views on inclusive economic growth and poverty alleviation. In many ways, his commitment to rural development, welfare policies, and economic reforms in India echoed these deeply held values, seeking to reduce inequality and uplift marginalized communities.

His belief in creating a society that provides opportunities for all individuals, regardless of their background or socio-economic status, was informed by these principles. The cultural milieu of Punjab, which has historically been a melting pot of various religious and cultural traditions, also influenced Dr. Singh's world view. The province's long history of resilience in the face of adversity—whether it be the invasions during the Mughal period, the challenges posed by the Partition, or the agricultural transformation post-Independence—instilled a sense of perseverance and adaptability in him. These qualities were crucial in his later career as he navigated the complex political landscape of India and responded to the challenges posed by economic reform. Dr. Singh's upbringing in Punjab also exposed him to the importance of agriculture in India's economy. The region's agricultural sector, particularly the Green Revolution, was a source of inspiration and a model for the kind of economic growth he hoped to see across the country.

The agricultural community's struggles, resilience, and drive for progress became an enduring influence on his policy focus, particularly in ensuring that economic development was not limited to urban areas but reached the rural heartlands as well. In conclusion, Dr. Singh's early education and the cultural influences he encountered growing up in Punjab were foundational to his development as an economist, statesman, and leader. The combination of rigourous academic discipline and the deeply rooted cultural values of justice, equality, and community service shaped his world view and influenced his approach to economic reform and public service. His educational background in Punjab, coupled with the cultural ethos of the region, helped lay the groundwork for his vision of an inclusive, equitable, and sustainable economic future for India. These early experiences would continue to inform his policies and actions throughout his distinguished career.

• Higher Education Abroad

Dr. Manmohan Singh's higher education abroad played a critical role in shaping his intellectual foundation and providing him with the theoretical and practical tools to navigate the complex landscape of economic development. His educational journey took him to some of the world's most prestigious academic institutions, where he was exposed to a variety of economic theories and global economic challenges. His time abroad not only shaped his economic philosophy but also laid the groundwork for his later success as an economist and statesman.

Cambridge: Exposure to Keynesian Economics

Dr. Manmohan Singh's pursuit of higher education took him abroad, where he sought to refine his intellectual foundations and expand his understanding of economic theories. One of the most formative phases of his academic journey occurred at Cambridge University, one of the world's most prestigious institutions. In the early 1950s, Dr. Singh moved to the United Kingdom to pursue his graduate studies, and it was here that he encountered the economic ideas that would go on to shape his intellectual and policy outlook. At Cambridge, Dr. Singh was deeply exposed to the ideas of John Maynard Keynes, one of the twentieth century's most influential economists. Keynesian economics, which advocates for government intervention in the market to stabilize economic fluctuations, was particularly relevant during the post-Second World War period. The world was grappling with the aftermath of the war, and countries were searching for ways to rebuild their economies and address issues such as unemployment, inflation, and poverty. Keynes's theories on aggregate demand, government spending, and fiscal policies provided an alternative to the *laissez-faire* capitalist ideas that had dominated the nineteenth century.

Dr. Singh, in particular, became attuned to the idea that markets alone might not always be sufficient to ensure full employment or balanced economic growth. The role of government in managing the economy through policies that influence demand, investment, and employment became a key concept in Dr. Singh's understanding of economics. He appreciated the emphasis Keynes placed on public investment as a tool to stimulate demand and alleviate economic crises. This exposure to Keynesian economics was critical in shaping Dr. Singh's later economic philosophy, especially in relation to economic planning and the role of the state in development. As an economist in independent India, Dr. Singh often advocated for state intervention to correct market failures, promote growth in key sectors, and reduce poverty.

The experience at Cambridge helped form his belief in a mixed economy, where both the private and public sectors play complementary roles in the economic development of a nation. Moreover, the influence of Keynesian thought was evident in his later policies, particularly in times of economic crisis. During the 1991 balance of payments crisis in India, Dr. Singh's approach reflected a blend of Keynesian principles, emphasizing macro-economic stabilization, fiscal reforms, and the need for government action to address the nation's economic challenges. Thus, Cambridge was a transformative phase in Dr. Singh's academic career, providing him not just with theoretical knowledge, but also with the critical intellectual tools to approach economic policy with a pragmatic understanding of government's role in achieving balanced and sustainable growth.

Oxford: Doctoral Thesis on Trade and Development

After completing his studies at Cambridge, Dr. Manmohan Singh continued his academic journey at Oxford University, another premier institution in the UK. It was at Oxford that he pursued his doctoral studies, focusing his research on the field of international trade and economic development. Dr. Singh's doctoral thesis, which was centred on the topic of trade and development, explored the relationships between trade policies, industrialization, and economic growth in developing countries. This area of study was particularly important given the post-Second World War focus on global development, with countries in the Global South struggling to modernize their economies while maintaining sovereignty over their economic policies. Dr. Singh's research at Oxford delved into the complexities of trade policies in developing countries, analysing how international trade could be leveraged to spur domestic economic development.

His thesis examined the dynamics between protectionist trade policies and the promotion of domestic industries, with a focus on how developing nations could balance the need for self-sufficiency with the need to engage in global trade. The thesis also explored the concept of import substitution industrialization (ISI), a policy that many newly-independent countries, including India, adopted in the 1950s and 1960s. The basic premise of ISI was that developing countries could reduce their dependence on foreign goods by fostering domestic industries and protecting them from international competition. The research Dr. Singh conducted at Oxford laid the foundation for many of his later policy views. His doctoral thesis provided a nuanced understanding of the challenges faced by developing economies in the global trading system.

He recognized that countries in the Global South often found themselves at a disadvantage in the international economic order, and that for these nations to grow and prosper, their trade and industrial policies needed to be designed in ways that aligned with their developmental goals. Moreover, Dr. Singh's time at Oxford deepened his understanding of global economic institutions and their role in shaping trade policies. He became increasingly aware of the ways in which organizations such as the World Trade Organization (WTO), the International Monetary Fund (IMF), and the World Bank influenced the economic trajectories of developing nations. This understanding would later inform his approach to India's engagement with international financial institutions and his role in global economic diplomacy. Dr. Singh's exposure to these theories and his rigourous academic training at Oxford helped him develop a pragmatic and balanced approach to trade and development, one that was grounded in the realities of the global economy but also sensitive to the needs of developing nations.

This intellectual grounding would influence his decisions as India's finance minister and later as prime minister, particularly in the context of India's own trade and economic liberalization policies in the 1990s. In conclusion, Dr. Singh's doctoral studies at Oxford provided him with deep insights into the complexities of trade, industrialization, and development, especially as they pertain to the challenges faced by emerging economies. The academic training he received during this time helped him formulate a set of policies that sought to balance the benefits of global integration with the imperatives of national development. His thesis, which emphasized the importance of strategic trade policies, industrial growth, and self-reliance, would serve as a cornerstone for his future work in economic policy and governance.

Shaping an Economist

Dr. Manmohan Singh's journey to becoming one of the foremost economists of his time was shaped not just by formal education, but also by the intellectual influences of academic mentors and global thinkers. His academic and professional life was deeply intertwined with the ideas and guidance of those who pushed him to think critically, engage with diverse economic perspectives, and develop a unique approach to policymaking. These mentors and thinkers provided Dr. Singh with the tools to blend theoretical knowledge with pragmatic solutions to India's developmental challenges.

- **Inspirations from Academic Mentors and Global Thinkers Each Heading**

Academic Mentors

From the early stages of his education, Dr. Singh had the privilege of being mentored by some of the most distinguished economists and academics of his time. At Cambridge University, he had the opportunity to interact with renowned economists and scholars who helped him shape his intellectual curiosity. One of the most influential figures during his time at Cambridge was Sir Richard Stone, a British economist known for his work on national income accounting and his contributions to the development of macroeconomic theory. Stone's mentorship provided Dr. Singh with a solid foundation in economic theory, which would serve him well in his future work in both academia and policymaking. Dr. Singh's exposure to Sir Richard Stone's work on national accounts and the role of data in economic planning was crucial in developing his understanding of the importance of economic measurement and statistical rigour in policymaking.

As a policymaker, Dr. Singh would often emphasize the need for accurate data and evidence-based decision-making, qualities that were fostered through his early academic experiences. Similarly, Professor Joan Robinson, another influential economist at Cambridge, had a profound effect on Dr. Singh's intellectual development. Robinson was a key figure in the development of post-Keynesian economics, and her work on imperfect competition and economic planning influenced Dr. Singh's understanding of the role of government in fostering economic stability and growth. She encouraged him to think beyond traditional economic frameworks and consider the complexities of economic systems, particularly in the context of developing economies like India. Dr. Singh's academic journey was further enriched by his time at Oxford University, where he was mentored by a range of distinguished economists.

His doctoral research on international trade and economic development brought him into contact with scholars who helped him refine his thoughts on the intersection between trade policy and industrialization. These academic mentors instilled in Dr. Singh a sense of intellectual rigour and encouraged him to develop a holistic approach to understanding economic problems. They also pushed him to consider the ways in which economic theories could be applied to address the real-world challenges faced by countries in the Global South, like India.

Global Thinkers

In addition to his direct mentors, Dr. Singh was influenced by a broader range of global thinkers, whose ideas had a significant impact on his intellectual development. These thinkers shaped Dr. Singh's understanding of economics, both in terms of its theoretical foundations and its practical application in the context of a developing economy. One of the most influential global thinkers who shaped Dr. Singh's economic philosophy was John Maynard Keynes, whose ideas on government intervention and fiscal policy became foundational for Dr. Singh's later policy decisions. Keynesian economics, with its emphasis on the importance of aggregate demand, government spending, and macroeconomic stabilization, resonated strongly with Dr. Singh. Keynes's work offered a framework for understanding how economies could recover from depressions and avoid the perils of economic instability. This exposure would profoundly influence Dr. Singh's approach to managing India's economic crises, especially during the 1991 balance of payments crisis, when he played a central role in advocating for liberalization and macroeconomic stabilization policies.

Another key global thinker whose influence can be traced in Dr. Singh's economic philosophy is Amartya Sen, a fellow Indian economist who won the Nobel Prize in Economics. Sen's work on welfare economics and his focus on poverty, development, and social choice theory had a lasting impact on Dr. Singh's understanding of economic development. Dr. Singh was deeply influenced by Sen's emphasis on the importance of inclusive development and his advocacy for human capabilities as a measure of economic progress. This intellectual influence is evident in Dr. Singh's commitment to poverty alleviation and his focus on ensuring that the benefits of economic growth were broadly distributed across Indian society, particularly to marginalized communities. Dr. Singh was also influenced by the ideas of Robert Solow, an American economist known for his work on economic growth theory. Solow's model of exogenous growth emphasized the importance of technological progress and capital accumulation in fostering long-term economic growth.

This framework helped Dr. Singh understand the factors that drive economic development in the long-term and shaped his approach to industrial policy and investment in India's infrastructure and human capital. Furthermore, Dr. Singh was influenced by the work of Albert Hirschman, a German-born economist known for his theories on economic development and the role of social capital in fostering growth. Hirschman's ideas on linkages between different sectors of the economy and the importance of investing in human resources resonated with Dr. Singh as he sought ways to boost India's industrialization and economic diversification. Hirschman's work on the role of incremental change and path dependence in development provided Dr. Singh with a more nuanced understanding of how economic progress could unfold in complex, heterogeneous societies like India.

Integration of Ideas

Dr. Singh's intellectual journey was characterized by a blending of different schools of thought, and he was adept at synthesizing insights from various global thinkers to shape his own economic philosophy. While Keynes's ideas on government intervention and macroeconomic management were influential, Dr. Singh also incorporated elements of free-market economics and global integration into his thinking. His ability to synthesize these ideas allowed him to create a balanced economic strategy that sought to combine the benefits of market liberalization with the need for state-led interventions to address poverty, unemployment, and infrastructure deficits. The influence of global thinkers such as Amartya Sen and Robert Solow also reinforced Dr. Singh's commitment to development policies that prioritized poverty reduction, inclusive growth, and human capital investment.

These thinkers provided Dr. Singh with a framework for understanding development that went beyond traditional economic indicators like GDP growth, emphasizing the importance of human well-being and social equity. In conclusion, Dr. Manmohan Singh's intellectual development as an economist was shaped by a combination of academic mentors and global thinkers whose ideas helped him refine his understanding of economics and its role in development. His exposure to the work of influential economists such as John Maynard Keynes, Amartya Sen, and Robert Solow, along with the guidance of his academic mentors at Cambridge and Oxford, helped him develop a nuanced and pragmatic approach to economic policy.

These influences provided Dr. Singh with the tools to craft policies that balanced market forces with the need for government intervention, ensuring that the benefits of economic growth were widely shared and that India's development challenges were addressed with thoughtful, evidence-based solutions.

REFERENCES

Adams, K.M. (2016). "Tourism and ethnicity in insular Southeast Asia: Eating, praying, loving and beyond." *Asian Journal of Tourism Research, 1*(1). https://doi.org/10.12982/ajtr.2016.0001

Alagar, G., Premkumar, L. & Ishita. (2017). "Sagarmala: Myth or Reality?", In *Occupation of the Coast: Blue Economy in India* (pp. 42-73). Programme for Social Action.

Alden, C. & Sidiropoulos, E. (2015). "Silk, Cinnamon and Cotton: Emerging Power Strategies for the Indian Ocean and the Implications for Africa." *South African Institute of International Affairs Policy Insights, 18*. https://saiia.org.za/research/silk-cinnamon-and-cotton-emerging-power-strategies-for-the-indian-ocean-and-the-implications-for-africa/

______(2015). "Silk, Cinnamon and Cotton: Emerging Power Strategies for the Indian Ocean and the Implications for Africa." *South African*

Institute of International Affairs Policy Insights, 18. https://www.jstor.org/stable/resrep25964

_____(2015). "Silk, Cinnamon and Cotton: Emerging Power Strategies for the Indian Ocean and the Implications for Africa." *South African Institute of International Affairs Policy Insights, 18*. https://archive.ids.ac.uk/eldis/document/A73586.html

_____(2015). "Silk, Cinnamon and Cotton: Emerging Power Strategies for the Indian Ocean and the Implications for Africa." *South African Institute of International Affairs Policy Insights, 18*. https://www.academia.edu/114431157/Silk_Cinnamon_and_Cotton_Emerging_Power_Strategies_for_the_Indian_Ocean_and_the_Implications_for_Africa

_____(2015). "Silk, Cinnamon and Cotton: Emerging Power Strategies for the Indian Ocean and the Implications for Africa." *South African Institute of International Affairs Policy Insights, 18*. https://www.polity.org.za/article/silk-cinnamon-and-cotton-emerging-saiia-policy-insights-no-18-power-strategies-for-the-indian-ocean-and-the-implications-for-africa-2015-06-09

_____(2015). "Silk, Cinnamon and Cotton: Emerging Power Strategies for the Indian Ocean and the Implications for Africa." *South African Institute of International Affairs Policy Insights, 18*. https://www.accord.org.za/ajcr-issues/silk-cinnamon-and-cotton-emerging-power-strategies-for-the-indian-ocean-and-the-implications-for-africa/

_____(2015). "Silk, Cinnamon and Cotton: Emerging Power Strategies for the Indian Ocean and the Implications for Africa." *South African Institute of International Affairs Policy Insights, 18*. https://www.saiia.org.za/research/silk-cinnamon-and-cotton-emerging-power-strategies-for-the-indian-ocean-and-the-implications-for-africa/

2

Early Professional Career

Dr. Manmohan Singh's early professional career was marked by a series of formative experiences that helped shape his future path as a distinguished economist and leader. After completing his education at prestigious institutions like Cambridge and Oxford, Dr. Singh returned to India in the early 1960s. Armed with a strong academic background, he quickly immersed himself in the field of economic planning and policymaking, beginning his career as an economist with the Government of India. His first notable role was at the Reserve Bank of India (RBI), where he served in various capacities from 1957 to 1966. During his time at the RBI, Dr. Singh contributed to the formulation of the country's monetary policy and its efforts to modernize the banking system. It was here that he gained critical insights into the functioning of India's financial institutions and the challenges they faced in the context of a developing economy.

His deep understanding of fiscal and monetary issues earned him a reputation as a highly competent economist, with an ability to analyse complex economic scenarios and propose practical solutions. In 1966, Dr. Singh transitioned to the Planning Commission of India, where he worked on various projects related to India's economic development. This role was crucial in expanding his influence in India's economic policymaking apparatus. The Planning Commission, established in 1950, was central to the government's strategy for economic development through five-year plans. Dr. Singh's work focused on analysing India's industrial and agricultural sectors, as well as improving the overall allocation of resources.

His approach emphasized the importance of building a strong economic foundation through public sector investments, as well as promoting industrialization to create jobs and improve living standards. During his time at the Commission, he played a key role in shaping the policies that would guide India's development trajectory. In the 1970s, Dr. Singh's career took a significant turn when he joined the Indian government's ministry of finance, first as an advisor and later as the Chief Economic Advisor. It was in these positions that he gained significant experience in handling macroeconomic issues at the national level, including budget formulation, taxation policies, and international economic relations. Dr. Singh's work in these roles demonstrated his ability to balance economic theory with practical policy execution, which became a hallmark of his leadership style in later years.

Throughout his early professional career, Dr. Singh was consistently involved in global economic discussions, participating in international forums such as the International Monetary Fund (IMF) and the World Bank. This international exposure further enriched his understanding of global economic dynamics and reinforced his belief in the importance of integrating India's economy into the global system. His involvement in these global institutions not only helped him develop an appreciation for multilateralism but also allowed him to advocate for the needs of developing nations in a rapidly changing world order. By the late 1970s and early 1980s, Dr. Singh had established himself as one of India's foremost economists, admired for his expertise and pragmatic approach to solving complex economic problems. His early professional career, marked by a combination of academic knowledge and practical experience, laid the groundwork for his later achievements as a key architect of India's economic liberalization in the 1990s. In many ways, his early career was a precursor to the broader economic reforms that would come to define his legacy as a leader committed to transforming India's economy from a closed, protectionist model to one that embraced the opportunities and challenges of globalization.

▪ Academic Contributions in India

Dr. Manmohan Singh's academic career in India laid a strong foundation for his later role as a policymaker and economist. Before transitioning to a full-fledged career in government, Dr. Singh made significant contributions to the field of economics through his academic work. His deep understanding of economic theory, combined with his exposure to global economic ideas, enabled him to make valuable contributions to India's academic and intellectual landscape. His work in academia not only helped shape the next generation of economists but also played a key role in the formulation of India's economic policies. Dr. Singh's academic journey in India began at prestigious institutions like the Delhi School of Economics (DSE) and Panjab University, where he served in various capacities, including as a faculty member, researcher, and advisor. He was involved in teaching and research that focused on issues central to India's economic development, including economic planning, growth, and trade policy. His academic contributions in India played a vital role in framing economic debates in post-Independence India, especially in the context of its transition from a colonial economy to a newly-independent nation grappling with the challenges of industrialization, economic planning, and poverty alleviation.

As an economist, Dr. Singh contributed significantly to the theoretical understanding of India's economic problems, particularly in the fields of trade, growth, and development economics. His work addressed pressing economic issues that were central to India's policy debates in the 1960s and 1970s. He became known for his deep analytical approach and his ability to apply global economic theories to the Indian context, ensuring that economic strategies were both practical and grounded in sound theory. Dr. Singh's time at the DSE, where he worked alongside some of the brightest minds in the country, allowed him to further develop his ideas on development economics. This was also the period when he began to gain recognition as a leading economist who understood the intricacies of economic growth and poverty alleviation, and his academic career would serve as a springboard for his later success as an economic reformer in the Indian government.

His time at institutions such as DSE helped him influence and mentor numerous students, many of whom would go on to become prominent figures in academia, policy, and governance. Through his research, lectures, and academic contributions, Dr. Singh also helped shape India's approach to economic policy formulation and economic planning, both of which became crucial areas of focus during his later tenure in the government. His role in academic institutions was crucial in preparing a generation of economists and policymakers who would later support the economic reforms and liberalization strategies that he championed in the 1990s. In this section, we explore Dr. Singh's academic contributions in more detail, examining his role in shaping the intellectual discourse on India's economic challenges, his teaching career, and his influence on both the academic and policy communities. His work in academia laid the groundwork for the policies he would later implement as India's finance minister and prime minister, highlighting his commitment to bridging the gap between economic theory and practical policy solutions.

Roles at Delhi School of Economics and Panjab University

The DSE is one of India's leading academic institutions in the field of economics, and it was here that Dr. Singh's academic career truly began to take shape. He joined DSE in the early years of his career, where he worked as a faculty member in the Department of Economics. His academic work at DSE focused primarily on development economics and trade theory, areas in which he would go on to make significant contributions both in his research and through policy implementation.

Dr. Singh's tenure at DSE was instrumental in developing his understanding of India's economic structure and its development needs. He worked alongside some of the country's brightest economists and scholars, which further enriched his academic experiences. This environment provided Dr. Singh with an opportunity to collaborate with leading economists, and he contributed to the growing discourse on India's economic development. At DSE, Dr. Singh not only focused on economic theory but also actively engaged with the practical challenges faced by India in the post-Independence period. He worked on understanding India's economic conditions, including issues like industrialization, agricultural policy, and foreign trade. His work often revolved around the idea of economic planning and state intervention to address the challenges of poverty and underdevelopment. He contributed to various research projects that focused on these issues and helped lay the groundwork for the economic policies that India would later adopt, particularly in the areas of trade policy and economic planning.

Dr. Singh's role at DSE also allowed him to mentor future generations of economists. Many of his students would later become prominent economists and policymakers in their own right. His teaching at DSE was known for its rigour, where he combined his knowledge of economic theory with a practical understanding of the socio-economic realities of India. The emphasis on critical thinking and empirical analysis in his teaching style influenced his students, many of whom would go on to contribute to India's economic development in various capacities. Dr. Singh's work at DSE was not just limited to the classroom. He was also involved in research projects that contributed to the broader academic understanding of India's economic challenges. His research at DSE was grounded in the issues facing the Indian economy, and he was particularly interested in exploring growth models that could be applied to developing countries. His work would later influence his policy thinking, as he developed an understanding of how India could harness its economic potential through careful planning and international trade.

▪ Role at Panjab University

In addition to his time at the DSE, Dr. Singh also had a significant role at Panjab University, another key institution in his academic journey. At Panjab University, he served as a professor and advisor in the Department of Economics, where he furthered his research interests and expanded his academic reach. Dr. Singh's time at Panjab University allowed him to work with a diverse group of scholars and engage in critical economic research on India's development.

At Panjab University, Dr. Singh's academic contributions were primarily focused on issues related to economic development, particularly in the context of trade and international economics. His work involved deep analysis of India's trade policy and its impact on the nation's economic growth. He emphasized the need for India to engage more actively with the global economy and increase its focus on trade liberalization and foreign exchange management. These ideas were ahead of their time and laid the intellectual groundwork for the economic liberalization reforms of the 1990s. His role at Panjab University also involved teaching and mentoring students, many of whom would go on to become prominent in the field of economics.

Dr. Singh's academic approach, which combined a solid grounding in economic theory with practical insights into India's developmental challenges, helped shape the economic thinking of many students and academics in the region. Moreover, at Panjab University, Dr. Singh was part of a broader academic community that was concerned with addressing India's economic and social issues. His work there focused on formulating solutions that could foster inclusive growth and reduce poverty. These themes would later become central to his policy agenda when he entered the public sphere. His experience at Panjab University reinforced his belief in the importance of education and research in economic policy formulation, and it played a crucial role in shaping his approach to governance and economic reform.

Contribution to Academic Discourse

Both at DSE and Panjab University, Dr. Singh contributed to the development of economic policy frameworks that would later be adopted at the national level. His work on trade policy, economic planning, and industrialization influenced the economic thinking of the time. Through his research, Dr. Singh helped to advocate for a more market-oriented approach to India's development, a view that would become more pronounced in his later career as a policymaker. Dr. Singh's academic contributions were also instrumental in fostering a deeper understanding of India's economic challenges among scholars and policymakers. His work in these institutions helped shift the discourse on India's economic policy from a purely theoretical perspective to one that was deeply rooted in the realities of the nation's development needs. His work in the classroom, coupled with his research contributions, made him a respected voice in academic circles.

Furthermore, his time at DSE and Panjab University allowed Dr. Singh to develop relationships with key figures in India's academic and policy communities, many of whom would later become important allies when he moved into government. The academic networks he built during these years provided him with the support and intellectual resources necessary to navigate the complexities of economic policymaking later in his career. Dr. Manmohan Singh's roles at the DSE and Panjab University were pivotal in shaping his career as an economist and policymaker. These institutions provided him with the academic environment to home his ideas on economic development and trade, which would later form the basis of his reformist agenda. His work at these institutions was not only influential in the academic community but also laid the intellectual foundations for the economic policies he would champion as India's finance minister and prime minister. Dr. Singh's academic journey was critical in preparing him to address the challenges of India's economy and ultimately contribute to its growth and global integration.

■ International Exposure

Dr. Manmohan Singh's international exposure played a crucial role in shaping his economic philosophy and policy approach. His work at renowned global institutions such as the United Nations Conference on Trade and Development (UNCTAD), the International Monetary Fund (IMF), and the World Bank provided him with invaluable experience and insights into global economic issues. This exposure helped him build a robust understanding of international economic systems, trade, financial markets, and the challenges faced by developing nations, particularly in the context of economic development, trade policy, and financial management. These experiences laid the groundwork for his later contributions to India's economic policy and reform efforts.

Role at UNCTAD: Early International Experience

Dr. Singh's involvement with UNCTAD in the early years of his career provided him with significant exposure to global trade issues and the challenges facing developing countries. UNCTAD is an organization within the United Nations that focuses on issues related to trade, investment, and development. It works to formulate policies that promote the integration of developing countries into the global economy while ensuring sustainable economic growth. Dr. Singh's role at UNCTAD involved engaging with the economic challenges faced by developing nations and finding ways to address their issues in the international economic system.

One of the key areas he focused on was the issue of trade and development—specifically, how developing countries could improve their terms of trade and increase their participation in global markets. His work in this area helped shape his views on the need for trade liberalization and the importance of developing countries having greater bargaining power in international trade negotiations. At UNCTAD, Dr. Singh gained experience working on policy issues that directly impacted India's economic challenges. He was involved in analysing how developing countries could manage their balance of payments, foreign exchange, and debt issues in the face of the global economic system. His work here reinforced his belief in the necessity of sound economic management and the importance of global cooperation in addressing the economic challenges of the developing world. This early exposure to international trade and development policy proved formative in shaping Dr. Singh's views on economic globalization and the need for India to engage more actively in the international economy.

Role at the IMF: Expertise in Financial Management and Crisis Management

Dr. Singh's time at the IMF was another key chapter in his international exposure. The IMF is a global organization that provides financial assistance to member countries facing balance of payments crises, as well as technical assistance and policy advice. Dr. Singh's work at the IMF involved analysing global economic conditions, particularly with respect to macroeconomic stability, exchange rates, and fiscal policy. During his time at the IMF, Dr. Singh gained valuable experience in dealing with the complexities of international finance. He worked on issues related to monetary policy, exchange rate management, and fiscal discipline, and he advised countries on how to stabilize their economies during times of financial distress. This experience provided Dr. Singh with insights into the critical importance of macroeconomic stability for economic growth and development. It also gave him a deeper understanding of how global financial markets operate and how national policies interact with the international economy. Dr. Singh's exposure to the IMF's work in crisis management and economic stabilization had a direct impact on his approach to economic policymaking in India. As India faced economic challenges in the 1980s, Dr. Singh drew on his IMF experience to shape his thinking about how the country could better manage its finances, stabilize its economy, and integrate into the global financial system. His IMF tenure helped solidify his belief in the importance of economic discipline and the role of international financial institutions in fostering global economic stability.

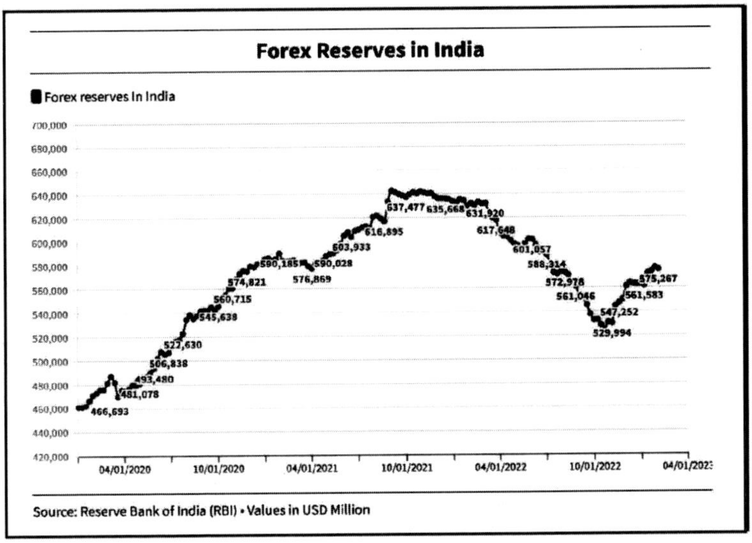

Fig. 2.1: India's Foreign Exchange Reserves: A Buffer against the Global Recession.

Role at the World Bank: Focus on Development and Economic Growth

Dr. Singh's time at the World Bank, the global development institution that provides loans and grants to developing countries for development projects, was another crucial phase in his international career. At the World Bank, Dr. Singh worked on development policy, particularly focusing on poverty alleviation, economic growth, and infrastructure development. His work at the World Bank reinforced his belief in the critical importance of inclusive development that could lift people out of poverty and promote sustainable economic growth. At the World Bank, Dr. Singh was involved in formulating and implementing development projects that aimed to improve the living standards of people in developing countries. His work focused on how financial resources could be used efficiently to foster economic growth and social development. He was particularly interested in how developing countries could use external capital—whether through loans, grants, or investments—to finance infrastructure projects that would facilitate economic development and improve living standards. Dr. Singh's experience at the World Bank also deepened his understanding of the interlinkages between economic policy, poverty alleviation, and sustainable development. He became a strong advocate for development finance that prioritized long-term goals over short-term economic stabilization.

This perspective would later influence his policy decisions as India's finance minister, particularly during the economic reforms of the 1990s, when he emphasized the need for inclusive growth that would benefit all segments of society.

Learning from International Institutions: Key Influences on Policy Thinking

Dr. Singh's roles at UNCTAD, the IMF, and the World Bank had a profound impact on his approach to economic policymaking. The experience he gained at these global institutions provided him with a deep understanding of the global economic system, the challenges faced by developing nations, and the ways in which economic policies can address those challenges. His exposure to international economic thinking helped him refine his views on issues like trade liberalization, global financial integration, poverty reduction, and the importance of sound economic management. Dr. Singh's time at these institutions also reinforced his belief in the need for global economic cooperation. He became a strong proponent of multilateralism, advocating for the involvement of developing countries in global decision making processes. This belief in global cooperation would later influence India's position in international forums such as the WTO, G20, and BRICS. Dr. Singh's time at the IMF and World Bank also deepened his understanding of how global financial systems and development assistance could be leveraged to foster economic growth in the developing world.

Conclusion: Shaping Dr. Singh's Economic Philosophy

The international roles Dr. Singh held at UNCTAD, the IMF, and the World Bank played a critical role in shaping his views on economic development, global integration, and policy management. His exposure to global economic issues and the challenges faced by developing countries gave him a nuanced understanding of how economic policies could be designed to address both national and global concerns. These experiences not only broadened his intellectual horizons but also prepared him to take on the monumental task of economic reforms and policy leadership upon his return to India. Dr. Singh's international exposure helped him develop a comprehensive and pragmatic approach to economic policymaking, which he would later apply in his roles as finance minister and prime minister of India. His work at UNCTAD, the IMF, and the World Bank not only gave him a strong foundation in international economic policy but also influenced his vision for India's economic growth and development in the globalized world.

▪ Return to India

Dr. Manmohan Singh's return to India marked a pivotal shift in his career, transitioning from an academic and international economist to a policymaker at the helm of India's economic reforms.

After gaining valuable international experience at prestigious institutions like the UNCTAD, IMF, and World Bank, Dr. Singh returned to India in the late 1970s, where he took on a new role that would shape his legacy as one of the most influential economic policymakers in the country's modern history. This transition was not only professional but also philosophical, as he moved from the realm of academic economic theory to the practical world of economic policymaking in a country that was grappling with stagnation, fiscal deficits, and a highly protected economy.

Moving Beyond Academia: A Shift in Focus

Before his return, Dr. Singh had spent a significant amount of time teaching at prestigious institutions, contributing to economic research, and advising global bodies on trade, development, and fiscal policy. His work at the DSE and Panjab University had equipped him with a thorough understanding of economic theory, particularly in the fields of development economics, international trade, and financial management. However, his return to India marked a transition from the theoretical to the practical. Upon his return, Dr. Singh was faced with the daunting task of applying his global expertise to a real-world economic landscape that was grappling with significant challenges. The Indian economy in the late 1970s and 1980s was under immense pressure due to a combination of low growth rates, fiscal deficits, a burgeoning public sector, and an over-reliance on imports.

The country was still pursuing a largely state-controlled economic model that emphasized protectionism, import substitution, and industrial licencing. These policies, though initially successful in promoting self-sufficiency, had stifled industrial growth, created inefficiencies, and led to chronic foreign exchange shortages. Dr. Singh's initial entry into policymaking was driven by his desire to address these systemic issues through economic reforms. His academic background gave him the tools to understand the complexities of India's economic challenges, while his international exposure provided him with a clear vision of how India could benefit from greater integration with the global economy. However, the policy environment in India at the time was deeply entrenched in socialist economic ideals, and any shift towards a market-driven approach would face significant resistance.

Joining the Indian Government: Economic Advisory Roles

Dr. Singh's transition from academia to policymaking began with his appointment to key positions within the Indian government. In 1971, he was appointed as an Economic Adviser to the Ministry of Finance, marking his formal entry into policy formulation. In this role, Dr. Singh provided advice on economic matters, including fiscal management, taxation, and trade policies. His role was to analyse India's economic performance and propose strategies to overcome stagnation and inefficiencies in the economy. The early years of his policy career were challenging. Despite his academic credentials and international experience, Dr. Singh had to navigate the political landscape of India, which was dominated by socialist ideals and a protectionist economic stance.

India's policymakers were still largely influenced by the Nehruvian model of state-led development, where the government played an extensive role in managing key industries and controlling trade and finance. Dr. Singh's economic philosophy, which emphasized the importance of market forces and global economic integration, was at odds with the prevailing views of the time. His work within the government began to make an impact when, in the mid-1980s, he was appointed as the Deputy Chairman of the Planning Commission, a body responsible for formulating India's long-term economic plans. This role gave him greater responsibility in shaping the country's economic policies and allowed him to influence decisions on key areas such as industrial policy, fiscal policy, and foreign trade.

The Call to Action: Economic Crisis of the Late 1980s

The turning point in Dr. Singh's career came during India's economic crisis in the late 1980s and early 1990s. By this time, the country was facing a severe balance of payments crisis, with mounting fiscal deficits, inflation, and a near-empty foreign exchange reserve. The crisis was compounded by a global decline in demand for India's exports, rising oil prices, and the growing debt burden. India's foreign debt had ballooned, and the country was unable to meet its obligations, putting severe pressure on the government's ability to finance essential imports, including oil and industrial materials. The economic conditions required urgent policy intervention, and Dr. Singh's international experience and economic expertise made him a natural candidate to address these issues. In 1991, he was appointed as finance minister in the government of Prime Minister P. V. Narasimha Rao. This role was not just a significant career milestone for Dr. Singh; it also marked the beginning of his most consequential work as an economic policymaker in India.

Shaping India's Economic Policy: The 1991 Reforms

Dr. Singh's appointment as finance minister occurred at a critical juncture in India's history. Faced with a dire economic crisis, he spearheaded a series of economic reforms that would transform India's economy and open it up to the world. His academic background, combined with his practical experience in global economic institutions, allowed him to introduce policies that moved India away from state control and towards a more market-oriented economy. The 1991 economic reforms, which included measures such as trade liberalization, industrial deregulation, and privatization of state-owned enterprises, were a radical departure from the protectionist policies of the past. Dr. Singh, alongside Prime Minister Narasimha Rao, faced considerable political opposition from both within the ruling party and from other political parties. However, his ability to sell these reforms as a means of ensuring India's economic survival in the face of the crisis helped him overcome these challenges. The reforms were not just about liberalizing trade and encouraging foreign investment; they also focused on building a robust economic infrastructure, improving fiscal discipline, and enhancing the efficiency of government institutions. Dr. Singh's international exposure, especially his experiences at the IMF and World Bank, helped him advocate for global integration and economic liberalization as key drivers of India's economic growth.

Transitioning to a Visionary: A Legacy of Economic Transformation

Dr. Singh's transition from academia to policymaking was a defining moment in his career. It was a shift from being an observer and theoretician to becoming a practitioner and leader. His experiences as an academic economist, along with his roles at international financial institutions, provided him with the insights and knowledge needed to understand the complexities of India's economy and the global economic system. His return to India allowed him to channel this expertise into policies that would eventually lead to one of the most significant economic transformations in India's modern history. The economic reforms he championed laid the foundation for India's subsequent economic growth, and his legacy continues to shape India's economic policies today. Dr. Singh's transition from academia to policymaking was not just a professional shift but also a philosophical transformation. He moved from the realm of theory to the world of practical policymaking, where he used his global insights to bring about real change in India's economic landscape.

His return to India and his role in economic policymaking marked the beginning of a new chapter in India's economic history—one that would lead to greater economic integration with the global economy, a stronger private sector, and improved living standards for millions of people.

REFERENCES

Alden, C. & Sidiropoulos, E. (2015). "Silk, Cinnamon and Cotton: Emerging Power Strategies for the Indian Ocean and the Implications for Africa." *South African Institute of International Affairs Policy Insights, 18*. https://www.saiia.org.za/research/silk-cinnamon-and-cotton-emerging-power-strategies-for-the-indian-ocean-and-the-implications-for-africa/

Andersson, L., Farrell, K., Moshkovich, O. & Cranbourne, C. (2016). *Implementing Virtual Design and Construction Using Bim: Current and Future Practices*. Routledge.

Benedict, M.A. & McMahon, E.T. (2012). *Green Infrastructure: Linking Landscapes and Communities*. Island Press.

Carroll, J.E. (2012). *Sustainability and Spirituality*. State University of New York Press.

3

Economic Philosophy and Vision

Dr. Manmohan Singh's economic philosophy and vision have been fundamental in shaping India's economic trajectory, particularly during his tenure as the finance minister in the early 1990s. His approach to economic policy has been characterized by a firm belief in liberalization, free markets, and globalization while maintaining a strong commitment to social equity and inclusive development. This balance between fostering economic growth and ensuring that the benefits of that growth reached all segments of society has been the hallmark of Dr. Singh's economic thinking. At the core of Dr. Singh's economic philosophy was his deep commitment to modernization and reform. He believed that India's economic growth was constrained by outdated policies, restrictive regulations, and a pervasive reliance on state control.

This view was shaped by his academic exposure to Keynesian economics and the ideas of classical liberal economists, who emphasized the importance of free markets, trade liberalization, and reducing the role of the state in economic activities. Dr. Singh was a strong proponent of transforming India's socialist-inspired planning model, which had been in place since the 1950s, into a more market-driven, open, and competitive economy. One of the key tenets of Dr. Singh's economic philosophy was the belief in the power of markets to drive growth and innovation. He argued that India's economic potential would only be fully realized if the state reduced its intervention in sectors such as industry, trade, and finance, allowing private enterprise to flourish.

This vision of a more market-oriented economy was at the heart of the economic liberalization reforms of the 1990s. However, while Dr. Singh was an advocate for reducing state control in economic activities, he was equally concerned with ensuring that growth was equitable and inclusive. For him, economic liberalization did not mean the abandonment of social responsibility. On the contrary, he believed that the state had a crucial role in creating the infrastructure and providing the social safety nets necessary for people to benefit from a market-driven economy. Dr. Singh's vision for economic growth was also deeply rooted in the idea of global integration. He understood that the world economy was becoming increasingly interconnected, and for India to prosper, it had to be a part of the global economic system.

He advocated for a more open trade policy, foreign direct investment (FDI) inflows, and greater engagement with international financial institutions such as the International Monetary Fund (IMF) and the World Bank. His belief in multilateralism and the benefits of international economic cooperation was evident in his push for India's greater participation in global trade and investment flows. Dr. Singh's vision was not just about opening up the economy but also about ensuring that India could leverage its strengths—such as its large, youthful population and its growing services sector—on the global stage. Equally important in Dr. Singh's economic philosophy was his focus on social equity. While he was deeply committed to the principles of market-driven growth, he was equally aware of the need to address the disparities in income, education, health care, and access to basic services that were prevalent across India.

He believed that growth should be inclusive, ensuring that the most marginalized sections of society, particularly those in rural areas, benefited from the country's economic progress. This commitment to inclusive growth became evident in his efforts to promote programmes aimed at improving rural infrastructure, increasing employment opportunities, and reducing poverty. Dr. Singh's belief in balancing growth with social equity guided his policy decisions and helped ensure that India's economic transformation was not just about economic aggregates but also about improving the lives of its people. Dr. Singh's vision for India was also characterized by a commitment to long-term planning. He was not one to advocate for quick fixes or short-term gains; instead, he focused on building the foundations for sustained economic growth over the coming decades.

His emphasis on investing in education, health care, and infrastructure was aimed at creating the conditions for long-term prosperity and social development. Dr. Singh's approach was pragmatic and long-term, aiming to secure India's position as a global economic power while ensuring that its benefits were widely shared. In sum, Dr. Singh's economic philosophy and vision have been integral to shaping India's path toward becoming an emerging economic powerhouse. His focus on liberalization, global integration, and social equity provided the guiding principles for his policy decisions. His emphasis on market-driven growth, balanced with a commitment to inclusive development, has made him one of India's most influential economic leaders. Through his visionary leadership, Dr. Singh not only transformed India's economic landscape but also laid the groundwork for future generations to continue building on his achievements.

▪ Belief in Liberalization

Dr. Manmohan Singh's belief in liberalization was one of the core pillars of his economic philosophy, which he carried throughout his career. This belief was not simply about advocating for a reduction in state control over the economy but about fostering a shift towards a more open, competitive, and market-driven economic system. At a time when India's economy was largely controlled by the state,

Dr. Singh's views on liberalization were considered revolutionary. India's economy before the 1990s was dominated by state control, with the government playing a significant role in almost every aspect of economic life. The Nehruvian model, which emphasized central planning and state ownership of key industries, was considered the foundation of India's economic structure. This model aimed at promoting self-sufficiency and reducing dependence on foreign nations. However, over the decades, it became evident that this approach had several shortcomings.

The state control mechanism created inefficiencies, stifled competition, and hindered innovation. Moreover, it resulted in an economy characterized by slow growth, bureaucratic inefficiencies, and limited integration with global markets. The era of licence raj, with its complex regulations and controls, also fostered corruption and inefficiencies in the system. Dr. Singh's liberalization philosophy, in contrast, aimed at shifting India's economic strategy from state control to a more market-oriented approach. He believed that a market economy, driven by the forces of supply and demand, competition, and entrepreneurship, would be a far more effective model for generating growth, employment, and innovation. Under this philosophy, the role of the state should be to regulate, not control, the economy. The state's function should be to create a level playing field, set clear rules for the market, and ensure that competition is fair and that there are safeguards for the most vulnerable sections of society.

The Market Economy: A New Vision

Dr. Singh argued that India's economy could no longer afford to be insulated from global economic forces. The protectionist policies of the past, which relied on import substitution and self-sufficiency, had failed to deliver sustained growth. In fact, the country's lack of integration into the global economy had left it isolated from the waves of technological innovation, capital inflows, and access to global markets. India's industries were inefficient, and its trade and financial systems were outdated. Dr. Singh envisioned a shift towards a market-driven economy, where competition could stimulate efficiency and innovation.

Central to his belief was the idea that market forces should drive decisions about production, investment, and trade. Rather than the government dictating which industries should thrive and which should fail, Dr. Singh argued that entrepreneurs and businesses should be allowed to compete freely, creating opportunities for innovation, job creation, and wealth generation. This shift, according to him, would lead to an economy that was not just more efficient but also better integrated into the global economic order.

Privatization and the Role of the State

One of the key aspects of Dr. Singh's liberalization philosophy was privatization. He believed that state-owned enterprises (SOEs), which were the backbone of India's industrial sector, were often inefficient and poorly managed. The government's ownership and control over these enterprises created an environment that discouraged innovation and held back the growth potential of key sectors. Therefore, one of Dr. Singh's main policy objectives was to privatize many of these state-owned enterprises, allowing them to operate in a more competitive, market-driven environment. However, Dr. Singh also recognized that the state would still have an important role in certain sectors, particularly those that had strategic or national importance, such as defence, energy, and infrastructure. For him, liberalization did not mean abandoning the state's role entirely, but rather redefining it. The state should focus on creating a regulatory framework that would allow the private sector to thrive, while also ensuring that the benefits of growth were shared equitably among all sections of society.

Industrial Deregulation and Foreign Investment

Dr. Singh's belief in liberalization was also evident in his efforts to deregulate the industrial sector. In the years leading up to the 1991 reforms, India's industries were heavily regulated through a complex web of laws, controls, and restrictions. The Industrial Licensing Policy required businesses to obtain licences for nearly every aspect of their operations, from setting up new plants to expanding existing ones. These regulations, while designed to protect domestic industries, had the effect of stifling growth and innovation, making it difficult for businesses to compete globally. Dr. Singh, as part of his broader liberalization agenda, moved to dismantle these controls, allowing businesses greater freedom to operate. This process of industrial de-licencing and deregulation was one of the cornerstones of the 1991 reforms. By removing restrictions on private enterprise, Dr. Singh believed that Indian industries would become more competitive, capable of improving their productivity and quality, and better positioned to compete in global markets.

Another significant part of Dr. Singh's liberalization vision was his advocacy for FDI. He recognized that foreign investment was critical to modernizing India's industries, transferring technology, and creating jobs. As part of the 1991 reforms, he relaxed regulations around FDI, making it easier for foreign companies to invest in India. This move not only helped to boost India's industrial output but also signalled to the world that India was open for business. The influx of FDI played a crucial role in shaping India's emergence as a global economic player.

The State's Role in a Liberalized Economy

Although Dr. Singh was a strong advocate of a market-driven economy, he did not believe in *laissez-faire* capitalism. He recognized that markets, left unchecked, could lead to inequality, environmental degradation, and exploitation. Therefore, he advocated for a balanced approach where the state continued to play an important role in providing public goods such as education, health care, and infrastructure, while also ensuring that the benefits of liberalization were equitably distributed across society. Dr. Singh's approach emphasized the need for inclusive growth—economic growth that benefited not just the rich and powerful but also the poor and marginalized sections of society. For him, liberalization was not just about opening up the economy to global competition but about using the power of the market to create a more prosperous and equitable society. This vision was reflected in his advocacy for policies such as poverty alleviation programmes, financial inclusion, and targeted social welfare.

Legacy of Liberalization

Dr. Singh's belief in liberalization laid the foundation for a significant shift in India's economic trajectory. The 1991 reforms, which he helped architect, were a turning point in India's economic history. By moving towards a market economy and reducing state control, Dr. Singh helped India unlock its economic potential, leading to rapid growth, increased foreign investment, and the emergence of India as a global economic power. His belief in liberalization remains one of his most enduring contributions to India's economic development. Today, India is one of the world's fastest-growing economies, and much of this success can be attributed to the liberalization policies that Dr. Singh championed in the 1990s. His vision of a market economy, supported by a regulatory framework that promotes competition, innovation, and inclusivity, has shaped the economic landscape of modern India.

▪ Commitment to Poverty Alleviation

Dr. Manmohan Singh's approach to economic policy was deeply rooted in his commitment to poverty alleviation. While he was a strong advocate for liberalization and the market economy, his economic philosophy always emphasized the importance of ensuring that growth was not only robust but also inclusive. For him, economic growth had to be coupled with equitable distribution of its benefits across different segments of society, particularly the disadvantaged and marginalized groups. Dr. Singh's stance on poverty alleviation was not just about boosting the overall size of the economy but about ensuring that the gains of growth reached those at the bottom of the socio-economic ladder. This commitment became more apparent during his tenure as finance minister in the early 1990s, when he helped steer the country through a period of economic crisis, and later during his time as prime minister.

Poverty Alleviation and Economic Growth: A Dual Objective

Dr. Singh consistently argued that economic growth and poverty alleviation were not mutually exclusive. Rather, he believed that they could be pursued simultaneously, with the right policies in place. Economic growth, in his view, was essential for creating jobs, increasing incomes, and generating resources that could be used for social welfare programmes aimed at alleviating poverty. Growth could provide the necessary funds for targeted interventions, such as in education, health care, infrastructure, and rural development, all of which were crucial in improving the living standards of the poor. However, Dr. Singh also acknowledged that growth alone would not automatically lead to poverty alleviation. Without a conscious effort to ensure that the benefits of growth were distributed equitably, there was a risk that economic development would lead to widening income inequality. Therefore, his approach was not just about growth for growth's sake but about ensuring that the growth model he championed was both sustainable and inclusive.

Strategies for Inclusive Growth

Dr. Singh's commitment to poverty alleviation was manifest in several of the key policies and reforms he championed throughout his career. These were aimed at making growth more inclusive and ensuring that the disadvantaged groups—particularly the rural poor, women, and Scheduled Castes and Scheduled Tribes—could benefit from India's economic progress.

1. **Rural Development and Agriculture:** One of the major focal points of Dr. Singh's poverty alleviation strategy was rural development, given that a significant portion of India's poor lived in rural areas. Agriculture, being the mainstay of the rural economy, was central to his vision of inclusive growth. Dr. Singh recognized that for India to achieve sustainable poverty reduction, it was imperative to modernize agriculture and improve the productivity of small and marginal farmers. During his tenure, several initiatives were introduced to improve rural infrastructure, boost agricultural productivity, and provide better access to markets. Programmes aimed at rural credit, irrigation, and rural employment were prioritized, with the aim of enhancing the income and living conditions of rural households. A more direct manifestation of this was the National Rural Employment Guarantee Act (NREGA), which was launched during his time as prime minister. The programme provided guaranteed employment to rural households, which was a significant step towards reducing rural poverty.
2. **Social Welfare Programmes:** Dr. Singh's commitment to equity was further reflected in his endorsement of social welfare programmes aimed at addressing the needs of the most disadvantaged segments of society. One such programme was the Targeted Public Distribution System (TPDS), which sought to provide subsidized food grains to low-income households, thus alleviating hunger and malnutrition. The system, while facing challenges in terms of implementation, was a step in the right direction towards improving the food security of the poor. Additionally, programmes aimed at education, health care, and basic infrastructure were expanded to ensure that growth was

not limited to a select few. He believed that economic development had to be accompanied by investments in human capital to ensure that the benefits of growth were sustainable and enjoyed by all.

3. **Financial Inclusion:** Another key element of Dr. Singh's strategy to balance growth with equity was his commitment to financial inclusion. He understood that for economic growth to be truly inclusive, the poor and marginalized sections of society had to have access to financial services, including savings accounts, credit, and insurance. Under his leadership, efforts were made to expand banking services to rural areas, ensuring that even those in the most remote corners of India could participate in the financial system. This also helped empower women and small entrepreneurs, providing them with the means to improve their livelihoods.
4. **Addressing Regional Disparities:** Dr. Singh's vision for inclusive growth also focused on addressing the regional disparities that existed within India. There were vast differences in economic development between states, and Dr. Singh was keen on ensuring that development was not confined to only a few regions. His policies aimed at creating a more balanced approach to economic development, ensuring that states and regions with lower levels of development received the attention and resources they needed to catch up with more prosperous areas.
5. **Social Safety Nets:** In addition to direct poverty alleviation programmes, Dr. Singh was committed to creating a system of social safety nets that would protect the most vulnerable sections of society from economic shocks. This included old age pensions, unemployment benefits, and other welfare programmes that would act as a buffer in times of crisis. Dr. Singh recognized that in a rapidly changing economy, where market forces were increasingly dominant, it was essential to have mechanisms in place that would

provide a safety net for those who could not keep pace with the changes.

Dr. Singh's Commitment to Equity in Global Context

Dr. Singh's commitment to poverty alleviation was not only confined to India's borders. On the global stage, he was an ardent advocate for the development needs of the global south. He consistently emphasized that economic globalization should not just benefit the already wealthy nations but should be inclusive and provide opportunities for the developing world. This was reflected in his advocacy for fair trade and his support for global initiatives aimed at alleviating poverty in developing countries. He also championed the cause of debt relief for the poorest countries, arguing that external debt was a major barrier to development and poverty alleviation in many low-income nations. His views on poverty alleviation were shaped by his belief that economic growth could not be meaningful unless it led to the improvement of the lives of the poor. This global vision of inclusive development was a key aspect of his leadership and legacy, both within India and internationally.

Legacy of Poverty Alleviation

Dr. Singh's commitment to balancing growth with equity had a lasting impact on India's economic policies and development trajectory.

The social welfare programmes, financial inclusion measures, and rural development initiatives that were implemented during his tenure laid the foundation for the country's future progress in poverty reduction. Though challenges remain, India's sustained economic growth and reduction in poverty over the past few decades can be traced back to the emphasis on inclusive growth that Dr. Singh championed. While liberalization played a crucial role in transforming India's economy, it was Dr. Singh's equity-focused policies that ensured the benefits of growth were shared by the broadest sections of society. His legacy is thus one of balancing the imperative of economic growth with the moral and social imperative of reducing poverty and inequality.

• Focus on Inclusive Development

Dr. Manmohan Singh's economic philosophy was underpinned by a vision of inclusive development, which was aimed at ensuring that the benefits of economic growth were shared across all sections of society. One of the most pressing challenges in India was the stark disparity between its rural and urban areas. This rural-urban divide was characterized by significant differences in income, infrastructure, access to services, and overall quality of life. Dr. Singh, in his capacity as finance minister and later as prime minister, recognized that addressing this disparity was crucial for ensuring that India's growth story was truly inclusive.

Understanding the Rural-Urban Divide

Before the economic reforms of the 1990s, India's economy was highly agrarian, with the majority of its population living in rural areas. However, economic progress was largely concentrated in urban centres, where industrialization, services, and commerce were more pronounced. This urban-centric model of development led to an unequal distribution of resources and opportunities, further exacerbating the differences between rural and urban populations. The rural economy was characterized by stagnant agricultural growth, low productivity, and limited access to modern technologies. Moreover, basic infrastructure such as roads, electricity, clean drinking water, and health care was underdeveloped. Rural areas also faced social exclusion and poor educational standards, which hindered the potential for upward mobility. In contrast, urban areas, especially major cities like Mumbai, Delhi, and Bengaluru, experienced rapid industrialization, high economic growth, and better access to education and health care.

This created a growing chasm between the urban elite and the rural poor. Dr. Singh, as a proponent of inclusive growth, sought to address these rural-urban disparities by ensuring that the development strategies were not only urban-centred but also incorporated the needs of rural areas. His approach aimed at ensuring that growth in urban sectors would not leave behind the rural population but instead create synergies between both.

Key Strategies to Address Rural-Urban Disparities

Dr. Singh's focus on addressing rural-urban disparities was reflected in the policies and programmes he initiated, both during his tenure as finance minister and later as prime minister. These efforts were aimed at fostering balanced growth and reducing the income gap between urban and rural India.

1. **Investment in Rural Infrastructure:** One of the central pillars of Dr. Singh's approach to inclusive development was the improvement of rural infrastructure. Inadequate infrastructure was one of the primary reasons for the backwardness of rural areas. Without reliable roads, access to markets, electricity, and sanitation, it was difficult for rural communities to thrive. Dr. Singh's policies emphasized investments in rural infrastructure to improve connectivity between villages and towns, facilitate trade, and provide essential services. Programmes like the Pradhan Mantri Gram Sadak Yojana (PMGSY) aimed at building all-weather roads in rural areas were initiated under his leadership. This initiative helped to reduce the isolation of rural communities, enabling them to access markets, health care, and education more easily. Additionally, improving electricity distribution in rural areas and ensuring irrigation facilities for farmers were key areas of focus. These measures

directly addressed the agricultural stagnation in rural areas and laid the foundation for improving the quality of life in the villages.

2. **Rural Employment Programmes:** Dr. Singh's government introduced several employment-generation programmes targeted at rural areas to address the problem of underemployment and poverty. One of the most significant initiatives in this regard was the National Rural Employment Guarantee Act (NREGA), which was introduced during his tenure as prime minister in 2005. The NREGA guaranteed 100 days of employment to every rural household in India. This was a major step towards poverty alleviation and social security in rural areas, providing a safety net for families in times of need.

   The programme not only helped improve income levels but also contributed to rural infrastructure development, as the work undertaken under the scheme often involved the construction of roads, water conservation projects, and other public works that benefited rural communities. In addition to NREGA, there were other initiatives aimed at promoting self-employment and entrepreneurship in rural areas, such as the Rural Development Fund, which provided credit and financial support to small and medium enterprises in the rural sector.

3. **Promoting Agricultural Growth:** Agriculture was the backbone of the rural economy, but for decades, it had suffered from low productivity and poor technological adoption. Dr. Singh recognized that improving the agricultural sector was critical to bridging the rural-urban divide. His policies focused on enhancing agricultural productivity through modernization and technological advancements. Under his leadership, the government made efforts to improve access to high-yielding seeds, fertilizers, and irrigation techniques. Additionally, the National Agricultural Policy was introduced in 2000 to promote

sustainable agricultural growth. Dr. Singh also advocated for better agricultural credit facilities to help farmers, many of whom had limited access to formal financial institutions. This approach was designed to improve the livelihoods of rural farmers and boost agricultural output, thereby contributing to both rural prosperity and overall economic growth.

4. **Education and Skill Development:** Another critical aspect of Dr. Singh's strategy to address rural-urban disparities was his emphasis on education and skill development. He recognized that education was the key to breaking the cycle of poverty in rural areas and promoting upward social mobility. Under his leadership, there was a significant increase in investment in primary and secondary education, particularly in rural areas. Programmes like Sarva Shiksha Abhiyan aimed to provide universal elementary education to all children, with a special focus on rural and disadvantaged children. Dr. Singh also supported vocational education and skill development programmes that aimed to equip rural youth with the skills required for non-agricultural employment, thereby broadening their opportunities in urban sectors as well.
5. **Decentralization of Development:** Dr. Singh also emphasized the need for decentralization in governance, where local bodies such as panchayats and municipalities would play a larger role in decision making and resource allocation. By empowering local communities to take control of their development, rural areas could address their unique challenges in a more targeted and effective manner. This decentralization approach was aligned with the Bottom-Up Development strategy, which sought to create more localized and inclusive development models that were tailored to the needs of specific rural communities, rather than relying on a one-size-fits-all approach dictated from the centre.

6. **Access to Financial Services:** Dr. Singh also emphasized improving financial inclusion as a means to bridge the rural-urban divide. He recognized that rural areas often lacked access to banking services, which severely restricted economic opportunities for rural entrepreneurs, farmers, and households. The National Rural Financial Inclusion Plan (NRFIP) was introduced to increase the penetration of banking services in rural areas. Furthermore, Dr. Singh supported microfinance institutions (MFIs) and self-help groups (SHGs), which helped provide rural women and small-scale entrepreneurs with access to credit and other financial services, thereby empowering them economically.

Legacy of Addressing Rural-Urban Disparities

Dr. Singh's efforts to bridge the rural-urban divide laid the foundation for India's inclusive growth model. His policies in rural infrastructure development, agricultural growth, employment generation, education, and financial inclusion significantly improved the living standards of rural populations. Though challenges remain, particularly in addressing persistent regional disparities, his approach to inclusive development remains a cornerstone of India's development strategy. By focusing on reducing rural-urban disparities, Dr. Singh not only helped improve the welfare of rural populations but also created a more balanced and sustainable economic growth model that sought to lift all sections of society.

REFERENCES

Costanza-Chock, S. (2020). *Design Justice: Community-Led Practices to Build The Worlds We Need.* The MIT Press.

Ching, F.D. (2023). *Architecture: Form, Space, and Order.* John Wiley & Sons.

Dameri, R.P. & Rosenthal-Sabroux, C. (Eds.). (2014). *Smart City: How to Create Public and Economic Value with High Technology in Urban Space.* Springer.

Doran, D. & Cather, B. (Eds.). (2013). *Construction Materials Reference Book*. Routledge.

Dover, J.W. (2015). *Green Infrastructure: Incorporating Plants and Enhancing Biodiversity in Buildings and Urban Environments*. Routledge.

Elliot, J.A. (2006). *An Introduction to Sustainable Development*. Routledge.

Forbes, L.H. & Ahmed, S.M. (2010). *Modern Construction: Lean Project Delivery and Integrated Practices*. CRC Press.

Grober, U. & Cunningham, R. (2012). *Sustainability: A Cultural History* (p. 156). Cambridge: Green Books.

Hardi, P. & Zdan, T. (1997). *Assessing Sustainable Development: Principles in Practice*. International Institute for Sustainable Development.

Ingram, J. (2020). *Understanding BIM: The Past, Present and Future*. Routledge.

4

The 1991 Economic Reforms

The 1991 Economic Reforms under Dr. Manmohan Singh's leadership as finance minister were a pivotal moment in India's economic history, marking a decisive break from the protectionist policies that had shaped the country's economic trajectory since its independence. Prior to these reforms, India's economy was largely closed off from the rest of the world, characterized by a controlled market with state ownership over many sectors and an emphasis on self-sufficiency. The 1991 crisis acted as the catalyst for the sweeping reforms that followed, leading to a dramatic restructuring of India's economic system, with the country moving from a socialist-style economy to a more market-oriented one.

These reforms not only transformed India's economy but also laid the groundwork for the nation's growth over the next several decades. The immediate backdrop to the 1991 reforms was a deep economic crisis. India faced a severe balance of payments crisis, with foreign exchange reserves plummeting to such a low point that they were barely sufficient to cover three weeks' worth of imports. The fiscal deficit had risen sharply, inflation was high, and the country's external debt burden was becoming unsustainable. A major reason for this crisis was the inefficiency of a highly protected and state-controlled economy, where heavy regulation and import restrictions stifled competition, innovation, and growth. Moreover, the world economy was also evolving rapidly, and India's protectionist policies were increasingly at odds with the trend toward globalization.

In response to the crisis, the Indian government, led by Prime Minister P.V. Narasimha Rao and supported by Dr. Singh, introduced a comprehensive set of economic reforms aimed at liberalizing the economy. These reforms were designed to shift India from a state-dominated economy to one driven by the forces of market competition, with a focus on integrating India more deeply into the global economy. The first major aspect of the 1991 reforms was the liberalization of trade. Prior to 1991, India followed an import substitution strategy, which aimed to reduce foreign dependence by promoting domestic industries through tariffs, quotas, and state protection. This approach, while initially useful in protecting nascent industries, eventually led to inefficiencies, low productivity, and a lack of global competitiveness. As part of the reforms, India reduced tariffs and opened up sectors to foreign trade. Import licencing was abolished, and quantitative restrictions on imports were relaxed.

Fig. 4.1: Public Sector Banks in India: The Backbone of Financial Stability during the Crisis.

This opened the Indian economy to global markets, allowing Indian companies to source cheaper raw materials and technologies while enabling consumers to access a wider array of goods at competitive prices. A crucial aspect of the 1991 reforms was the emphasis on attracting foreign direct investment (FDI). Prior to the reforms, India had stringent restrictions on FDI, with most foreign companies unable to enter Indian markets without joint ventures with domestic firms, and foreign ownership was capped at 40 per cent in most industries. The 1991 reforms significantly relaxed these restrictions. The government introduced a more liberal policy that allowed for greater foreign participation, including in key sectors such as manufacturing, telecommunications, and retail.

This policy shift encouraged an inflow of foreign capital, which helped modernize Indian industries and facilitated the transfer of technology and expertise, ultimately boosting the country's industrial output and productivity. Another major change introduced by the 1991 reforms was the devaluation of the Indian rupee. The rupee had been artificially overvalued for many years due to the country's protectionist policies, which made Indian exports uncompetitive on the global market. The devaluation of the rupee made Indian goods more affordable abroad, stimulating export growth. This was an important move that helped India integrate into the global economy by encouraging exports, particularly in sectors such as textiles, software, and engineering goods. Devaluation also helped reduce India's trade deficit, as it made imports more expensive, thereby encouraging domestic production. In addition to trade and currency liberalization, the 1991 reforms also focused on liberalizing the domestic industrial sector.

India's industrial policy had been heavily regulated, with strict licencing requirements, government control over production levels, and a lack of competition. The Industrial Policy of 1991 moved away from this model, with the government dismantling the Licence Raj and removing restrictions on investment and production. This allowed for greater private sector participation in industries that were previously dominated by the state, leading to more efficient and innovative businesses. The policy also included measures to encourage small and medium-sized enterprises (SMEs) by simplifying regulatory procedures and removing barriers to entry. Financial sector reforms were another key component of the 1991 economic reforms. The financial system in India had long been characterized by state control, with banks heavily regulated by the government.

As part of the reforms, Dr. Singh introduced measures to enhance the efficiency and competitiveness of the banking sector. The government began to encourage privatization, reducing the dominance of public sector banks, and promoting the entry of private and foreign banks. The Reserve Bank of India (RBI) was given greater autonomy, and banking regulations were relaxed to promote competition and innovation. This led to greater access to credit for businesses and individuals, which in turn contributed to higher levels of investment and consumption. In the tax sector, the 1991 reforms focused on simplifying the tax system and improving compliance. The Indian tax system had been notorious for its complexity and inefficiency, with a high level of evasion and corruption. The government introduced a new tax structure, with reduced tax rates and broader tax bases, making it easier for businesses and individuals to comply with the law.

The reforms also included measures to improve the efficiency of tax administration, which helped increase government revenues and reduce fiscal deficits. Despite the significant improvements brought about by the 1991 economic reforms, challenges remained. The pace of privatization and deregulation was initially slow, and some sectors remained heavily protected. The reforms also created winners and losers, as certain industries and regions benefited disproportionately, while others were left behind. Additionally, the focus on growth and liberalization often led to concerns about inequality, as the benefits of the reforms were not always equally distributed across society. However, in the years following the 1991 reforms, India witnessed a remarkable period of economic growth. The liberalization measures led to increased foreign investment, faster industrial growth, and greater exports, particularly in the services sector, including information technology and business process outsourcing.

India became one of the world's fastest-growing economies, with a rapidly expanding middle class, improved infrastructure, and higher standards of living. The reforms also contributed to a reduction in poverty, as the benefits of economic growth trickled down to the poorer segments of society. In conclusion, the 1991 economic reforms, initiated by Dr. Manmohan Singh, played a central role in transforming India's economy. By dismantling the Licence Raj, promoting trade liberalization, devaluing the currency, and encouraging foreign investment, India shifted from a closed, state-controlled economy to a more open and competitive market economy. The success of these reforms was not immediate, but over time they catalyzed India's rise as one of the world's major emerging economies. The reforms continue to shape India's economic landscape today, providing a foundation for future growth and prosperity. Dr. Singh's leadership during this period remains one of the most significant milestones in India's post-Independence economic history.

Table 4.1: Fiscal Deficit Trends (2004–2014)

Year	Fiscal Deficit (% of GDP)
2004	3.9
2006	3.4
2008	5.9
2010	4.8
2012	5.7
2014	4.1

■ The Crisis Context

In the early 1990s, India faced a severe balance of payments crisis that threatened to derail its economic stability. The country was grappling with a dire fiscal and external debt situation, which was compounded by low foreign exchange reserves. This crisis marked a turning point in India's economic history, forcing the government to implement sweeping economic reforms. Understanding the causes of this crisis, along with the international pressures that accompanied it, is crucial to grasp the profound impact it had on India's economic policies and trajectory.

Causes of the Balance of Payments Crisis

The balance of payments (BoP) crisis in India in 1991 was primarily triggered by a combination of domestic economic mismanagement and external factors that had severely strained India's economic fundamentals. The key causes can be outlined as follows:

1. **Rising Fiscal Deficits:** One of the most significant contributors to India's balance of payments crisis was the rising fiscal deficit. In the years leading up to 1991, the Indian government had been running large fiscal deficits, primarily due to increased public spending on subsidies, welfare programmes, and defence. This unsustainable fiscal expansion led to a growing gap between government revenues and expenditures. To finance this deficit, the government relied heavily on borrowing, both domestically and from international lenders, which placed additional pressure on India's foreign exchange reserves.
2. **Inefficient Economic Structure:** India's economy in the pre-1990s period was largely characterized by a state-controlled economic model. The government had a central role in regulating the economy through policies of import substitution and protectionism, which discouraged competition and market efficiency. The industrial sector

was heavily regulated, and there were significant barriers to entry, which led to low productivity and inefficiency. The agriculture sector also faced stagnation, with poor infrastructure and outdated technologies. This inefficient structure created significant pressure on India's foreign exchange position. High levels of import dependency for essential goods, combined with low export growth, created an imbalance in the current account of the balance of payments. The country's foreign exchange reserves were insufficient to cover the import bills, leading to an acute shortage of dollars.

3. **Increase in External Debt:** During the 1980s, India had increasingly relied on external borrowing to finance its fiscal deficit and development programmes. This led to a rapid rise in India's external debt. However, a growing burden of debt service payments (interest and principal repayments) became unsustainable by 1991, particularly as the global interest rates began to rise, further stressing India's financial position.
4. **Decline in Foreign Exchange Reserves:** By 1991, India's foreign exchange reserves had dwindled to alarming levels. The country's reserves were only sufficient to cover about three weeks of imports, a dangerously low threshold. As a result, India faced the threat of defaulting on its external debt obligations, which in turn led to a loss of confidence among international investors and lenders.
5. **Political Instability and Governance Issues:** The political environment in India also contributed to the crisis. The early 1990s witnessed political instability, with frequent changes in leadership and governance. This instability weakened the country's ability to implement long-term, consistent economic policies. Moreover, the policy paralysis in addressing economic inefficiencies and pursuing reforms contributed to the crisis.

6. **Global Economic Shocks:** The global economic environment in the late 1980s and early 1990s also played a role in triggering the crisis. The oil price shock of the early 1990s led to an increase in India's import bill, particularly for crude oil, which further strained its foreign exchange reserves. Additionally, the Gulf War and the associated increase in oil prices in 1990 placed additional pressure on the Indian economy, contributing to the balance of payments crisis.

International Pressure for Reforms

The severe balance of payments crisis in India in 1991 attracted significant international attention and pressure. India had already sought financial assistance from international organizations such as the International Monetary Fund (IMF) and the World Bank in the past, but the scale of the crisis in 1991 forced the country into a position where it had little choice but to accept substantial international intervention and reform programmes.

1. **IMF and World Bank Involvement:** Faced with a rapidly deteriorating economic situation, the Indian government sought assistance from the IMF and the World Bank to avert an economic collapse. In July 1991, the Indian government, led by then-Finance Minister Dr. Manmohan Singh, entered into a structural adjustment programme (SAP) with the IMF. This agreement involved India agreeing to adopt a set of economic reforms that would align the country with the broader principles of global economic liberalization. The IMF's assistance package was tied to India's commitment to implementing key reforms, including trade liberalization, privatization, and market-oriented economic policies. These reforms were meant to address the country's fiscal deficits, boost foreign exchange reserves, and increase economic efficiency by opening up the economy to global competition.

2. **Devaluation of the Rupee:** One of the key recommendations from the IMF was to devalue the Indian rupee, which was seen as overvalued in the international markets. The devaluation aimed to make India's exports more competitive and to reduce the gap between the demand for foreign currency and India's foreign exchange reserves. The devaluation, although controversial, was a key element in the broader economic reforms that India undertook.
3. **Liberalization and Structural Reforms:** The international community, particularly the IMF and World Bank, pushed for India to liberalize its economy and adopt a more market-oriented approach. The global economic context of the early 1990s, characterized by the rise of neoliberalism and the Washington Consensus, favoured policies that prioritized privatization, trade liberalization, and market deregulation. The international pressure was significant, as India had limited room for manoeuvring given its dire economic situation and the impending threat of a default on external debt obligations.
4. **Foreign Investment and Global Integration:** The IMF and World Bank also pushed for India to create a more favourable environment for FDI. In exchange for financial assistance, India was required to open up sectors such as manufacturing, telecommunications, and banking to foreign investors. The international community emphasized the need for India to integrate more deeply into the global economy by reducing trade barriers and adopting more liberal economic policies.
5. **Political and Economic Reforms:** The international pressure also extended to the political and economic governance structures within India. The IMF insisted on reforms to improve the efficiency and accountability of government institutions. This involved implementing measures to reduce corruption, streamline bureaucratic

inefficiencies, and enhance transparency in the economic decision making process.

The balance of payments crisis of 1991 was a watershed moment in India's economic history. The causes of the crisis were multifaceted, including fiscal mismanagement, inefficiencies in the economic structure, external debt burdens, and global economic shocks. However, the crisis also acted as a catalyst for deep-rooted economic reforms. The international pressure from institutions like the IMF and World Bank played a pivotal role in shaping India's transition from a state-controlled economy to a more market-driven one. These reforms, which included trade liberalization, devaluation of the rupee, privatization, and a shift toward greater economic globalization, not only addressed the immediate crisis but also set the stage for India's economic transformation in the following decades.

▪ Appointment as Finance Minister

In 1991, Dr. Manmohan Singh was appointed as the Finance Minister of India during one of the most turbulent economic periods in the country's history. The balance of payments crisis, the depletion of foreign exchange reserves, and rising fiscal deficits had pushed the Indian economy to the brink of collapse. Singh's appointment marked a pivotal moment in the Indian economic landscape, as he was tasked with addressing these severe challenges and leading the country through a transformative period. Dr. Singh's appointment was not just a response to the immediate crisis but also a strategic move to reorient India's economic policies toward liberalization and global integration.

Vision for India's Economic Future

Dr. Manmohan Singh's vision for India's economy was fundamentally anchored in the belief that the country could no longer afford to follow the same state-controlled economic model that had prevailed since Independence. Singh, with his exposure to global economic thought and his experiences in international organizations like the World Bank and IMF, saw that India's economic policies needed to undergo a paradigm shift if the country was to achieve sustainable growth and global competitiveness.

1. **Economic Liberalization:** At the heart of Dr. Singh's vision was the belief that India needed to move away from its import substitution model and embrace economic liberalization. He strongly advocated for the opening up of markets, reducing trade barriers, and fostering a more competitive economy. Singh's vision was grounded in the understanding that India's industrial and economic growth was stifled by excessive state control and bureaucratic inefficiency. He argued that the country needed to liberalize its economy in order to unleash the potential of the private sector, foreign investment, and global trade relations.
2. **Integration into the Global Economy:** Dr. Singh saw the global economy as an arena where India could compete and thrive if it opened its doors to foreign investment and embraced globalization. He recognized that India's relative economic isolation in the post-Independence period had hindered its growth potential. Under Singh's leadership, the goal was to make India an attractive destination for FDI and to ensure that India's industries were competitive on the global stage. He believed that by reducing trade barriers, promoting exports, and opening up various sectors to international players, India could fuel its growth engine.
3. **Addressing Structural Economic Inefficiencies:** A crucial component of Singh's vision was addressing India's structural economic inefficiencies. The state-controlled model had resulted in economic stagnation, bureaucratic red tape, and a lack of innovation in several sectors. Singh was determined to streamline India's industrial

policies, reduce Licence Raj, and encourage private sector participation. His goal was to create a more dynamic and flexible economy that could attract new technologies and ideas, particularly from the fast-developing Asian Tigers and other emerging markets.

4. **Fiscal Responsibility and Financial Reforms:** Another priority for Dr. Singh was addressing India's severe fiscal imbalances. The country's fiscal deficit was unsustainable, and the government had been borrowing excessively to fund its spending. Singh emphasized the importance of fiscal discipline and advocated for measures that would bring the fiscal deficit under control. In his view, fiscal responsibility was critical not only to stabilize India's macro-economic environment but also to build investor confidence and pave the way for more robust economic growth.
5. **Poverty Alleviation and Inclusive Growth:** While Dr. Singh was a strong proponent of economic liberalization, he also believed that growth should be inclusive and focused on poverty alleviation. Singh's vision incorporated a balanced approach that ensured economic liberalization did not come at the cost of the country's poor. He strongly believed in the reduction of poverty through equitable growth, which would involve investments in rural areas, social infrastructure, and welfare schemes that would uplift the marginalized segments of society. This focus on inclusive development, which continued throughout his tenure, became an essential component of India's post-1991 economic trajectory.
6. **Industrial and Agricultural Growth:** Dr. Singh understood that economic liberalization needed to go hand in hand with industry modernization and agricultural development. He recognized the central role of both sectors in India's overall economic health. In particular, Singh emphasized the importance of fostering industrial growth

through deregulation, privatization, and the reduction of trade barriers. At the same time, he also focused on revitalizing agriculture, ensuring that rural development was given priority, and that farmers had access to better tools, technologies, and markets.

7. **Privatization and Market-Oriented Reforms:** One of Singh's most ambitious goals was to initiate a programme of privatization for state-owned enterprises, many of which were financially inefficient and weighed down by outdated management practices. He believed that reducing government control over industries would allow for more private sector-led growth and better resource allocation. The aim was not only to reduce the fiscal burden on the government but also to make India's industries more competitive and efficient in the global market.

Priorities in the First Budget

In July 1991, Dr. Singh presented his first budget as finance minister, a landmark moment that laid the groundwork for India's economic reforms. Some of the key priorities and steps taken in the budget reflected his broader vision:

1. **Tax Reforms:** The budget included significant tax reforms, aiming to broaden the tax base, reduce tax evasion, and streamline the tax structure. The Goods and Services Tax (GST), which would later be introduced in 2017, had its conceptual roots in these early reforms.
2. **Trade Liberalization:** Singh's budget focused on reducing tariffs and import duties, aligning India more closely with global trade standards. The goal was to make Indian goods more competitive internationally, while also encouraging foreign imports to introduce greater competition in the domestic market.

3. **Industrial Reforms:** Dr. Singh announced a series of measures to dismantle the Licence Raj. These included relaxing restrictions on new industrial projects, removing some of the red tape involved in starting businesses, and allowing greater foreign investment.
4. **Foreign Investment and Privatization:** The budget laid the foundation for opening key sectors of the economy to foreign investment, setting the stage for privatization initiatives in sectors like telecommunications, energy, and banking.
5. **Economic Stabilization:** With an eye on stabilizing the Indian economy, Singh also prioritized policies aimed at reducing inflation, strengthening the currency, and stabilizing the stock market.

Dr. Manmohan Singh's appointment as finance minister in 1991 came at a time of great economic turmoil for India. The balance of payments crisis, fiscal imbalances, and global pressures had pushed the country to the brink, and Singh's vision for India was crucial in steering the country through this crisis. His priorities focused on liberalizing India's economy, integrating it into the global market, and ensuring that growth was inclusive and sustainable. Dr. Singh's foresight, economic expertise, and political pragmatism set the stage for India's economic transformation in the 1990s, and his policies would shape the nation's economic trajectory for decades to come.

• Landmark Reforms

The landmark reforms initiated by Dr. Manmohan Singh in 1991 played a pivotal role in transforming India's economic landscape. Among the most significant of these were the industrial de-licencing and foreign direct FDI policies, which shifted India away from the restrictive policies of the past and opened the economy to greater competition and innovation. Under the previous Licence Raj system, starting a business in India was a bureaucratic nightmare, with companies required to obtain government approval for nearly every aspect of their operations. This system stifled entrepreneurship and industrial growth, leading to inefficiency and stagnation. The industrial de-licencing reforms removed many of these restrictions, thereby promoting a market-driven economy and encouraging private sector participation.

This move not only boosted industrial growth but also attracted significant foreign investment, which helped modernize India's manufacturing base and spurred the development of key industries. Alongside industrial de-licencing, the liberalization of FDI policies marked another critical reform. By allowing greater FDI in key sectors, such as telecommunications, automobiles, and retail, the Indian government sought to integrate India into the global economy. These reforms allowed foreign companies to establish a stronger foothold in India, bringing in capital, technology, and managerial expertise, all of which played a crucial role in boosting the country's economic growth and creating jobs. As a result, India became an increasingly attractive destination for global investors, and the economy began to experience accelerated growth.

In addition to industrial and FDI reforms, Dr. Singh also spearheaded significant changes in banking, taxation, and trade liberalization. The banking reforms focused on improving the efficiency and stability of India's financial system. This included measures to modernize the banking sector, such as introducing new technologies and improving the capital adequacy ratio of banks, making them more resilient to external shocks. In the taxation sector, Dr. Singh's government undertook reforms aimed at simplifying the tax structure, broadening the tax base, and reducing the tax burden on businesses. The introduction of a more streamlined tax system helped increase compliance and created a more conducive environment for business growth. On the trade front, the government drastically reduced import tariffs and trade barriers, shifting from an import-substitution approach to a more open, export-oriented model.

By fostering a more competitive environment and integrating India into the global economy, these reforms helped stimulate exports, improve industrial competitiveness, and drive economic growth. Together, these landmark reforms represented a transformative shift in India's economic policies, laying the foundation for the modern, globally integrated economy that India is today. The industrial de-licencing and FDI policies, combined with banking, taxation, and trade liberalization, created a robust framework that spurred growth, fostered innovation, and integrated India into the global market.

Industrial De-licencing and FDI Policies

The industrial de-licencing policy introduced in 1991 was one of the most significant economic reforms under Dr. Manmohan Singh's leadership. Prior to these reforms, India's industrial sector was heavily regulated under the Licence Raj, which required businesses to obtain government licences for virtually every aspect of production, expansion, and pricing. This system created inefficiencies, stifled entrepreneurship, and limited the growth potential of industries. In 1991, as part of the economic liberalization process, the Indian government moved to dismantle these bureaucratic controls, allowing the private sector to operate more freely and efficiently. The move to de-licence industries enabled Indian businesses to make decisions based on market demand and competition, rather than being bogged down by government regulations. This resulted in increased industrial growth, better resource allocation, and enhanced competitiveness.

It opened up numerous opportunities for small and medium enterprises (SMEs) to grow and thrive, and larger firms were able to expand their operations without unnecessary bureaucratic hurdles. The industrial de-licencing policy also helped India integrate its manufacturing sector into the global supply chain, fostering innovation and technological advancement. Alongside industrial de-licencing, the FDI policies were significantly liberalized. The government allowed greater foreign investment in key sectors, including automobiles, telecommunications, and consumer goods, thereby facilitating the influx of capital, technology, and managerial expertise. By relaxing FDI restrictions, India attracted international companies, which not only provided much-needed capital but also brought in advanced technologies and global best practices. The presence of multinational corporations also helped create jobs, improve skills, and increase exports. India's economic environment became more competitive, and its global economic integration was accelerated.

This move towards more open FDI policies marked a significant departure from the protectionist policies of the past and was a driving force behind India's economic modernization.

Banking, Taxation, and Trade Liberalization

Alongside industrial de-licencing and FDI liberalization, Dr. Manmohan Singh also oversaw comprehensive reforms in the banking, taxation, and trade sectors, which collectively helped modernize India's economic infrastructure and made it more competitive on the global stage. In the banking sector, reforms focused on improving the efficiency and stability of financial institutions. Prior to 1991, India's banking system was underdeveloped, inefficient, and heavily controlled by the government. Banks were often plagued by non-performing assets (NPAs) and lacked the capital needed for growth. To address these issues, Dr. Singh's government introduced measures to modernize and restructure the banking sector. These included the liberalization of interest rates, reform of the public sector banks, and the introduction of capital adequacy norms, aligning Indian banks with international standards. These reforms improved the health of the banking system, making it more robust and better able to support economic growth. The banking sector was also given the freedom to innovate and compete, allowing for the introduction of new banking products and services, which helped improve access to finance for businesses and individuals alike.

In the taxation sector, the government focused on simplifying the tax structure, eliminating many of the complex indirect taxes, and moving towards a more transparent and efficient tax regime. The introduction of indirect tax reforms reduced the multiplicity of taxes and helped broaden the tax base. This shift was aimed at creating a more favourable environment for businesses, reducing the tax burden on entrepreneurs, and ensuring that the government could generate the necessary revenue to fund economic development. These tax reforms, along with the streamlining of the tax administration system, improved tax compliance, reduced the scope for corruption, and made it easier for businesses to operate and expand. The trade liberalization policies introduced in 1991 were another cornerstone of the economic reforms. India had long maintained a protectionist trade regime, with high tariffs, import restrictions, and a range of quotas. These barriers hindered the growth of industries and limited India's access to global markets. In 1991, as part of the broader economic liberalization process, India drastically reduced its import tariffs, dismantled non-tariff barriers, and opened up key sectors to foreign competition.

The goal was to shift India from an import-substitution model to an export-oriented one, where industries could compete globally and take advantage of global markets. By lowering tariffs and reducing trade restrictions, India not only fostered a more competitive environment for domestic industries but also encouraged the growth of exports. Indian companies began to look beyond their domestic markets, exporting more goods and services to international markets. This helped to improve the balance of payments, increase foreign exchange reserves, and position India as a more integrated player in the global economy. Trade liberalization also opened the door to a wider variety of goods in the Indian market, providing consumers with better choices and promoting the development of a more competitive retail sector. Together, these reforms in the banking, taxation, and trade sectors contributed to making India's economy more efficient, globally integrated, and competitive. The liberalization policies not only opened up opportunities for foreign investors but also set the stage for sustained economic growth and development, transforming India into one of the world's leading emerging economies.

▪ Initial Resistance

The economic reforms initiated by Dr. Manmohan Singh in 1991 faced substantial initial resistance, both from political factions and segments of the public. Despite the necessity of these reforms for India's long-term growth and development, they were met with scepticism, apprehension, and outright opposition. Politically, the reforms were seen as a departure from the Nehruvian economic model, which had emphasized state control and protectionist policies. The Congress party, while supportive of the reforms at the top level, faced opposition within its ranks. Many party members were concerned about alienating the traditional voter base primarily the working class and the rural population who had benefited from the welfare-oriented policies of the past. Some Congress leaders were wary that embracing market-driven policies could undermine the party's historical commitment to social welfare and equitable development. Opposition parties, such as the BJP, also strongly criticized the reforms. They viewed the liberalization measures as an imposition of foreign interests, particularly from the World Bank and the IMF. They feared that opening up India's economy to foreign investments and privatizing state-owned enterprises would lead to job losses, industrial decline, and increased inequality, disproportionately affecting the poorest sections of society. Public scepticism was equally widespread. For much of the population, particularly those accustomed to the Licence Raj system and the protectionist policies of the past, the shift to a market-driven economy seemed unsettling.

Many feared that FDI and privatization would lead to the domination of Indian industries by multinational corporations, further deepening economic disparities. The idea that liberalization would benefit the economy was difficult to accept for many who were unfamiliar with the concept of market-driven policies. There were also concerns about the immediate consequences of the reforms. The devaluation of the rupee, a key part of the stabilization measures, led to rising inflation and higher prices, particularly for imported goods. This created a sense of economic discomfort among the public, as many felt the reforms would reduce their purchasing power and standard of living. The privatization of state-owned enterprises, which was a central element of the reforms, also led to fears of widespread job cuts and redundancies, particularly in public sector industries. Labour unions, in particular, expressed concern that the changes would lead to poor working conditions and diminished job security for workers.

The middle class and certain sectors of the business community who had long operated within the protectionist environment of the Licence Raj were also apprehensive. Many were uncertain how the new market-oriented policies would impact their businesses and livelihoods. This uncertainty contributed to a climate of resistance to the reforms, as the move toward liberalization was seen as a threat to established business practices and interests. Despite these challenges, the political leadership of Prime Minister P.V. Narasimha Rao and Dr. Singh's determination played a crucial role in pushing the reforms through. While the immediate effects were met with resistance, the long-term benefits of the reforms began to become evident as India experienced improved economic performance, marked by an increase in foreign exchange reserves, accelerated industrial growth, and a surge in the IT sector.

The initial resistance gradually softened as people began to recognize the positive changes brought about by the liberalization measures, such as increased employment opportunities, higher living standards, and greater access to goods and services. In conclusion, the initial resistance to the 1991 economic reforms highlights the significant political and public challenges associated with transforming an economy steeped in state control and protectionism. The liberalization process was not a smooth one, and it required careful navigation of internal political opposition and public fears. However, as the benefits of the reforms became clearer, the opposition diminished, and India's economy was set on a path of sustained growth and global integration.

Political Opposition

Politically, the 1991 reforms were seen by many as a break from the Nehruvian economic model, which emphasized state control over key sectors of the economy. The Congress party, which spearheaded the reforms, faced internal opposition. Many Congress members were concerned that embracing market-oriented policies would alienate the party's traditional support base—especially the working class and the rural population—who had benefited from state-led welfare policies. Within the party, there were also voices of concern about losing the support of trade unions and other social groups who benefited from the existing welfare system. Moreover, opposition parties, including the BJP, were vocal in their criticism. They viewed the liberalization measures as an imposition of foreign interests and neo-liberal economic practices that would compromise India's sovereignty. They feared that opening up India's economy would increase dependence on foreign capital and corporations, and lead to an unequal distribution of wealth. Political opponents also argued that the reforms would undermine India's self-sufficiency and expose the country to global market forces that could disadvantage India's poorer and vulnerable sections.

Public Scepticism

The public scepticism surrounding the reforms was also considerable. Many Indians, particularly those who had grown up under the Licence Raj system, viewed liberalization with suspicion. The economic liberalization agenda, which included the privatization of state-owned enterprises, reduction of trade barriers, and opening the economy to FDI, seemed radical to a population accustomed to protectionist policies. The fear was that these changes would lead to job losses, increased inequality, and the displacement of local industries by foreign companies. The devaluation of the rupee, an essential part of the reforms, sparked concerns about inflation and rising costs of goods, particularly imported items. The public feared that this would lead to a decrease in purchasing power and a decline in their standard of living. Additionally, the privatization of public sector enterprises was seen as a threat to the job security of workers in state-run industries. Many feared that such privatization would lead to layoffs and deterioration in working conditions, further alienating the working class.

Resistance from Labour Unions

Labour unions were particularly vocal in their opposition. They feared that the push for privatization and market reforms would result in job cuts, lower wages, and exploitation of workers. The protests against privatization were widespread, with labour unions fearing that their members would lose the social security benefits and protections they had enjoyed under the state-controlled economic system.

Middle-Class and Business Community Concerns

The middle class, especially those who had enjoyed the benefits of a controlled economy, were also apprehensive. Some feared that the opening up of the economy would lead to increased foreign competition, making locally produced goods less competitive. Small businesses, which were often protected from international competition under previous policies, were particularly uncertain about the impact of market liberalization. Moreover, certain sectors of the business community, who had operated within the protectionist framework, were concerned about how the reforms would affect their enterprises. They were used to the Licence Raj system, which gave them a certain degree of control over their industries. The sudden shift to a more globalized market was unsettling for these business interests, and many feared that it would disrupt their existing business models.

Overcoming Resistance

Despite these political and public challenges, Dr. Singh's commitment to the reforms, combined with Prime Minister P.V. Narasimha Rao's leadership, ensured the successful implementation of these policies. While initial opposition was high, the gradual positive outcomes of the reforms, such as increased foreign exchange reserves, industrial growth, and the emergence of the IT sector, helped reduce scepticism. Over time, the public began to see the benefits of the reforms as the economy showed signs of recovery and growth. As India's economic landscape transformed, with the country moving from a stagnant economy to one of the fastest-growing nations in the world, many of the initial fears began to dissipate. The reforms eventually gained widespread acceptance as they demonstrated their potential to unlock India's economic potential, although the political and public resistance initially posed a considerable challenge.

Conclusion

In summary, the initial resistance to the 1991 economic reforms in India was significant, both politically and publicly.

It stemmed from a variety of factors, including fears of economic inequality, job losses, and the loss of national sovereignty. However, despite the initial scepticism, the leadership of Dr. Singh and Prime Minister Rao, combined with the gradual positive effects of the reforms, helped India overcome these challenges. Over time, the country embraced the new economic model, which set the stage for India's transformation into one of the world's leading emerging markets.

REFERENCES

Aga Khan Development Network. (2015). *Nizamuddin Urban Renewal Initiative*. Retrieved September 2016, from http://annualreport2015.nizamuddinrenewal.org/index.php

Aga Khan Trust for Culture. (2007). *Walled City of Lahore Conservation*. Retrieved on 3 March 2017, from http://www.akdn.org/where-we-work/south asia/pakistan/culturaldevelopment/walled-city-of-lahore-conservation

Jenks, M. & Jones, C. (Eds.). (2009). *Dimensions of the Sustainable City*.

Kibert, C.J. (2016). *Sustainable Construction: Green Building Design and Delivery*. John Wiley & Sons.

Lawson, M., Ogden, R. & Goodier, C. (2014). *Design in Modular Construction*. CRC Press.

Lechner, N. (2014). *Heating, Cooling, Lighting: Sustainable Design Methods for Architects*. John Wiley & Sons.

Smith, R.E. (2010). *Prefab Architecture: A Guide to Modular Design and Construction*. John Wiley & Sons.

Vale, L. (2014). *Architecture, Power and National Identity*. Routledge.

Vezzoli, C. & Manzini, E. (2008). *Design for Environmental Sustainability*. London: Springer.

Wang, S. (2009). *Intelligent Buildings and Building Automation*. Routledge.

5

Post-1991 Economic Stabilization

The period following India's 1991 economic reforms marked a critical juncture in the nation's economic history, shifting from a largely closed and state-controlled economy to one that was more market-oriented and integrated with the global economy. The stabilization phase, which followed these reforms, was crucial for consolidating the gains achieved during the initial liberalization period and for ensuring long-term, sustainable growth. Dr. Manmohan Singh, as the finance minister at the time, played a pivotal role in orchestrating these stabilizing measures that aimed to mitigate the effects of the economic crisis and lay the groundwork for India's future growth trajectory.

A primary area of focus during the stabilization period was the management of India's external sector and fiscal health. In the early 1990s, India was facing an acute balance of payments (BoP) crisis, with foreign exchange reserves plummeting and the country unable to meet its external payment obligations. To address this, Dr. Singh's government devalued the rupee, which helped make Indian exports more competitive and reduced the country's trade deficit. The rupee's depreciation, however, had both positive and negative consequences: while it boosted exports, it also made imports more expensive, leading to inflationary pressures. Alongside the devaluation of the rupee, the government took decisive steps to stabilize the fiscal situation. The introduction of fiscal reforms sought to reduce India's fiscal deficit, which had reached unsustainable levels.

Public sector enterprises were identified for privatization and divestment, and subsidies were rationalized in an effort to reduce government spending. These measures were difficult politically, given the strong resistance from labour unions and other political factions, but they were crucial in restoring confidence in India's economic management. Over the following years, fiscal deficits were brought down, and India regained the trust of international investors and credit agencies, contributing to more stable macroeconomic conditions. Alongside fiscal reforms, India's monetary policy underwent significant changes to ensure stability. The Reserve Bank of India (RBI) played a key role in managing inflation and exchange rate stability. Interest rates were adjusted to balance inflationary pressures and encourage investment, while also controlling excessive credit growth.

The central bank's role in managing liquidity became increasingly important as India opened up its markets to foreign investment and capital flows. Inflation, which had been a persistent issue in the years before 1991, was brought under control during the stabilization phase. Measures to reduce fiscal deficits, along with the government's efforts to encourage private sector participation in various industries, helped stabilize price levels. Despite challenges, such as fluctuations in international oil prices and the volatility in global financial markets, the Indian economy emerged from the 1991 crisis with greater resilience. The post-1991 stabilization period also focused on deepening India's integration with the global economy. Trade liberalization measures introduced earlier, such as the reduction in import tariffs and the removal of quantitative restrictions, were complemented by efforts to improve the ease of doing business in India.

To attract foreign investment, particularly in the manufacturing and services sectors, India implemented investor-friendly policies, relaxed restrictions on foreign direct investment (FDI), and provided incentives for joint ventures with international companies. India's foreign exchange reserves began to grow as a result of increased foreign investment and export growth, enabling the government to manage external shocks more effectively. By the mid-1990s, India had built a more diversified economy with strong sectors in technology, services, and manufacturing. These reforms not only helped stabilize the economy but also set the stage for India's economic growth over the next two decades. While the liberalization policies focused on industry and services, the agriculture sector was also an important area for stabilization. The 1991 reforms emphasized the need to address the inefficiencies within agriculture, which had long been a stagnant sector despite its crucial role in India's economy.

Agricultural reforms sought to improve productivity, ease regulatory burdens, and encourage private sector participation in agriculture, which was critical for reducing rural poverty. In addition, structural reforms within India's industrial sector played a crucial role in post-1991 stabilization. The dismantling of the Licence Raj allowed for private sector investment to flourish in industries that had previously been dominated by state-owned enterprises. The government also focused on improving infrastructure, which was critical to boosting industrial output. Efforts to improve the power, transport, and telecommunications sectors were instrumental in creating a conducive environment for business growth, particularly in urban areas. One of the most significant aspects of post-1991 stabilization was the rapid growth of India's information technology (IT) sector.

The liberalization of trade, along with the removal of restrictions on foreign investments and services, played a key role in making India an attractive destination for global outsourcing and software development. India's software and IT services industry became one of the fastest-growing sectors in the country, propelling India onto the global stage as a leader in information technology services. This not only boosted India's economic growth but also created millions of jobs, particularly for skilled workers in urban areas. The emphasis on education and human capital development during the post-1991 period helped India build a competitive edge in global markets. The rise of India's IT and services sector also encouraged a shift in the economic structure, with services accounting for a growing share of the GDP.

Social and Institutional Reforms: While economic stabilization focused largely on market reforms, it was also crucial to ensure that the benefits of growth were more broadly distributed across society. India faced significant challenges in terms of poverty, unemployment, and inequality, particularly in rural areas. Dr. Singh's policies emphasized the need for inclusive development, recognizing that economic reforms had to be accompanied by social and institutional changes. Post-1991, the Indian government worked on implementing targeted welfare programmes to address poverty and improve social indicators such as literacy, health, and employment. Schemes such as the National Rural Employment Guarantee Act (NREGA), which provided employment opportunities for rural households, aimed to provide a social safety net for those who were left behind by the broader economic transformation.

These programmes were crucial in balancing the economic liberalization with social equity. Despite the successes of the post-1991 stabilization period, the reforms were not without challenges. The liberalization process led to increased inequality, as the benefits of growth were not evenly distributed. While urban areas and the services sector boomed, rural areas and traditional sectors like agriculture faced challenges. There was also criticism of the pace and depth of the reforms, as some segments of society, particularly the agrarian sector and small industries, felt left behind by the broader market-oriented policies. Moreover, India's infrastructure continued to face significant bottlenecks, despite improvements in some sectors. The lack of adequate infrastructure in transportation, energy, and urban services remained a challenge for sustained growth. The government's capacity to implement and manage the reforms effectively also came under scrutiny, with some reforms perceived as incomplete or inadequately executed.

Post-1991 economic stabilization, led by Dr. Manmohan Singh, was critical in consolidating the gains of liberalization and fostering long-term economic growth. The reforms initiated during this period helped India move from a state-dominated, inward-looking economy to a more outward-facing, market-driven economy. This transformation not only stabilized the country's macroeconomic environment but also set the stage for India's emergence as one of the world's fastest-growing economies in the subsequent decades. Although the period was not without challenges, it laid the foundations for India's rise as a global economic power in the twenty-first century.

▪ Macroeconomic Recovery

The macroeconomic recovery that followed the 1991 economic reforms in India marked a turning point in the country's economic history. At the time, India faced a severe balance of payments crisis, characterized by dwindling foreign exchange reserves and a rapidly deteriorating fiscal situation. However, through a combination of liberalization policies, structural reforms, and external assistance, the country was able to stabilize its economy and embark on a path of sustained economic growth.

Growth in GDP

One of the most notable achievements of India's macroeconomic recovery was the substantial growth in its Gross Domestic Product (GDP). Prior to the 1991 reforms, India's economic growth had been sluggish, with average GDP growth rates hovering around 3.5 per cent per year during the 1980s, often referred to as the "Hindu rate of growth". The economy was burdened by state control, inefficiency, and a lack of competition. However, with the liberalization of markets, industrial de-licencing, and the opening up of the economy to foreign investments, the country witnessed a marked acceleration in growth. Post-reform, India's GDP growth surged. Between 1991 and 2000, India experienced an average annual growth rate of about 6 per cent, and by the mid-2000s, this figure had risen to nearly 8 per cent. The reforms unleashed new potential in the Indian economy, particularly in sectors such as IT, telecommunications, and services, which became major drivers of GDP growth. The country's transition to a market economy stimulated entrepreneurship, encouraged foreign direct investment (FDI), and led to the development of a more competitive industrial base. Economic diversification also played a critical role, as the economy moved away from the over-reliance on agriculture and state-owned industries. India's embrace of globalization brought with it access to foreign markets and new technologies, further driving its economic growth.

Table 5.1: Comparison of Global and Indian GDP Recovery Rates

Year	Global GDP Growth Rate (%)	India GDP Growth Rate (%)
2009	-0.1	8.5
2010	5.4	10.3
2011	3.9	6.6

Foreign Exchange Reserves

Another major aspect of India's macroeconomic recovery was the substantial improvement in the country's foreign exchange reserves. In 1991, India was on the brink of default, with only about $1 billion in foreign exchange reserves, which was barely enough to cover three weeks' worth of imports. The balance of payments crisis and the resulting external debt posed a severe threat to the country's ability to meet its international obligations and import essential goods like oil and raw materials. However, the introduction of reforms, coupled with an influx of FDI, foreign portfolio investments, and external assistance from institutions like the IMF and the World Bank, rapidly stabilized India's financial position.

India's foreign exchange reserves increased dramatically over the next few years. By the mid-1990s, India's foreign exchange reserves had grown to approximately $20 billion, and by the early 2000s, the figure had surpassed $50 billion. The growth in foreign exchange reserves helped boost investor confidence in the Indian economy. It also provided the government with the economic buffer needed to withstand external shocks, such as fluctuations in global oil prices. Additionally, the increase in reserves gave India greater flexibility in monetary policy and allowed the Reserve Bank of India (RBI) to strengthen the Indian rupee and manage inflation more effectively.

Impact of Reforms on Growth

The reforms that contributed to this macroeconomic recovery were multifaceted. Key changes included the liberalization of the economy, which reduced barriers to trade, and the privatization of state-owned enterprises, which improved efficiency and productivity. The opening of India's markets to foreign competition encouraged Indian industries to become more competitive and globally integrated. Furthermore, the reduction of tariffs and deregulation of the industrial sector allowed businesses to operate with more freedom and access to international markets. In particular, the IT sector experienced exponential growth as a result of these reforms. Policies such as the establishment of Software Technology Parks of India (STPI) and the introduction of tax incentives for IT companies allowed India to become a global hub for software development and services. This sector alone played a crucial role in propelling India's GDP growth during the post-reform period, contributing billions of dollars in export revenues and creating millions of jobs.

The services sector, which was underdeveloped prior to 1991, also became a significant contributor to India's GDP growth. Industries like telecommunications, banking, and financial services flourished, thanks in part to foreign investments and the liberalization of regulations governing these sectors. Additionally, reforms in agriculture and trade policies helped improve the efficiency of India's agricultural sector, contributing to higher productivity and more robust economic output. The macroeconomic recovery that India experienced after the 1991 reforms was a result of several factors working in tandem. The most visible outcomes of the recovery were the growth in GDP and the substantial increase in foreign exchange reserves. These developments laid the foundation for a new era of economic expansion, turning India into one of the world's fastest-growing economies. While challenges remained, particularly in terms of inequality and infrastructure development, the overall success of the reforms was undeniable.

India's improved economic standing on the global stage was a direct outcome of the bold decisions made in the early 1990s, reshaping the trajectory of the country's economic future.

■ Banking Reforms

The banking reforms initiated in India in the early 1990s were a critical component of the broader economic liberalization process. These reforms aimed to modernize and strengthen the financial system, making it more competitive, efficient, and responsive to the needs of a rapidly growing economy. The financial sector, particularly banking, was a significant area of focus because it was plagued by inefficiencies, poor governance, and an outdated infrastructure that had long hindered economic progress. The reforms addressed these issues, leading to a series of significant changes in the banking landscape.

Expansion and Modernization of the Banking Sector

Before the 1991 reforms, the Indian banking system was characterized by state control, a lack of competition, and heavy regulation. The public sector banks had a monopoly, and most of them were not able to effectively meet the needs of the emerging market economy. The banks were burdened with high levels of non-performing assets (NPAs), and the financial infrastructure was not well-developed to support the rapid expansion of the economy. In response, the government introduced reforms aimed at modernizing the financial sector by bringing in more competition and improving the management and efficiency of banks. A major initiative in the reform process was the liberalization of interest rates.

Prior to 1991, the government regulated the interest rates that banks could offer on deposits and loans, leading to inefficiencies and misallocation of capital. Under the new regime, interest rates were deregulated, allowing banks to set rates according to market conditions. This liberalization spurred greater competition among banks, incentivized them to become more efficient, and attracted more private investment into the sector. The liberalization of interest rates helped create a more dynamic financial market, with more competitive lending rates and improved returns on savings for consumers. The privatization of the banking sector was another crucial element of the reforms. The government introduced policies that allowed private players to enter the banking industry, breaking the monopoly of state-owned banks. The entry of private and foreign banks introduced modern banking practices, better customer service, and a wider array of financial products.

These changes significantly transformed the banking landscape, leading to the rise of well-managed, customer-centric private banks that were able to offer competitive products and services. The introduction of private sector banks increased the overall efficiency of the banking system by introducing competition, modern technology, and better management practices. Private banks such as ICICI Bank, HDFC Bank, and Axis Bank became leaders in innovation, offering a range of services such as retail banking, corporate banking, and wealth management. The presence of foreign banks, such as Standard Chartered and Citibank, further increased competition and introduced global best practices. Another key reform in the banking sector was the restructuring of public sector banks. The government undertook a series of measures to improve the financial health of these banks by injecting capital, reducing their non-performing assets, and improving their management practices. A key part of this was the introduction of prudential norms by the RBI, which required banks to maintain minimum capital reserves and implement stringent risk management practices. The reforms also aimed at making public sector banks more autonomous and professional, enabling them to compete more effectively in a liberalized economy.

Technological Advancements in Banking

A major thrust of the reforms was the adoption of technology to modernize the banking infrastructure. The introduction of computerization in banks was one of the most transformative changes in the banking sector. Prior to the reforms, banking operations were largely manual, and transactions were slow and inefficient. The introduction of computerized systems allowed banks to process transactions more quickly, reduce errors, and offer a wider range of services to customers. This shift not only improved operational efficiency but also allowed banks to offer innovative products such as ATM services, electronic funds transfer, and Internet banking. The advent of ATMs allowed customers to access their bank accounts 24/7, making banking more convenient and accessible. This was particularly significant in a country as large as India, where physical bank branches were often scarce in rural areas. ATMs allowed people in remote regions to access their accounts, withdraw cash, and even conduct other transactions without needing to visit a branch. Internet banking and mobile banking further revolutionized the banking experience in India. These technologies allowed customers to perform banking transactions online, transferring money, paying bills, and accessing other services from the comfort of their homes or offices. As the use of smartphones grew, mobile banking became a powerful tool for financial inclusion, allowing millions of Indians to access banking services who were previously excluded from the formal banking system.

Strengthening Regulatory Frameworks

One of the cornerstones of the banking reforms was the strengthening of the regulatory framework under the RBI. The RBI introduced a series of measures to bring Indian banks in line with international standards of financial management, risk assessment, and transparency. These included the introduction of Basel norms for capital adequacy, which required banks to maintain a minimum ratio of capital to risk-weighted assets. This was aimed at ensuring that banks had enough capital to absorb losses and protect depositors' funds in case of financial shocks. The RBI also introduced measures to reduce NPAs, which were a major issue for Indian banks, especially public sector banks. The central bank required banks to implement asset classification systems and set aside specific provisions for bad loans. In addition, the RBI's stricter loan recovery mechanisms helped banks recover dues from defaulters, thereby improving the overall health of the financial system.

Deepening Financial Inclusion

An essential goal of the banking reforms was to deepen financial inclusion by making banking services accessible to a larger portion of the population, especially in rural areas. Before the reforms, a significant portion of the Indian population remained unbanked and had limited access to financial services. The liberalization of the banking sector allowed for the establishment of new branches, especially in remote areas, and the creation of more financial products tailored to the needs of underserved populations. Banks were also incentivized to extend microfinance and small loans to low-income families, thereby promoting financial inclusion. The introduction of Pradhan Mantri Jan Dhan Yojana (PMJDY) in 2014, long after the initial reforms, was another milestone in India's financial inclusion journey.

This initiative aimed at providing bank accounts to every Indian household, with a focus on rural areas, helping millions of people who had previously been excluded from the banking system. The success of this programme demonstrated the lasting impact of the banking reforms initiated in the 1990s, which laid the groundwork for these efforts. The banking reforms of the early 1990s were a critical part of India's economic liberalization process. They not only modernized the banking sector but also helped foster economic growth by improving the efficiency of the financial system. These reforms made banks more competitive, technologically advanced, and financially stable, while also improving accessibility for a larger section of the population.

The liberalization of interest rates, introduction of private sector banks, adoption of new technologies, and strengthening of regulatory frameworks laid the foundation for India's robust financial sector today. These changes not only facilitated the growth of businesses and industries but also played a key role in transforming India into one of the fastest-growing economies in the world. The banking reforms are one of the most enduring legacies of India's economic liberalization, contributing significantly to the country's economic success in the years that followed.

■ Impact on Industries

The economic reforms of the early 1990s had a transformative effect on various sectors of the Indian economy, with industry being one of the most significantly impacted areas. Prior to the reforms, India's industrial sector was marked by inefficiencies, stagnation, and limited growth due to a heavily regulated environment that restricted competition, innovation, and investment. The liberalization policies of 1991 sought to revitalize India's industrial base, promote export growth, and foster competition, both domestically and internationally.

Industrial Growth Post-Liberalization

The liberalization reforms initiated in 1991 drastically altered the landscape of Indian industries. Prior to this period, industrial growth was heavily constrained by Licence Raj—a system of licencing and bureaucratic control that limited the ability of businesses to expand, innovate, or diversify. With the dismantling of the licencing system and the reduction of trade barriers, industries in India found themselves operating in a much more dynamic environment. The policy changes allowed for greater freedom of operation, encouraging both domestic and international investment in the country's industrial sectors. The most immediate effect of the reforms was the increased competition in Indian industries.

Domestic industries were now exposed to the global market, and many businesses had to improve their productivity, quality, and efficiency to survive. This competition led to the modernization of many industries, as companies embraced new technologies and improved production techniques. Many firms, particularly in the automotive, electronics, and consumer goods sectors, invested heavily in upgrading their manufacturing processes and adopting world-class standards of quality control and production efficiency. One of the key sectors that benefited from the reforms was the automobile industry. In the years following liberalization, the Indian automobile sector saw a dramatic transformation, driven by both foreign investment and the entry of global players into the Indian market.

Major global automakers like Toyota, Honda, and Ford set up manufacturing plants in India, while Indian companies like Maruti Suzuki and Tata Motors expanded and modernized their operations to meet global standards. The opening up of the sector allowed India to become one of the largest producers of automobiles in the world, while also generating millions of jobs in manufacturing and ancillary industries. The consumer goods sector also experienced significant growth after liberalization. Companies in sectors like electronics, home appliances, and telecommunications saw a boom in demand due to increased disposable income, improved access to credit, and the influx of foreign brands. The mobile phone industry, for instance, witnessed explosive growth with the arrival of global players like Nokia and Samsung, which introduced affordable, high-quality products that were well-suited to the Indian market. The domestic industry also flourished, with companies like Bharti Airtel and Reliance Communications transforming the telecommunications landscape.

Impact on Exports

In addition to boosting industrial growth, the 1991 reforms were crucial in promoting exports and integrating India into the global trading system. Before the reforms, India's export sector was heavily restricted by protectionist policies, including high tariffs, quotas, and foreign exchange controls. These policies limited India's access to international markets and reduced the competitiveness of Indian products abroad. The liberalization measures, including the removal of trade barriers, devaluation of the rupee, and the introduction of export incentives, had a profound impact on India's export sector. The devaluation of the rupee, in particular, made Indian goods cheaper and more competitive in international markets, which led to a significant increase in the volume of exports.

Indian industries, particularly those in manufacturing, textiles, pharmaceuticals, and software services, found new opportunities in global markets. The pharmaceutical sector was one of the most successful beneficiaries of these export-driven reforms. India's generic drug industry became a global leader, providing affordable medications to markets in Africa, Latin America, and Europe. The removal of restrictions on FDI in the sector allowed global pharmaceutical giants to collaborate with Indian firms, driving innovation and the expansion of the industry. Similarly, the textile and garment industries experienced a boost, with India becoming one of the leading exporters of textiles and garments to the United States and the European Union.

The country's competitive advantage in labour costs, combined with the government's export promotion policies, helped the textile industry grow rapidly, leading to significant increases in both production and employment. India's software and IT services sectors also saw phenomenal growth in the post-reform era. The liberalization policies, particularly the focus on technology and information technology-enabled services (ITES), paved the way for India to become a global hub for outsourcing and software development. Indian firms like Infosys, Tata Consultancy Services (TCS), and Wipro expanded their operations globally, providing services to multinational companies and gaining a significant share of the international market for IT and business process outsourcing (BPO) services. This sector, in turn, became a major contributor to India's export earnings, as IT exports grew exponentially over the next few decades.

Foreign Direct Investment (FDI) and Industrial Growth

The liberalization reforms were also pivotal in attracting FDI into India. The opening up of key sectors like automobiles, telecommunications, retail, and finance allowed multinational corporations to establish operations in India. FDI played a crucial role in driving industrial growth by providing much-needed capital, technology, and management expertise to domestic industries. The entry of global companies brought with it not only investment but also opportunities for joint ventures and collaborations, which helped Indian industries modernize and become more competitive on the global stage. The automotive sector, for example, attracted significant FDI, which helped establish India as a major manufacturing hub for global automotive giants. Similarly, the electronics industry witnessed a surge in foreign investment, with companies like Samsung and Sony setting up manufacturing facilities in India to take advantage of its cost-effective labour force.

Policy Reforms to Promote Exports

To encourage export growth, the Indian government introduced a series of measures aimed at reducing the costs and barriers to international trade. Key reforms included the introduction of special export zones, such as Export Processing Zones (EPZs) and Special Economic Zones (SEZs), which provided tax exemptions, infrastructure support, and regulatory incentives to companies engaged in export activities. These zones became important centres for manufacturing and export, providing a competitive edge to industries such as textiles, electronics, and automobiles.

The government also introduced export credit schemes to provide financing to exporters, helping them manage risks associated with international trade. Additionally, the Development Commissioner's Office played a vital role in assisting exporters with information and resources related to global markets, trade regulations, and financing. The industrial reforms and export promotion policies of the early 1990s were crucial in shaping India's modern industrial and economic landscape. The removal of restrictive controls, the liberalization of trade, and the opening up of markets to global competition revitalized India's industrial sector, leading to significant growth in key industries such as automobiles, textiles, pharmaceuticals, and IT.

The surge in exports, fuelled by a combination of policy incentives and increased global demand, transformed India into an important player in international trade. These reforms not only helped India become more competitive globally but also laid the foundation for a more diverse and dynamic industrial sector. The increased industrial output and export growth created millions of jobs, fuelled innovation, and facilitated the integration of India into the global economy. The legacy of these reforms continues to shape India's industrial development, as the country continues to experience robust economic growth and plays an increasingly important role in the global marketplace.

• Foreign Investment Boom

The Foreign Investment Boom in India post-1991 represents a pivotal moment in the country's economic history. Prior to the liberalization of the Indian economy, foreign investment was minimal due to strict controls, high tariffs, and a policy environment that was not conducive to the free flow of capital. However, with the reforms introduced in the early 1990s, India began to emerge as a preferred destination for foreign investment, dramatically transforming its economic landscape.

The Context for Foreign Investment

Before the 1991 economic reforms, India was largely closed to foreign investment. The country's policy was focused on import substitution and protectionism, where the government shielded domestic industries from foreign competition. The restrictions were rooted in concerns over national sovereignty, as well as a desire to promote indigenous industries. However, this approach led to economic stagnation, inefficiency, and a reliance on imports for many goods, including capital and technology. India's economic balance of payments crisis in 1991, which was triggered by a combination of rising fiscal deficits, low foreign exchange reserves, and a large current account deficit, marked the turning point.

In response to the crisis, the Indian government, led by Finance Minister Dr. Manmohan Singh, shifted its economic policy to liberalization, privatization, and globalization, opening the country's doors to foreign investment.

The Key Drivers of Foreign Investment

The reforms implemented in 1991 were designed to liberalize the economy and promote a market-oriented approach, and they included a range of measures that made India more attractive to foreign investors. These included the removal of restrictions on FDI, the devaluation of the rupee, the reduction of tariffs and trade barriers, and the privatization of state-owned enterprises. These moves signalled a major departure from the previous economic model, encouraging foreign investors to see India as a growing, competitive, and promising market. A central aspect of the reforms was the introduction of a simplified FDI policy, which allowed greater foreign ownership in Indian businesses, particularly in sectors such as automobiles, telecommunications, retail, and information technology.

Previously, foreign companies were limited in the extent of their ownership in Indian ventures, but the new policies opened up various sectors to greater foreign participation. Additionally, foreign investors were offered incentives such as tax breaks, investment guarantees, and export-oriented incentives. The Indian government also undertook major efforts to enhance the ease of doing business in the country, implementing legal and regulatory reforms that streamlined business procedures. The establishment of SEZs, with tax exemptions and infrastructure support, further encouraged both domestic and foreign companies to invest in manufacturing and export activities. The privatization of state-owned enterprises was another critical move in attracting foreign investment. As industries were privatized, foreign investors had the opportunity to acquire stakes in profitable businesses, particularly in the energy, mining, and telecommunications sectors. This not only brought in fresh capital but also helped to improve efficiency and competitiveness within these industries.

India as a Preferred Destination for Foreign Investors

The combination of these factors made India an increasingly attractive destination for foreign investment. A key factor was India's vast consumer market, which was expanding rapidly as the middle class grew. The removal of trade barriers and the opening up of India's economy meant that foreign companies could now tap into this enormous market.

In particular, global companies in sectors like automobiles, consumer electronics, retail, and IT saw India as an ideal location to expand their operations and supply chains. India's young, educated, and relatively low-cost labour force also made it an attractive place for companies looking to establish production and manufacturing bases. Many multinational companies, particularly in electronics, textiles, and automotive manufacturing, were drawn to India due to its cost competitiveness and availability of skilled labour. This was especially true for sectors that involved low-margin, high-volume production, where India's labour costs were significantly lower than those in developed countries. The Indian government also began fostering close economic ties with other countries and international institutions, further enhancing India's reputation as a favourable destination for foreign investment. India's growing trade relations with countries such as the United States, Japan, South Korea, and members of the European Union attracted more investment and business partnerships. The Indian economy's integration into global supply chains and its growing influence in regional trade forums also served as a powerful signal to foreign investors that India was a safe and profitable place to invest.

Sectors that Benefited Most

Several sectors saw a significant influx of foreign investment, which played a critical role in their growth and modernization. The automobile sector was one of the largest beneficiaries of foreign investment, with global automobile giants like Honda, Ford, General Motors, and Hyundai establishing manufacturing plants in India. This brought not only capital but also cutting-edge technology and management practices, enabling India to become one of the world's largest automobile producers. The information technology (IT) and business process outsourcing (BPO) industries experienced exponential growth as well.

India became a global hub for IT services, with companies like Infosys, Wipro, and Tata Consultancy Services (TCS) benefiting from foreign investment in both the form of capital and market access. The IT sector attracted foreign venture capital and partnerships with global firms, and Indian IT companies expanded their operations worldwide, becoming leaders in the global outsourcing market. The telecommunications sector also saw significant foreign investment following liberalization. International telecom giants such as Vodafone, AT&T, and Orange entered the Indian market, leading to greater competition, improved services, and reduced costs for consumers.

India's rapid mobile phone penetration, aided by the entry of these multinational firms, helped fuel the country's growth into one of the world's largest mobile markets. The retail sector also experienced a boom, particularly with the entry of global retail chains like Wal-Mart, Carrefour, and IKEA, who set up large-scale operations in India to capitalize on its burgeoning consumer market. Although the Indian retail sector remained heavily regulated for a period, the gradual relaxation of restrictions paved the way for these companies to invest in the country.

Impact on India's Economic Growth

Foreign investment played a significant role in driving India's economic growth in the post-liberalization period. As foreign companies brought in capital, technology, and expertise, they helped India's industrial sector modernize and become more competitive on the global stage. The inflow of FDI contributed to the creation of new jobs, increased exports, and enhanced industrial productivity. Moreover, the growth in foreign investment helped in improving India's foreign exchange reserves and balance of payments, as the country became a significant beneficiary of global capital flows. The increase in exports, driven by both domestic industries and foreign companies, further bolstered the country's economic standing, turning India into a net exporter and enhancing its credit rating.

The Foreign Investment Boom in India following the 1991 economic reforms was one of the most important drivers of the country's economic transformation. By liberalizing the economy and opening up to global markets, India became a preferred destination for foreign investors, who recognized the potential of the Indian market, its growing consumer base, and its competitive labour force. Foreign investment led to the growth and modernization of key sectors like automobiles, IT, telecommunications, and retail, contributing significantly to India's overall economic growth. As a result, foreign investment not only played a critical role in accelerating India's industrial and technological progress but also positioned the country as a key player in the global economy. The policies of liberalization and globalization laid the foundation for India to become one of the world's largest and fastest-growing economies, and foreign investment remains a cornerstone of this ongoing success.

REFERENCES

Arenstein, S. (1969). "A Ladder of Citizen Participation." *Journal of the American Institute of Planners, 35*(4): 216-224.

Asia Europe Network of Urban Heritage for Sustainable Creative Economies. (2015). *Understanding Creative Economies.* New Delhi: Indian National Trust for Art and Cultural Heritage (INTACH).

Beebe, J. (1995). "Basic Concepts and Techniques of Rapid Appraisal." *Human Organisation, 54*: 42-51.

Chan, P.Y. (2016). *Community Participation in Heritage Management: A Case in Macau.* Columbia: Graduate School of Architecture, Planning and Preservation, Columbia University.

Council of Europe (2005). *Council of Europe Framework Convention on the Value of Cultural Heritage for Society.* Faro.

Girard, T.B. (2011). *Heritage in Socio-economic Development: Direct and Indirect Impact.* Paris: ICOMOS-International Council on Monuments and Sites.

Greffe, X. (2012). *Getting into Business.* Oslo: Norwegian Institute of Cultural Research.

Lindblom, I. & Paludan-Müller, C. (2012). *Harnessing the Hidden Potential of Cities.* Oslo: The Norwegian Institute for Cultural Heritage Research.

INTACH (2012). Achieving economic and environmental goals through heritage preservation initiatives: Pondicherry experience, *Asia Urbs Programme*: 2002-2004. Puducherry: INTACH Pondicherry.

Krishna, A. (2012). "The Business of Heritage." *Journal of the Development and Research Organisation for Nature, Arts and Heritage*, 9(2): 13-21.

6

Architect of India's IT Revolution

Dr. Manmohan Singh, as the architect of India's information technology (IT) revolution, played a pivotal role in transforming the country's economic landscape by leveraging the potential of the IT sector. At the time of India's economic liberalization in the early 1990s, India's IT industry was in its infancy, but under Dr. Singh's guidance, it grew into a global powerhouse. His vision was instrumental in positioning India as a major player in the global IT services market, driving both economic growth and social development. The foundation for this transformation was laid through a series of policy reforms that sought to modernize the country's infrastructure, streamline regulations, and foster an environment conducive to the growth of the IT sector.

One of the first key steps was the establishment of the Software Technology Parks of India (STPIs) in 1991, a vital move that provided IT companies with the necessary resources, including uninterrupted power supply, world-class communication infrastructure, and tax incentives. This initiative ensured that Indian companies could compete on a global scale and attracted numerous international firms to establish operations in India. Furthermore, Dr. Singh recognized the need to create a robust legal and regulatory framework to protect digital commerce and intellectual property. The Information Technology Act of 2000 was a significant milestone in this regard, providing a legal foundation for electronic transactions, digital signatures, and online business activities.

Additionally, the liberalization of India's telecommunications sector under Dr. Singh's leadership played a crucial role in expanding access to the Internet and reducing communication costs, making it easier for IT firms to expand their global presence. Alongside these infrastructural and regulatory reforms, Dr. Singh's government also focused on improving the country's educational framework, particularly in technical disciplines. Recognizing the immense potential of India's large, English-speaking, and educated workforce, the government promoted the expansion of technical education to meet the growing demand for IT professionals. This emphasis on skills development created a highly-trained workforce that was central to the success of India's IT sector.

Moreover, the strategic shift towards embracing globalization and opening the economy to foreign direct investment (FDI) allowed India to attract global IT companies, which in turn boosted India's stature in the global economy. Dr. Singh's policies not only helped create a thriving IT ecosystem within India but also led to the emergence of several Indian IT giants such as Infosys, Wipro, and Tata Consultancy Services (TCS), which became globally recognized brands. These companies went on to provide high-quality IT services to clients worldwide, generating significant revenue and providing millions of jobs in the process. The IT sector's growth also had a cascading effect on other sectors of the economy, further contributing to India's rise as an economic power.

The successful integration of India into the global IT industry helped the country weather economic recessions, such as the 2008 global financial crisis, and emerge as one of the fastest-growing economies in the world. In conclusion, Dr. Manmohan Singh's leadership and vision were instrumental in transforming India into a global IT leader. His focus on building the right infrastructure, fostering a competitive regulatory environment, and empowering the nation's youth with skills made India an attractive destination for global IT investment and outsourcing. The lasting impact of these policies continues to shape India's economic growth and its position in the global digital economy today.

▪ Early Recognition of IT Potential

Dr. Manmohan Singh's role in shaping India's economic landscape also extended to the early recognition of the potential of IT, which would later become one of the cornerstones of India's economic growth. In the early 1990s, as the country was undergoing economic liberalization, Dr. Singh understood that the IT sector could be a major driver of growth, innovation, and job creation. He was one of the key figures behind India's efforts to establish itself as a global leader in IT services. His policies and initiatives paved the way for India's transformation into an IT powerhouse, and the decisions made during this time have had long-lasting effects on the global tech industry.

Key Policies and Initiatives for IT Development

1. National Policy on Software and Information Technology (1998)

A significant policy initiative was the formulation of the National Policy on Software and Information Technology in 1998. This policy aimed to foster a favourable environment for IT growth in India. The key elements of this policy were:

- **Promotion of IT Exports**: The policy encouraged software exports by offering a range of tax incentives to IT companies. One of the key incentives was the establishment of STPIs, which offered duty-free imports of equipment, tax exemptions on exports, and other business-friendly provisions. This provided a substantial boost to the IT export sector.

- **Creation of an IT Infrastructure**: The policy also focused on building the necessary infrastructure for IT development, including telecommunication networks and Internet connectivity, which were essential for the development of the software industry. Improved infrastructure helped create an environment conducive to the growth of IT businesses.
- **Development of Human Capital**: Recognizing that skilled manpower was the key to success in the IT industry, the government-initiated efforts to develop a workforce capable of meeting the demands of the global IT market. This led to an increase in educational programmes focused on software engineering, computer science, and IT in both public and private institutions across India.

2. Information Technology Act, 2000

Another key policy initiative that supported India's IT growth was the Information Technology Act of 2000. This legislation was a landmark step toward establishing the legal and regulatory framework necessary for the digital economy in India. The Act laid down the foundation for electronic commerce, digital signatures, and the legal recognition of electronic records. This move was crucial in making India's IT infrastructure more reliable and trustworthy for both domestic and international investors. By setting up the legal and regulatory framework for e-commerce, the law helped attract global IT companies to establish operations in India. It also allowed Indian IT companies to engage in secure online transactions and business dealings, which were important for the growth of India's IT services industry.

3. Privatization and Liberalization of the Telecommunications Sector

The liberalization of the telecommunications sector was another key initiative that Dr. Singh championed during his tenure as finance minister. The policy aimed to increase competition, reduce prices, and improve the quality of telecommunication services across India.

As part of these reforms, the government allowed private players to enter the market, thereby enhancing infrastructure and reducing the cost of communication. The expansion of telecommunications was essential for the growth of the IT industry, as it provided the foundation for Internet connectivity, data transfer, and global communications. Improved telecom infrastructure helped Indian IT companies offer services to global clients, and the affordable, high-quality communication networks that emerged as a result of this liberalization were key enablers of India's outsourcing boom.

4. Promotion of Software Exports

Dr. Singh's economic vision for India involved tapping into the global demand for software development and IT services. Recognizing the growing trend of outsourcing and the need for cost-effective IT solutions, the Indian government launched a range of incentives to support IT exports. These included:

- **Tax Exemptions for IT Exporters**: One of the primary incentives for the export of software was the tax exemption granted to IT exporters under the STP scheme, which provided a 100 per cent exemption on profits for IT firms that focused on exports. This allowed Indian companies to become highly competitive in the global IT outsourcing market.
- **Promotion of Export-Oriented IT Hubs**: India witnessed the development of several IT hubs in cities like Bangalore, Hyderabad, Chennai, and Pune, which attracted significant foreign investment. These cities became global centres for software development, programming, and business process outsourcing (BPO), contributing massively to India's IT export growth.

5. Establishment of Software Technology Parks of India (STPI)

A key initiative to promote IT growth was the establishment of

STPIs. These parks were set up in different parts of India to create specialized zones for software development. The STPI policy allowed companies to avail themselves of tax benefits, duty-free imports, and modern infrastructure, which made these parks highly attractive to both Indian and foreign software firms.

The STPI model was designed to create a business-friendly environment by providing state-of-the-art infrastructure for IT companies and offering them the ability to export software without facing the typical regulatory and bureaucratic hurdles. This policy led to the rapid growth of India's IT services sector and helped transform cities like Bangalore into global IT hubs.

6. Fostering International Partnerships

Dr. Singh also recognized the importance of international collaboration in furthering India's IT growth. During the 1990s, India started to build strategic partnerships with countries like the United States and European Union to attract investments, foster technological exchanges, and integrate Indian firms into global supply chains. This global integration played a significant role in establishing India's competitive advantage in the IT sector. As part of India's efforts to promote the IT industry, government leaders and policymakers engaged with international investors and multinational corporations, positioning India as a leading player in the global outsourcing industry. India's English-speaking workforce, lower labour costs, and growing pool of skilled professionals made it an ideal destination for international companies to outsource their IT operations.

Dr. Manmohan Singh's foresight and leadership in recognizing the potential of the IT sector in the early 1990s were instrumental in shaping India into the global IT powerhouse it is today. The key policies and initiatives that he helped implement, such as the National Policy on Software and Information Technology, the Information Technology Act of 2000, and the promotion of software exports and telecom infrastructure, laid the groundwork for the IT revolution in India. These efforts attracted significant foreign investment, created millions of high-paying jobs, and positioned India as the global leader in IT services and outsourcing. Today, the IT sector continues to be one of India's most important economic engines, contributing to its GDP, exports, and global reputation as a hub for technology and innovation. Dr. Singh's recognition of the IT sector's potential and his ability to foster an environment conducive to its growth remains one of his most significant contributions to India's economic development.

▪ Building an IT Ecosystem

Dr. Manmohan Singh's tenure as finance minister in the early 1990s marked the beginning of significant efforts to build a sustainable and competitive IT ecosystem in India.

One of the central strategies for developing this ecosystem was the establishment of the STPIs and the introduction of several regulatory reforms that provided the necessary infrastructure and business environment for the IT sector to flourish.

Software Technology Parks of India (STPIs)

The STPIs, established in 1991, became one of the cornerstones of India's efforts to promote its IT sector. The STPIs initiative was part of Dr. Singh's broader vision to create a favourable environment for software development and IT services in the country. These parks were specifically designed to encourage software exports, promote technology innovation, and attract foreign investments by providing tax incentives and creating world-class infrastructure for IT companies.

1. Establishment and Growth of STPIs

The first STPIs were set up in Bangalore and Chennai, which were quickly followed by many other cities across the country, such as Hyderabad, Pune, and Delhi. These parks were equipped with high-tech infrastructure, offering companies the necessary physical space and resources to conduct software development. The idea behind the parks was to cluster software companies together in specialized zones, providing them with access to state-of-the-art technology, and the necessary connectivity to facilitate global business. STPIs also served as export-oriented zones, allowing IT companies to focus on developing software and services for international markets. This concept helped India become an attractive destination for international IT companies seeking low-cost, high-quality software development services. The park's infrastructure was designed to meet international standards, and it provided duty-free import of equipment for software development, enabling companies to reduce costs significantly.

2. *Tax and Incentive Policies for STPIs*

The government's tax policies played a crucial role in encouraging software companies to set up their operations in the STPIs. Companies located in STPIs were granted a 100 per cent tax exemption on their export income for a period of 10 years, and they were also given duty-free imports of machinery, equipment, and software for their operations. The STPIs model was designed to offer financial incentives and business-friendly policies that made it easier for IT companies to scale their operations, both domestically and globally.

In addition to these tax incentives, the parks provided access to specialized human resources, including skilled IT professionals, and ensured that companies operating within them had access to reliable telecommunication networks and global connectivity. This made the STPIs highly attractive to both Indian and multinational companies, helping India to become one of the most significant players in the global IT outsourcing market.

3. *Promoting India's IT Export Boom*

The creation of STPIs was an essential element in India's IT export boom. With the rapid growth of companies in the software sector, many of them began focusing on exporting their products and services to the global market, particularly to the United States and European countries. India's export-oriented IT industry gained momentum with the establishment of STPIs, which allowed companies to position themselves as global service providers. The STPIs also played an essential role in creating a strong Indian software services export industry, which became one of the largest in the world. Indian IT companies, particularly in cities such as Bangalore (now Bengaluru), became integral to global supply chains, and the country quickly gained a reputation for providing high-quality, cost-effective software services.

Regulatory Reforms for IT Growth

Along with the establishment of STPIs, Dr. Singh's government took significant steps to introduce regulatory reforms that would foster the growth of India's IT sector and promote an open, competitive market for IT services. These reforms were aimed at creating an environment where technology companies could thrive, build global partnerships, and compete effectively in the world market.

1. Deregulation of Telecommunications and Internet Access

A major hurdle to the growth of the IT industry in India was the poor quality of telecommunication infrastructure and the high cost of Internet access. Dr. Singh's government focused on liberalizing telecommunications by allowing the entry of private players, which significantly improved the quality of services and reduced costs. The government also facilitated Internet connectivity by supporting the establishment of a more robust national Internet infrastructure. As Internet access became more affordable and widespread, it became easier for Indian IT companies to engage in global outsourcing and remote software development.

Improved Internet access opened the door for new business models in the e-commerce and information services sectors, helping India to become an attractive outsourcing destination.

2. Legal and Institutional Reforms

The Information Technology Act of 2000 was another significant regulatory reform that helped boost India's IT growth. This Act provided the legal framework necessary for electronic commerce, digital signatures, data protection, and the legal recognition of electronic records, making it easier for businesses to operate in the digital economy. The Act was aimed at facilitating the growth of IT businesses by offering a secure environment for online transactions and fostering confidence in the use of digital platforms for business dealings. By creating a favourable legal framework, the IT Act of 2000 helped ensure that India's IT sector could integrate into global e-commerce and digital services ecosystems.

3. Human Resource Development and Skill Building

Another significant regulatory initiative was the emphasis on human resource development for the IT industry. The government took steps to upgrade educational programmes and vocational training in the fields of software engineering and computer science, both in government universities and private institutions. This was critical to meeting the growing demand for skilled IT professionals, and it helped India to build a highly-skilled workforce capable of meeting the needs of the global IT services market. The government also supported the establishment of private IT training institutions that provided specialized courses in programming languages, software development, and systems management. By investing in human capital, India was able to ensure a steady supply of skilled IT workers for its growing software and services sector.

4. Promotion of Foreign Direct Investment (FDI)

The liberalization policies introduced by Dr. Singh's government also focused on attracting FDI into India's IT sector. By offering a favourable investment climate, India became an attractive destination for foreign companies looking to capitalize on the country's cost-effective labour, skilled workforce, and growing infrastructure. Incentives such as tax breaks, investment allowances, and regulatory exemptions encouraged global IT firms to set up operations in India, either in joint ventures or wholly owned subsidiaries. This influx of FDI played a crucial role in expanding the capacity of India's IT sector, particularly in the areas of software development and IT-enabled services.

The establishment of STPIs and the various regulatory reforms introduced during Dr. Manmohan Singh's tenure as finance minister were critical in building the robust IT ecosystem that India has today. The STPIs model, combined with tax incentives, telecommunications deregulation, and the promotion of foreign investments, provided the foundation for India's rise as a global leader in the IT industry. These policies not only facilitated India's growth as a major player in the global software services and outsourcing markets but also positioned the country as an attractive destination for foreign investment and technological innovation. With these foundational policies, India's IT sector has continued to thrive, creating millions of jobs and driving the country's economic growth in the decades that followed.

▪ India as a Global IT Leader

Dr. Manmohan Singh's economic reforms in the early 1990s laid the foundation for India to emerge as a global IT leader, particularly in the area of software services and outsourcing. The establishment of STPIs, coupled with significant regulatory reforms, set the stage for a remarkable period of growth in the IT sector. As a result, India became one of the world's leading providers of IT services, with both export growth and job creation as key drivers of this transformation.

Export Growth

One of the most notable outcomes of India's IT revolution was the explosive growth in software exports. The Indian government's pro-business policies, such as tax exemptions for export-oriented businesses and the liberalization of the telecommunications sector, enabled companies to reach global markets. As a result, India became the preferred destination for international firms seeking to outsource software development, IT support, and business process outsourcing (BPO). In the early 1990s, India's IT exports were relatively modest. However, by the late 1990s and early 2000s, India began to see an exponential rise in IT-related exports, driven largely by the global outsourcing trend. Countries, especially in North America, began outsourcing non-core functions, such as customer service, technical support, and software development, to Indian firms. This was due to India's competitive labour costs, availability of skilled manpower, and growing expertise in areas like software engineering, programming, and IT-enabled services.

By the early 2000s, India had firmly established itself as the world's outsourcing hub, with software and services exports reaching billions of dollars. Key global players like IBM, Accenture, Cisco, and Microsoft began setting up operations in India, contributing to a massive rise in India's export figures. The country's export-oriented IT industry was soon driving economic growth and enhancing its position in the global supply chain. India's IT exports spanned a range of sectors, including custom software development, systems integration, data processing, call centres, and technical support services. The success of Indian IT firms in providing high-quality and cost-effective services gave the country a distinct competitive edge in the global market. By offering solutions that were not only economically attractive but also of high quality, India became a major player in the global IT landscape. The export growth in the IT sector also had significant ripple effects on other parts of the economy. As the demand for Indian software and IT services grew, the global market for Indian IT workers also expanded. Companies from various parts of the world increasingly turned to India to fulfil their IT needs, whether it was for simple coding tasks, complex systems integration, or support services.

Job Creation

The rapid expansion of India's IT sector under Dr. Manmohan Singh's economic policies also resulted in significant job creation across the country. By promoting software exports and providing incentives for domestic IT firms to grow, the government created a conducive environment for the rise of a vibrant IT services industry. As a result, millions of high-paying jobs were generated in the sector, with India's large pool of skilled workers becoming one of the primary reasons why the country excelled in IT outsourcing. In the early stages, the IT industry was concentrated in cities like Bangalore, Hyderabad, Pune, and Chennai, which became known as technology hubs. However, as the industry grew, so did the geographic spread of IT jobs. Smaller towns and cities across India also began to see the benefits of the IT boom, with companies opening new offices and creating job opportunities for local populations. This was particularly important for regional development, as it helped generate employment outside India's traditional economic centres, contributing to the overall growth of the economy. The job creation in the IT sector was not just limited to software engineers and developers. The IT ecosystem also generated employment in a range of related areas, such as human resources, project management, technical support, sales and marketing, administrative roles, and customer service.

With the rise of BPO, a whole new industry was born, creating millions of jobs for professionals in areas like telemarketing, data entry, back-office operations, and financial services. A significant portion of the job creation was in the form of white-collar jobs, which attracted young, educated professionals from all walks of life. The booming IT sector was seen as an avenue for upward mobility, with many individuals from middle-class families able to secure high-paying jobs in this burgeoning industry. The rise of the IT sector created a new middle class in India, which had access to higher wages, better living standards, and improved social mobility. For many young Indians, the IT industry became the gateway to a better future, offering opportunities that were previously unattainable in other sectors.

The Broader Socio-economic Impact

The IT sector's rapid growth also had a profound socio-economic impact on India. With the creation of millions of jobs, there was a notable increase in consumer spending, particularly in urban areas where IT jobs were concentrated. The rise in income levels translated into higher demand for goods and services, further driving India's economic growth. The influx of foreign exchange from IT exports boosted India's foreign reserves, strengthening the country's financial position on the global stage. The IT sector also contributed significantly to tax revenues, enabling the government to invest more in infrastructure development, education, health care, and other sectors crucial for national growth.

The Indian IT industry, with its burgeoning workforce and increasing export growth, became a major contributor to India's GDP growth. By the early 2000s, the IT sector was a key driver of India's economic rise, helping the country transition from a primarily agrarian economy to a more diversified one with a growing services sector. Moreover, the job creation in the IT sector had a direct positive impact on the education system. The demand for skilled IT professionals led to the creation of numerous educational institutions, training centres, and professional courses aimed at producing qualified candidates for the industry. As the sector grew, so did the number of graduates from engineering and computer science programmes, further contributing to the expansion of India's skilled workforce.

Conclusion

India's rise as a global IT leader can be attributed to Dr. Manmohan Singh's visionary economic reforms in the early 1990s.

Through policies that promoted software exports, job creation, and a strong regulatory framework, India was able to position itself as a global hub for IT services and outsourcing. This led to the creation of millions of jobs, not just in IT but across various related sectors, transforming India's economy and shaping the global perception of the country as an emerging economic power. The growth of India's IT sector has had long-lasting effects, creating a new middle class, fostering technological innovation, and positioning India as a global economic player. Today, the country continues to be a leading provider of IT services, with companies like Infosys, Tata Consultancy Services (TCS), Wipro, and HCL at the forefront of the global IT outsourcing industry. The success of India's IT sector has not only benefited the economy but has also had a transformative impact on the social and cultural fabric of the country, offering opportunities for millions of young Indians to realize their potential in the global marketplace.

REFERENCES

Patel, S. (2012). *Culture is Produced by People*. Oslo: The Norwegian Institute for Cultural Heritage Research.

Peacock, A. T. (1998). *Does the Past have a Future?: The Political Economy of Heritage*. Virginia: Institute of Economic Affairs.

PlaceEconomics. (2011). *Measuring Economic Impacts of Heritage Conservation*. Washington, DC.

Rojas, E. (2002). *Urban Heritage Conservation in Latin America and the Caribbean: A Task for all Social Actors*. Washington, DC: Sustainable Development Department, Inter-American Development Bank.

Shahjahanabad Redevelopment Corporation (2015). Re Siravo, F. (2011). "Conservation Planning: The Road Less Travelled." *Conservation Perspective; The GCI Newsletter, 26*(2): 4-10.

The Asian Development Bank. (2008). *Revitalization of Historic Inner City Areas of Asia: The Potential for Urban Renewal in Ha Noi, Jakarta and Manila*. Philippines.

The Economic Times (2016, 10 January). "How a Haveli in Dharampura is a Perfect Example of How Delhi's History can be Restored & Saved." Retrieved on 3 March 2017, from http://economictimes.indiatimes.com/news/politics-and-nation/how-a-haveli-in-dharampura-is-a-perfect-example-of-how-delhis-history-can-be-restored-saved/articleshow/50512470.cms

The Economic Times (2016, 13 July). "Probe Committee Formed after Complaints Over Quality of Restoration at Humayun's Tomb." Retrieved on 11 September 2016, from http://economictimes.indiatimes.com/news/politics-and-nation/probe-committee-formed-after-complaints-over-quality-of-restoration-at-humayunstomb/articleshow/53182399.cms

The Getty Institute (2002). *Assessing the Value of Cultural Heritage*. Los Angeles.

7

Economic Diplomacy Under Dr. Singh

Dr. Manmohan Singh's tenure as prime minister of India from 2004 to 2014 saw a marked shift in India's approach to economic diplomacy, a realm that became one of his defining contributions to the global stage. His leadership transformed India's foreign policy into one that actively sought to expand the country's economic influence, leveraging international partnerships, and strengthening India's role in the global economic governance. Economic diplomacy under Dr. Singh was characterized by pragmatic strategies aimed at enhancing India's global economic footprint, securing favourable trade agreements, and positioning India as a key player in global economic forums.

A crucial element of Dr. Singh's economic diplomacy was his focus on multilateral engagement. Recognizing the increasing interconnectedness of global economies, he made it a priority for India to actively participate in and influence multilateral institutions such as the World Trade Organization (WTO), the International Monetary Fund (IMF), and the World Bank. Dr. Singh's government consistently advocated for reforms in these institutions to ensure they reflected the interests of developing economies like India. Under his leadership, India positioned itself as a champion of the developing world, emphasizing issues such as trade liberalization, poverty reduction, and equitable economic growth in global forums. One of the most significant milestones in Dr. Singh's economic diplomacy was India's growing involvement in the G20.

Recognizing the need for a collective response to global economic challenges, India played a vital role in shaping the global economic agenda during the 2008 financial crisis and beyond. Dr. Singh's leadership at the G20 allowed India to push for global economic reforms that aligned with the interests of emerging markets, particularly in the areas of trade, investment, and financial regulations. His pragmatic approach to economic diplomacy was evident in his call for a more inclusive global financial system, one that better accounted for the realities of developing nations. In addition to multilateral engagements, Dr. Singh's government also sought to strengthen bilateral economic ties with key global players.

The Indo-US nuclear deal, signed in 2008, was a defining achievement of Dr. Singh's economic diplomacy, as it not only strengthened strategic ties with the United States but also opened up India's access to nuclear technology and global markets. This deal was a testimony to his skill in balancing India's economic and strategic interests, aligning national growth ambitions with international relationships. Dr. Singh's approach to economic diplomacy also extended to India's growing ties with other emerging economies. His leadership played a central role in shaping the BRICS (Brazil, Russia, India, China, South Africa) coalition, which became an important platform for advocating for the interests of the global South. Through BRICS, Dr. Singh helped promote a new paradigm of economic cooperation that challenged the dominance of Western-led economic institutions and provided a voice for developing economies on the world stage.

The strengthening of India's economic diplomacy during Dr. Singh's tenure was also seen in India's active participation in regional economic groupings. Dr. Singh was a strong proponent of enhancing regional economic integration, particularly within

South Asia and with East Asia. He played an instrumental role in the formation of the South Asian Free Trade Area (SAFTA) and was deeply involved in enhancing India's economic ties with ASEAN countries. These efforts helped increase India's trade with its neighbours and contributed to a broader strategy of regional economic cooperation. Moreover, Dr. Singh understood the strategic importance of foreign direct investment (FDI) in driving India's growth. His government worked tirelessly to improve India's investment climate, implementing reforms that aimed at attracting more FDI into key sectors such as manufacturing, infrastructure, and retail.

India's economic diplomacy, under his leadership, focused not only on trade but also on creating an environment that encouraged the inflow of capital and technology, essential for India's development in the twenty-first century. Dr. Singh's economic diplomacy was also defined by his strong belief in balancing India's national interests with global opportunities. He sought to ensure that India's rising economic influence was used to benefit both the country and the global community. Under his leadership, India emerged as an advocate for inclusive economic growth, focusing on poverty alleviation, sustainable development, and social equity in its foreign economic policy. In conclusion, Dr. Manmohan Singh's economic diplomacy was a hallmark of his tenure as prime minister. His strategic vision helped shape India's global economic role, elevating the country's standing on the world stage and fostering stronger relationships with key economic partners. Through his leadership, India not only participated in but also shaped key international economic policies and institutions, ensuring that the interests of emerging economies were represented. Dr. Singh's approach to economic diplomacy laid the foundation for India's continued rise as a global economic power.

• Shaping India's Global Trade Relations

Dr. Manmohan Singh's tenure as finance minister and later as prime minister saw a concerted effort to integrate India into the global economy, and one of the key strategies was shaping India's global trade relations through bilateral and regional agreements. These agreements were pivotal in transitioning India from an insular economy focused on self-sufficiency to one that actively participated in global trade networks. His focus was to expand India's economic footprint through trade relations with regional neighbours and global economic powers. Among the most significant were agreements with Association of Southeast Asian Nations (ASEAN) and SAFTA.

Bilateral Agreements with ASEAN

India's trade relations with ASEAN became a cornerstone of its Look East Policy, a strategic effort to enhance political, economic, and cultural ties with the countries of Southeast Asia. In 1991, India formally began engaging with ASEAN countries to increase economic cooperation, and Dr. Singh played a key role in these negotiations, recognizing the importance of ASEAN as a growing economic bloc. The regional organization, comprising nations such as Indonesia, Thailand, Singapore, and Malaysia, was increasingly seen as a critical player in the global economic order, especially after the Cold War.

One of the first major steps in this regard was the India-ASEAN Trade and Investment Agreement, signed in 2003. This agreement was a milestone, laying the foundation for greater trade relations, facilitating the exchange of goods, services, and investments between India and the ASEAN countries. The agreement aimed to reduce trade barriers, lower tariffs, and foster deeper economic integration, benefiting India by opening up new markets for Indian goods and services, especially in the areas of manufacturing, IT, and pharmaceuticals. Additionally, the ASEAN-India Free Trade Area (AIFTA), established in 2010, was another significant development. Under this agreement, tariffs on a variety of goods were slashed, and trade in goods, services, and investments flourished.

India became increasingly integrated into the ASEAN supply chain, with Indian textile, automobile, and IT services companies setting up operations in Southeast Asia. This partnership not only bolstered trade volumes but also contributed to enhancing regional economic cooperation and peace. Moreover, India's participation in ASEAN-led initiatives such as the ASEAN Regional Forum and the East Asia Summit further solidified its diplomatic and economic ties with Southeast Asia, creating a strategic alignment with one of the most economically dynamic regions in the world. As Dr. Singh believed in the long-term economic benefits of strengthening such relationships, India began to look toward ASEAN not only as a trading partner but also as a vital part of its broader geopolitical and economic strategy.

SAFTA: Strengthening Trade Relations within South Asia

While India's external economic relations with ASEAN were of strategic importance, Dr. Singh also sought to strengthen trade ties within the South Asian region through the establishment of the SAFTA. Signed in 2004, SAFTA aimed to create a free trade area within South Asian Association for Regional Cooperation (SAARC), which included Afghanistan, Bangladesh, Bhutan, India, Maldives, Nepal, Pakistan, and Sri Lanka. The goal of SAFTA was to reduce tariffs and promote trade within the region by creating a more open and cooperative trade environment. Dr. Singh's leadership was critical in shaping this agreement, as India recognized that stronger economic integration within South Asia could lead to economic growth, poverty reduction, and a more balanced development within the region. As one of the largest and most developed economies in SAARC, India stood to gain significantly from greater access to the markets of neighbouring countries.

By reducing trade barriers, India hoped to increase its export share to regional partners in sectors such as agriculture, manufacturing, pharmaceuticals, and consumer goods. Despite the benefits, the SAFTA agreement faced challenges, particularly due to political tensions and trade imbalances between India and Pakistan, as well as the sometimes divergent economic policies of member countries. However, Dr. Singh's commitment to regional economic integration was unwavering. He recognized that regional cooperation was essential for the stability and prosperity of South Asia, and that deeper trade ties within the region could help in addressing some of the economic disparities between countries. SAFTA also paved the way for other initiatives such as the SAARC Preferential Trading Arrangement (SAPTA), which sought to lower tariff rates and promote cross-border trade in agricultural products, manufactured goods, and services. Through this, India aimed to improve market access for its goods while fostering a sense of regional cooperation that transcended political divisions. Furthermore, India actively encouraged investment flows into South Asia, providing a boost to the infrastructure and industry sectors in countries such as Bangladesh, Sri Lanka, and Nepal, contributing to regional economic growth.

The Strategic Importance of Bilateral and Regional Agreements

Dr. Singh's push for bilateral and regional trade agreements was not just about economic growth; it was also about positioning India within a global framework. By fostering closer ties with ASEAN, SAARC, and other regional partners, India not only expanded its trade volume but also helped create a more stable and cooperative regional economic environment. These efforts aligned with Dr. Singh's broader vision of India being an active participant in global trade and economic governance.

India's participation in these agreements demonstrated a shift in policy from the insular approach of the past, which had focused on self-sufficiency and protectionism, to a more open-market approach focused on trade liberalization and economic integration. Through these efforts, India sought to bolster its position in the global economy, attract foreign investment, and gain access to new technologies, markets, and business opportunities. These agreements also signalled India's shift toward a more multilateral approach to international trade. Through ASEAN and SAFTA, India not only deepened its bilateral relations with neighbouring countries but also promoted regional stability and economic cooperation in a region that had long been marked by economic disparity and political tension.

Dr. Singh's approach to regional trade integration reflected his belief that economic cooperation would create a foundation for peace and security in South Asia, as well as position India as a leading global economic power in the coming decades. In conclusion, Dr. Manmohan Singh's emphasis on bilateral and regional agreements, such as those with ASEAN and SAFTA, played a pivotal role in shaping India's global trade relations. These agreements facilitated India's integration into the global economic system, promoted trade liberalization, and enhanced regional economic cooperation. Dr. Singh's forward-thinking approach helped transform India from a largely protectionist economy into an active player in the global market, fostering trade relationships that continue to benefit India's economy today. His vision for a more open and connected India helped lay the groundwork for the country's future economic success on the global stage.

▪ Advocacy for Developing Economies

Dr. Manmohan Singh's tenure as finance minister and later as prime minister was marked by a strong commitment to global economic cooperation and advocacy for the interests of developing economies on the world stage. His leadership in various international forums such as the World Trade Organization (WTO), G20, and the International Monetary Fund (IMF) helped reshape global economic policies, ensuring that the voice of developing countries was heard and considered in global economic decision making processes. His advocacy for developing economies centred around fair trade, inclusive growth, and economic justice in a world that was increasingly dominated by powerful economies and multinational corporations.

Role at the World Trade Organization (WTO)

The WTO, which was established in 1995, became one of the most important multilateral platforms for global trade negotiations and policy formulation. As India's finance minister and later prime minister, Dr. Singh played a crucial role in ensuring that the needs of developing countries were prioritized in global trade agreements. His approach to the WTO was grounded in the belief that trade should not just be about opening markets but also about ensuring that the benefits of globalization were equally distributed between developed and developing nations. Dr. Singh consistently advocated for trade justice at the WTO, pushing for reforms that would address the challenges faced by developing economies, particularly in the areas of agriculture, intellectual property rights, and subsidies. One of his key concerns was the agricultural trade barriers that hindered the ability of developing countries to compete in the global market.

He emphasized that developing countries needed special treatment in these sectors to ensure their farmers could compete on an even footing with the heavily subsidized agricultural sectors of developed economies, particularly the United States and the European Union. Dr. Singh's leadership was instrumental in securing the Doha Development Round in 2001, which was aimed at addressing the specific needs of developing countries. The focus was on reducing trade barriers, especially in agriculture, and ensuring that trade agreements considered the development needs of poorer nations. While the Doha round faced challenges, Dr. Singh remained a vocal advocate for a fairer global trading system, constantly reminding the global community of the importance of equity and inclusivity in trade negotiations. Moreover, under Dr. Singh's guidance, India became an important voice in the G20 discussions, pushing for reforms in global trade and finance that would benefit emerging economies. His strong stance at the WTO reflected his broader vision of a global economic order that was not skewed in favour of the developed world but one that empowered developing economies to take advantage of global trade and growth opportunities.

Role at the G20

The G20 (Group of Twenty) is an international forum that brings together the world's major economies, both developed and developing, to discuss and coordinate global economic policies. Dr. Singh played a pivotal role in representing India's interests at the G20, especially during the critical period of the global financial crisis in 2008. As a prominent member of the G20, India's participation under Dr. Singh's leadership was crucial in shaping the group's response to the global downturn and ensuring that the interests of developing countries were reflected in the policy responses. One of Dr. Singh's major contributions to the G20 discussions was his advocacy for global economic governance reforms.

He argued that the global financial system needed to be restructured to better represent the realities of a multi-polar world where developing economies were playing an increasingly important role. He called for greater representation of emerging markets in institutions like the IMF and the World Bank, which had historically been dominated by the US and European powers. His push for economic inclusivity was reflected in the G20's call for stronger global financial regulation and more balanced economic growth across both developed and developing nations. Dr. Singh's advocacy also focused on the need for fiscal stimulus packages to counter the impact of the financial crisis on developing countries.

While the developed world was quickly mobilizing rescue packages for its own economies, he argued that the global economic recovery had to be inclusive, with special attention paid to the needs of developing countries that were disproportionately impacted by the downturn. His emphasis on economic justice was central to his discussions at the G20, where he pushed for an economic system that did not prioritize the interests of the rich but rather created opportunities for all. Moreover, Dr. Singh was instrumental in pushing for reform of the international monetary system to reflect the new economic realities of the twenty-first century. He advocated for greater voting power for emerging economies in global financial institutions and emphasized the need for multilateral cooperation to address global challenges such as climate change, poverty reduction, and sustainable development.

Table 7.1: Infrastructure Projects Supported by Stimulus Packages

Project	Investment (INR Crore)
National Highways Development	40,000
Rural Electrification	15,000
Metro Rail Expansion	30,000

Role at the IMF

As prime minister, Dr. Singh also worked closely with the IMF, particularly in the context of India's growing influence on the world stage. Dr. Singh played a significant role in shaping India's relationship with the IMF, and he worked to ensure that the institution's policies would not adversely affect developing nations. He was a strong proponent of international financial reforms that would provide a more equitable and inclusive economic framework. Dr. Singh's approach to the IMF was deeply informed by his understanding of the global financial system and its impact on developing economies. He was one of the leading voices calling for the reform of IMF governance to give emerging economies a larger say in the decision making process.

This was part of a broader effort to reflect the growing influence of countries like India, China, and Brazil in the global economy. Under Dr. Singh's leadership, India became a vocal advocate for policies that promoted financial stability, sustainable economic growth, and poverty alleviation. He sought to ensure that the IMF's lending programmes were designed to help countries weather financial crises without imposing austerity measures that could exacerbate poverty and inequality. Dr. Singh emphasized that financial stability must be achieved through inclusive growth that benefited all segments of society, especially the most vulnerable. India's relationship with the IMF under Dr. Singh was one of active engagement and constructive criticism.

Dr. Singh's leadership ensured that India played a key role in the IMF's responses to the Asian financial crisis in the late 1990s and the global financial crisis in 2008, advocating for policies that protected the interests of developing countries and promoted global financial stability. Dr. Manmohan Singh's advocacy for developing economies at the WTO, G20, and IMF was central to India's increasing prominence in the global economic order. His work in these forums helped ensure that the interests of developing nations were not sidelined in the global economic decision making process. Through his leadership, India not only gained a more prominent voice in global economic governance but also helped shape policies that fostered fairer trade practices, inclusive growth, and economic justice for the world's poorer nations. His contributions to these international organizations reinforced his belief in multilateralism, equitable global trade, and the need for global economic reforms that took into account the realities of the developing world.

▪ Strengthening South Asia

Dr. Manmohan Singh's approach to strengthening economic cooperation in South Asia represented a bold and transformative vision for the region, one that aimed to foster integration, reduce poverty, and create a stronger collective presence on the global economic stage. As both the finance minister and prime minister of India, Dr. Singh played a pivotal role in pushing for greater regional collaboration, guided by the belief that regional economic ties could create a more stable, prosperous, and resilient South Asia.

Regional Integration and Trade Liberalization

One of the key pillars of Dr. Singh's vision for South Asia was economic integration, particularly through the promotion of regional trade agreements. His efforts were focused on creating an environment where the countries of South Asia could benefit from greater trade flows, investment opportunities, and infrastructure development. At the core of this vision was the SAFTA, which was aimed at reducing trade barriers, improving market access, and encouraging collaboration among member states of the SAARC. The SAFTA agreement was a historic step towards removing the economic barriers that had historically hindered intra-regional trade. Dr. Singh saw regional trade agreements as a way to counter the impact of protectionist policies that had long stifled economic growth in South Asia.

He understood that by opening markets, improving trade flows, and creating economic interdependence, countries in the region would be better positioned to weather global economic challenges and leverage each other's strengths. For instance, India, with its relatively more advanced industrial base, could benefit from greater access to markets in Bangladesh, Sri Lanka, and Nepal, while smaller economies could tap into India's vast consumer base. However, the path to deeper regional trade integration was not without obstacles. Dr. Singh's efforts to encourage greater economic cooperation within SAARC were met with resistance, particularly due to the historical tensions between India and its neighbours, especially Pakistan. The geopolitical realities of the region often led to diplomatic challenges, making it difficult to achieve the vision of seamless economic cooperation. Nevertheless, Dr. Singh remained steadfast in his belief that economic diplomacy could play a critical role in overcoming these tensions and building lasting economic partnerships.

India-Pakistan Economic Cooperation

A significant dimension of Dr. Singh's regional strategy was his focus on improving relations with Pakistan. Despite the political tensions between the two countries, Dr. Singh viewed economic cooperation as an essential pathway to peace and stability. He believed that economic interdependence could provide both nations with incentives for cooperation, reduce the risk of conflict, and enhance the overall stability of the region. Under his leadership, India made efforts to foster greater trade liberalization with Pakistan, including discussions on removing tariff and non-tariff barriers to trade. These efforts were seen as part of a broader strategy to build confidence and create a positive feedback loop, where economic ties would reduce hostilities and pave the way for long-term peace. Additionally, Dr. Singh encouraged bilateral initiatives focused on areas like agriculture, water resource management, and cross-border infrastructure projects, which could benefit both countries. However, the political situation often placed constraints on these initiatives, and progress was slow. Despite these setbacks, Dr. Singh's dedication to fostering a closer economic relationship with Pakistan remains an important aspect of his regional economic diplomacy.

Infrastructure Development: The Backbone of Regional Cooperation

Dr. Singh's vision for regional infrastructure development was another key component of his broader economic strategy for South Asia. He recognized that poor infrastructure was a major constraint to the growth of cross-border trade and regional economic integration. Without adequate transportation networks, energy supply systems, and telecommunication infrastructure, South Asia would continue to lag behind in its pursuit of sustainable development. As a result, Dr. Singh sought to improve infrastructure connectivity, focusing on projects that would facilitate the movement of goods, services, and people across borders. Key infrastructure initiatives during Dr. Singh's tenure included the development of road corridors linking India to Bangladesh, Nepal, and Myanmar, as well as enhancing rail connectivity within the region. These projects were aimed at reducing the cost of trade, improving access to markets, and boosting industrial growth in peripheral regions. Similarly, the development of energy pipelines and power grids connecting India with neighbouring countries, such as Nepal, Bhutan, and Bangladesh, was seen as a strategic way to ensure that all countries in the region had access to reliable energy supplies.

Dr. Singh's government also prioritized the expansion of port facilities and airports to improve connectivity with South Asian neighbours, recognizing that logistical infrastructure was key to promoting regional trade. These projects were crucial not only for boosting intra-regional trade but also for attracting FDI from global markets.

Addressing South Asia's Socio-Economic Challenges

Another fundamental aspect of Dr. Singh's approach to regional economic cooperation was the emphasis on inclusive development. Dr. Singh believed that South Asia, despite its collective growth potential, faced stark socio-economic disparities, particularly between urban and rural areas, and among its more and less developed nations. He was committed to ensuring that the fruits of economic growth were shared equally across the region, emphasizing the need for social equity, poverty reduction, and regional balance. For Dr. Singh, this meant not only focusing on the economic growth of India but also on helping smaller nations like Nepal and Bhutan to achieve their development goals.

He advocated for regional development initiatives that could reduce income inequality, improve access to basic services like education and health care, and address issues like hunger, malnutrition, and lack of employment opportunities. His policies sought to ensure that economic progress in South Asia was inclusive and that no country or community was left behind. One of the ways in which Dr. Singh sought to address these disparities was through the development of cross-border initiatives in sectors such as agriculture, where countries could collaborate on improving crop yields, developing irrigation systems, and addressing food security.

Similarly, he advocated for regional cooperation in education, recognizing the importance of building human capital in South Asia as a foundation for long-term growth.

Building Stronger Regional Institutions

Dr. Singh's efforts to promote economic cooperation also included the strengthening of regional institutions. He saw organizations like SAARC and BIMSTEC (Bay of Bengal Initiative for Multi-Sectoral Technical and Economic Cooperation) as vital to creating a platform for South Asian countries to collaborate on a wide range of issues, from trade to environmental sustainability. Strengthening these institutions would provide a framework for joint development projects, enabling countries in the region to pool resources, share knowledge, and collectively address issues that affected them all, such as climate change, natural disasters, and cross-border conflicts.

Dr. Singh also focused on fostering regional security cooperation, recognizing that peace and stability were essential for economic prosperity. By building stronger economic and security ties within South Asia, he believed the region could present a unified front in addressing common challenges, including terrorism, nuclear proliferation, and political instability. Dr. Manmohan Singh's contributions to strengthening South Asia's economic ties were profound and far-reaching. His emphasis on regional economic integration, infrastructure development, and inclusive growth shaped the trajectory of South Asia's economic landscape. Although challenges, such as political resistance, regional disparities, and geopolitical tensions, slowed progress, Dr. Singh's vision of a more interconnected, prosperous South Asia remains an important part of his legacy. His approach to economic diplomacy and his unwavering belief in the potential of regional cooperation continue to influence India's economic relations with its South Asian neighbours, and his efforts laid the groundwork for a more integrated and resilient region in the decades to come.

REFERENCES

Asian Relations Organization. (1948). *Asian Relations: Report of the Proceedings and Documentation of the First Asian Relations Conference.* New Delhi, March-April 1947. Asian Relations Organization.

Bhattacharya, B.B. (1992). *India's Economic Crises: Debt Burden and Specialisation.* Delhi: B.R. Publishing Corporation.

books.google.com

Ghosh, M. (2013). *Liberalization, Growth and Regional Disparities in India.* Springer India.

Gordon, S. (1995). "India and Southeast Asia: A Renaissance in Relations?" In S. Gordon & S. Henningham (Eds.), *India Looks East: An Emerging Power and Its Asia-Pacific Neighbours* (pp. 207-29). Australian National University.

The Sunday Standard (2016, 1 May). "A Lot of Delhi's History goes Missing in Broad Daylight." Retrieved on 11 September 2016, from http://www.newindianexpress.com/thesundaystandard/A-Lot-of-Delhis-History-Goes-Missing-in-Broad-Daylight/2016/05/01/article3408990.ece

The World Bank (2001). *Cultural Heritage and Development: A Framework for Action in the Middle East and North Africa.* Washington, DC: The World Bank.

_______ (2006). *Public Participation: Best Practices Principles.* The World Bank.

_______ (2012). *The Economics of Uniqueness.* Washington, DC.

_______ (2014). *Inclusive Heritage-based City Development Programme in India.* Delhi and Washington, DC: The World Bank Group.

8

Prime Ministerial Leadership (2004–2014)

Dr. Manmohan Singh's tenure as prime minister of India from 2004 to 2014 was marked by a unique leadership style that blended economic expertise, political pragmatism, and a calm demeanour. As India's prime minister during this period, Dr. Singh navigated a rapidly changing global economic landscape and steered the country through various challenges, while also making significant strides in domestic and foreign policy. His leadership was both transformative and stabilizing, shaping India's trajectory for the twenty-first century. Dr. Singh's leadership style was characterized by intellectual rigour and an unwavering commitment to economic liberalization, which was a hallmark of his career. His background as an economist and his extensive experience in managing India's economic policies enabled him to approach governance with a pragmatic outlook.

This was especially evident in his handling of the global financial crisis of 2008, where his background in economics played a pivotal role in formulating policy responses that shielded India from the worst impacts of the crisis. Under his leadership, India was one of the few major economies to maintain positive growth during the global recession, demonstrating the effectiveness of his approach to economic management. His leadership was also defined by a deep understanding of the political dynamics at play within the country. As a member of the Congress party, Dr. Singh was adept at navigating the complexities of coalition politics. Leading a government that was formed by a coalition of multiple parties (the United Progressive Alliance or UPA), he often had to balance the demands of diverse political actors.

Despite this, he managed to keep the focus on India's long-term economic growth and stability. His tenure saw significant economic reforms, including the continuation of the liberalization policies initiated in the 1990s, as well as targeted efforts in sectors such as infrastructure, health care, and education. One of the defining features of Dr. Singh's leadership was his quiet, unassuming demeanour. Unlike many political leaders known for their charisma and public flair, Dr. Singh's leadership was characterized by a calm, steady, and principled approach. He often let his work speak for itself, preferring to avoid the media spotlight and focusing on governance. His modesty and integrity earned him respect both within India and on the global stage. As prime minister, Dr. Singh became a symbol of intellectual leadership and governance based on principles rather than populism.

In terms of domestic policy, Dr. Singh's leadership contributed to significant strides in infrastructure development, poverty alleviation, and social welfare. Programmes like the National Rural Employment Guarantee Act (NREGA) were introduced to provide employment to millions of rural households, contributing to poverty reduction and enhancing rural development. The government also made significant progress in areas like education, health care, and the rural economy. However, despite these successes, Dr. Singh's government faced considerable challenges, particularly in addressing corruption scandals and managing the complexities of coalition politics. On the international front, Dr. Singh's leadership further elevated India's standing in the global community.

His economic diplomacy helped India build stronger trade and strategic relationships with key global powers, including the

United States, Russia, and China. Dr. Singh was instrumental in securing the 2008 Indo-US nuclear deal, which not only enhanced India's global stature but also had profound implications for its energy security. His leadership in global forums like the G20 and the United Nations also helped position India as an influential voice on global economic issues. Despite the challenges, Dr. Singh's leadership during the 2004-14 period laid the foundation for many of the economic and political transformations India is witnessing today. His focus on long-term growth, inclusive development, and global cooperation helped India emerge as a key player in the global economic and political order.

However, his tenure was not without criticism, especially in the latter years of his government. Scandals like the 2G spectrum case and allegations of governance failure tainted the final years of his leadership. Nonetheless, Dr. Singh's calm approach, intellectual rigour, and commitment to India's development ensured his legacy as one of the most respected prime ministers in India's history. In conclusion, Dr. Manmohan Singh's leadership from 2004 to 2014 left an indelible mark on India's development and global standing. His tenure demonstrated that effective leadership is not necessarily about personal charisma but about vision, principles, and the ability to make tough decisions in the face of adversity. Dr. Singh's tenure as prime minister was marked by significant economic growth, political stability, and a commitment to India's long-term progress. While his leadership faced several challenges, both political and economic, his contributions to India's growth trajectory and his emphasis on inclusive development continue to resonate in the country's ongoing journey towards becoming a global economic power.

▪ Major Policy Initiatives

Dr. Manmohan Singh's tenure as prime minister of India from 2004 to 2014 saw the implementation of several transformative policy initiatives aimed at addressing India's socio-economic challenges.

These policies, focusing on rural employment, governance transparency, and infrastructure development, were designed to bring about inclusive growth and uplift underdeveloped and marginalized communities. They represent some of the most ambitious reforms in modern Indian history and reflect Dr. Singh's vision for economic equity and sustainable development.

Rural Employment—MGNREGA

One of the hallmark initiatives of Dr. Singh's government was the Mahatma Gandhi National Rural Employment Guarantee Act (MGNREGA), passed in 2005. The programme aimed to provide guaranteed employment to rural households, particularly in backward areas where unemployment was rampant, and the traditional agricultural economy was in decline. The idea behind MGNREGA was to create rural employment opportunities by making it mandatory for the government to provide work to those who sought it, thereby improving livelihoods, reducing rural poverty, and contributing to the development of rural infrastructure. MGNREGA's design was a direct response to the agrarian distress and underemployment faced by a significant portion of India's rural population. The programme promised 100 days of wage employment annually to every rural household whose adult members were willing to take up unskilled manual labour.

The initiative targeted infrastructure creation at the grassroots level, focusing on building roads, water conservation systems, and rural housing. The impact of MGNREGA was profound in several ways. It provided a social safety net for millions of poor rural families who had previously faced prolonged periods of unemployment or underemployment. It also helped address rural migration, which had led many people to leave their villages in search of work in urban areas. By creating local employment opportunities, the programme helped reduce rural outmigration, stabilizing rural communities and curbing the increasing pressure on urban infrastructures. However, the initiative also faced some criticism for implementation challenges, such as poor monitoring, delays in payments, and instances of corruption in local administration. Despite these issues, MGNREGA remains a cornerstone of India's rural development policies.

Right to Information (RTI)

Another significant policy initiative under Dr. Singh was the Right to Information Act (RTI), passed in 2005, which revolutionized the relationship between the government and the citizens. The RTI Act empowered the public to access information from government bodies, thereby promoting transparency and accountability in governance. By allowing citizens to demand information about the functioning and decision making processes of government institutions, the RTI Act aimed to curb corruption, enhance public participation, and ensure that public resources were utilized efficiently. The RTI Act was also a significant step in strengthening democracy by enabling people to engage with the government in a more direct manner. It provided a legal framework for citizens to seek information on government spending, welfare schemes, and public service delivery, offering a tool to hold public officials accountable. The implementation of RTI became a powerful means for activists, journalists, and common citizens to expose corruption, inefficiency, and mismanagement within the bureaucracy. While the law's full potential has not been fully realized in some areas due to issues with bureaucratic resistance and slow processing of requests, the RTI Act remains a critical instrument for transparency in Indian governance.

Infrastructure Development

Infrastructure development was a key focus of Dr. Singh's government, reflecting his belief that robust infrastructure is essential for sustaining long-term economic growth and improving the quality of life for citizens. Under his leadership, there was an emphasis on improving infrastructure across rural, urban, and transport sectors. Investments in transportation, energy, and communication were seen as essential to supporting India's growing economy and improving its global competitiveness. The development of rural infrastructure was a key priority under Dr. Singh, with programmes like MGNREGA facilitating the creation of roads, water conservation projects, and rural housing. In addition to these efforts, the government launched initiatives like the Pradhan Mantri Gram Sadak Yojana (PMGSY), which aimed to build all-weather roads connecting villages to the national highway network. This programme significantly reduced the urban-rural divide by improving connectivity and accessibility to basic services such as health care, education, and markets. On the urban front, the government undertook significant investments in improving urban infrastructure as part of its broader vision to modernize India's cities and towns.

This included expanding urban housing, enhancing sanitation, improving water supply, and addressing traffic congestion. The government also launched several schemes to address urban slums and informal settlements, such as the Jawaharlal Nehru National Urban Renewal Mission (JNNURM), which aimed to rejuvenate city infrastructure and improve the quality of life in urban areas. Dr. Singh also prioritized energy sector reforms, recognizing the importance of energy security and the need for reliable electricity for both industrial growth and daily life. The government undertook major initiatives to expand the capacity of power plants, improve the efficiency of transmission and distribution networks, and increase the share of renewable energy in India's energy mix. Initiatives like the National Solar Mission were launched to tap into India's renewable energy potential and reduce the dependence on fossil fuels. Under Dr. Singh, India saw a marked improvement in its transportation networks.

The government focused on upgrading the national highways, expanding the railway network, and improving port and airport infrastructure. These efforts were designed to improve logistical efficiency and facilitate the movement of goods and services across the country, boosting trade and economic activity. Dr. Singh's vision for infrastructure development was closely tied to his belief in inclusive growth. He understood that infrastructure development was not only about building physical structures but also about ensuring that the benefits of development reached marginalized and underdeveloped regions. His government sought to balance urban and rural development, with a strong focus on creating opportunities for disadvantaged communities.

Dr. Manmohan Singh's major policy initiatives in the areas of rural employment, governance transparency, and infrastructure development were transformative and had far-reaching impacts. Through programmes like MGNREGA, the Right to Information Act, and large-scale infrastructure projects, Dr. Singh sought to create a more equitable society by empowering marginalized communities, promoting transparency in governance, and improving the country's overall development prospects. These policies not only aimed to address immediate socio-economic issues but also laid the groundwork for sustained growth in the future. While challenges remain, the legacy of these initiatives continues to shape India's development agenda, with many of the policies still playing a critical role in India's economic and social landscape.

▪ Balancing Politics and Policy

Dr. Manmohan Singh's tenure as prime minister of India from 2004 to 2014 was marked by complex coalition dynamics and significant challenges in balancing politics with economic reforms. As the leader of a coalition government, Dr. Singh had to navigate the often tumultuous political environment of a multi-party democracy while ensuring the continuity and success of his policy agenda. The coalition, which included parties with differing political ideologies, presented both opportunities and obstacles. Dr. Singh's ability to maintain political stability while pushing through crucial economic reforms was a testament to his diplomatic acumen, strategic thinking, and commitment to the nation's long-term development.

Coalition Government: Composition and Challenges

Dr. Singh led the United Progressive Alliance (UPA), a coalition of diverse political parties, which came to power after the 2004 general elections. The UPA was primarily anchored by the Indian National Congress (INC), with the Communist Party of India (Marxist) (CPI(M)) and several regional parties forming the crucial support base. The coalition was inherently fragile due to the wide ideological differences among its constituents. The presence of left-wing parties, such as the CPI(M), who were often ideologically opposed to market reforms, created significant tension with the more pro-reform policies championed by Dr. Singh, particularly in the areas of economic liberalization, privatization, and FDI.

Dr. Singh's leadership style, characterized by his quiet diplomacy, humility, and conciliatory approach, was crucial in managing these internal contradictions. He often had to strike a balance between his economic vision and the demands of his coalition partners, who were more cautious or even hostile toward certain reforms. The Communist Party of India (Marxist), for instance, vehemently opposed some of the government's economic liberalization policies and made it clear that they would not support measures that threatened India's public sector or social welfare programmes. To maintain the coalition's stability, Dr. Singh had to make several concessions and work closely with his partners, ensuring that the government's policies could garner wide political support despite their differences.

Strategic Compromises and Policy Shifts

The need for compromise in such a diverse coalition government often led to policy shifts that were more incremental than radical. One prominent example was the approach to FDI.

While Dr. Singh and his Congress party were keen to open up sectors such as retail and insurance to FDI, the Left parties were staunchly opposed to any such measures. This created a deadlock for several months, and in the end, the government was forced to delay or water down several policy proposals related to FDI to keep the Left in the coalition. This situation illustrated the political compromise that Dr. Singh had to make, balancing his pro-market reforms with the ideological constraints of his political allies. However, Dr. Singh's remarkable skill in political negotiation helped the UPA government to push through many key reforms without the coalition collapsing. His ability to engage stakeholders and win over critics was pivotal in keeping the government's legislative agenda on track. This period of coalition politics also saw the introduction of several important pieces of social welfare legislation, such as the National Rural Employment Guarantee Act (MGNREGA), which focused on rural employment, and the Right to Information (RTI) Act, which aimed to increase transparency in governance. These initiatives were not only part of Dr. Singh's commitment to inclusive development, but they also helped maintain the support of key coalition members such as the Samajwadi Party and Indian National Congress party, who prioritized social welfare.

Dealing with Political Opposition

Managing opposition from parties outside the coalition was another significant challenge during Dr. Singh's tenure. The Bharatiya Janata Party (BJP), the principal opposition party, consistently attacked the government on various fronts, including its handling of corruption scandals, economic liberalization, and foreign policy. The BJP accused Dr. Singh of being a weak leader who was unable to assert his authority within the coalition and was thus unable to govern effectively. The BJP's frequent criticism, particularly after the 2008 Mumbai attacks, created additional pressure on the government, forcing Dr. Singh to defend his policies and leadership in both the media and in parliament. Despite this, Dr. Singh maintained a firm stance on his economic agenda, believing that the long-term growth and prosperity of the nation should transcend short-term political setbacks. He was particularly focused on ensuring that the government's economic reforms would continue even amidst political challenges. Dr. Singh's tenure also coincided with global financial crises, and his handling of the crisis in 2008 was often cited as an example of his political foresight and economic prudence.

The Political Challenge of Managing Diverse Regional Interests

Another crucial element of Dr. Singh's political strategy was his ability to balance regional interests.

India's federal structure means that regional parties, which represent specific states and regions, often hold significant sway over national policies. During his tenure, Dr. Singh worked to ensure that regional demands were addressed while maintaining national cohesion. This included making financial allocations for regional development, as well as tailoring policies to the specific needs of different states. For example, Dr. Singh's government introduced the Special Category Status for certain states, which involved granting them financial assistance and tax exemptions to address regional imbalances. This was particularly important for states in the north-east and backward regions, where economic development had lagged behind the more prosperous areas. By doing so, Dr. Singh was able to secure the support of regional parties while maintaining his larger national and economic objectives.

The Role of Congress Party and UPA's Governance Philosophy

As the leader of the Congress party, Dr. Singh was also tasked with ensuring that the party's interests were aligned with the coalition's goals. This required managing the often-complex internal dynamics of the Congress party, which, like many large political parties, had its own factionalism and competing ideologies. Dr. Singh's personal integrity and detachment from the day-to-day politics helped him steer the Congress party through these challenges. His leadership style was more focused on policy implementation than political manoeuvring, which allowed him to stay relatively above the fray of political infighting. Under Dr. Singh, the UPA government emphasized the importance of long-term growth, even when it meant making difficult decisions.

This contrasted with the more populist approaches of other coalition members who often favoured immediate gratification for electoral gains. The UPA's approach to governance was defined by its focus on inclusive development and poverty reduction, which guided the government's policy initiatives, even if they occasionally alienated some political allies. Dr. Manmohan Singh's leadership in balancing politics and policy was a defining feature of his tenure as prime minister. His success in managing coalition dynamics, forging strategic compromises, and navigating the challenges posed by political opposition allowed him to push forward many of India's critical reforms. Despite the challenges, he remained focused on his economic vision and worked tirelessly to maintain political stability while ensuring that India's long-term growth trajectory was not derailed by short-term political pressures. His leadership in this context not only shaped India's economic policies but also played a crucial role in ensuring that the country remained on a path of progressive development.

• Governance Philosophy

Dr. Manmohan Singh's governance philosophy during his tenure as prime minister of India (2004–14) was deeply rooted in a commitment to long-term economic growth and national development. Unlike some of his political contemporaries, who often emphasized populist measures for immediate political gains, Dr. Singh prioritized policies that he believed would lead to sustainable growth and a stronger, more resilient economy over the long run. His focus was always on ensuring that India's economic reforms and development strategies would yield dividends in the years and decades to come, even if the immediate benefits were not as visible.

Vision of Long-term Growth

Dr. Singh believed that economic development was not an overnight process but required careful planning, foresight, and the political will to implement complex reforms. As a trained economist, he understood the importance of sound macroeconomic policies, fiscal discipline, and the need for structural reforms to ensure a robust and growing economy. His government's agenda was driven by the vision of transforming India into a global economic power, a vision that focused on laying the foundation for sustainable growth rather than seeking quick fixes to appeal to the electorate. This long-term focus became especially evident when Dr. Singh continued to pursue economic liberalization and market-oriented reforms despite the political risks and the opposition from certain sectors of the political spectrum. He believed that liberalizing the economy, fostering foreign investment, and enhancing trade would create the necessary conditions for job creation, industrial growth, and poverty reduction in the future. These policies, while sometimes controversial in the short-term, were ultimately designed to make India more competitive, both in regional and global markets.

Rural Development and Inclusive Growth

Dr. Singh's governance philosophy also reflected a strong commitment to inclusive growth. He understood that India's vast rural population needed to be uplifted through socio-economic reforms that would address both their immediate needs and their long-term economic security. Under his leadership, several social welfare initiatives were launched, including the MGNREGA, which aimed at providing guaranteed employment for rural households. While the programme had populist appeal, it was also aligned with Dr. Singh's long-term vision of poverty alleviation and rural development.

By providing rural citizens with a steady income and enhancing rural infrastructure, Dr. Singh was creating an environment for future growth, where rural areas could contribute meaningfully to the national economy. Similarly, his government's focus on financial inclusion was driven by the idea that access to banking, credit, and financial services would help uplift the marginalized and underserved sections of society. Initiatives such as Jan Dhan Yojana and microfinance programmes were aimed at bringing financial services to the poorest, ensuring that they could participate in the formal economy and, in the process, improving their livelihoods in the long-term.

Fiscal Responsibility and Economic Stability

Dr. Singh was also known for his commitment to fiscal responsibility, which he viewed as integral to achieving sustainable economic growth. His tenure saw a continued emphasis on controlling inflation, reducing fiscal deficits, and maintaining a stable macroeconomic environment. He understood that, for India to emerge as a competitive player in the global economy, it had to show fiscal discipline and credibility. During his time as finance minister in the early 1990s, he had implemented key reforms such as reducing government borrowing and bringing the economy under control. As prime minister, he continued these principles, ensuring that inflation rates remained manageable and that economic stability was maintained, even during times of global financial crises. This focus on long-term growth, however, was not without its challenges. Some of his policies, particularly those related to reforms in labour laws, foreign investment, and privatization of public sector enterprises, faced significant opposition from left-wing parties and trade unions. Critics argued that these measures would lead to social inequality and undermine the welfare state. However, Dr. Singh's approach was to advance economic reforms cautiously, explaining that they were necessary for India's future competitiveness and to create an investment-friendly environment that would eventually benefit the entire nation.

Balancing Short-term Political Gains with Long-term Goals

One of the core aspects of Dr. Singh's governance philosophy was his ability to balance the short-term political needs of his coalition government with his long-term policy goals. Leading a coalition of ideologically diverse political parties, Dr. Singh often had to make compromises on his economic reforms, but he ensured that these compromises did not significantly derail his vision for India's economic future.

For example, while he faced political pressure from certain groups to reverse liberalization measures or adopt more protectionist policies, Dr. Singh managed to remain committed to economic reforms by emphasizing their long-term benefits. His government continued to focus on improving India's industrial and export sectors, attracting FDI, and enhancing the country's global trade relations, even when these policies were not immediately popular among certain sections of society. This demonstrated Dr. Singh's belief in the principle of deferred gratification, understanding that the benefits of his reforms would only be fully realized after a period of investment and structural change.

Focus on Infrastructure Development

Dr. Singh also understood the importance of infrastructure development as a key enabler of long-term growth. During his tenure, the government made significant strides in improving India's infrastructure, particularly in sectors such as transportation, energy, and telecommunications. He believed that a modern, efficient infrastructure network was essential for fostering business development, attracting investment, and improving the quality of life for ordinary citizens. Key initiatives, including the Golden

Quadrilateral Project (which aimed to connect major cities through an extensive highway network) and the National Power Grid, were part of his broader vision to enhance India's infrastructure and industrial competitiveness. By focusing on infrastructure development, Dr. Singh aimed to create an environment that would facilitate long-term economic growth.

Modern infrastructure would not only benefit existing industries but also encourage new business opportunities in areas such as logistics, information technology, and renewable energy. Dr. Manmohan Singh's governance philosophy, characterized by a focus on long-term growth over populist policies, was a defining feature of his tenure as prime minister of India. His commitment to inclusive growth, fiscal responsibility, infrastructure development, and social welfare initiatives demonstrated his belief that the economic transformation of India required a steady, strategic approach that would endure beyond the immediate political pressures of the day. Despite facing challenges from political opposition and ideological factions within his own coalition, Dr. Singh's unwavering commitment to his vision ultimately shaped India's economic trajectory and laid the foundation for the country's emergence as a global economic power.

▪ Key Controversies

During Dr. Manmohan Singh's tenure as prime minister, his government faced several controversies that led to intense political and public scrutiny. Among the most prominent of these were the 2G spectrum scam and the coal allocation issues, both of which not only created a significant political storm but also cast a shadow over the governance of his administration.

2G Spectrum Scam

The 2G spectrum scam became one of the most significant scandals during Dr. Singh's leadership, raising serious concerns about the integrity of his government's decision making process. The controversy revolved around the allocation of 2G spectrum licences for mobile telecommunications in India, which took place in 2008. The licences were issued at 1999 prices, despite the rise in demand and value for the spectrum, resulting in a massive financial loss for the exchequer. The Central Bureau of Investigation (CBI) and the Public Accounts Committee (PAC) found that there was a lack of transparency in the way spectrum licences were allocated. The process was allegedly manipulated to benefit certain private companies, leading to an estimated 1.76 lakh crore ($40 billion) loss to the public treasury. The key figures involved in the scandal included A. Raja, the then telecommunications minister, who was arrested and later convicted for his role in the scam. The telecom companies involved, along with certain political allies, were accused of colluding to secure licences at below-market rates, further inflating the controversy. Dr. Singh, despite his reputation as an economist known for promoting economic transparency and integrity, found himself at the centre of this storm due to his association with the scandal, as A. Raja was a member of the Indian National Congress, the ruling party. While Dr. Singh himself was not directly implicated in the scandal, critics pointed to his lack of oversight in the matter, raising questions about his leadership style and whether he had fully exercised his responsibilities as the prime minister. Dr. Singh's response to the controversy was measured, as he denied any wrongdoing, but the scandal undoubtedly tarnished his government's image, especially in the context of his focus on reforms. His ability to maintain control over the administration despite such high-profile issues was a testament to his political acumen, but the 2G scam remained a contentious issue that haunted his tenure.

Coal Allocation Issues

Another key controversy that marred Dr. Singh's leadership was the coal allocation issue, which became public in 2012. This scandal, also known as the Coal Scam, involved the allocation of coal blocks to private companies by the government from 2004 onwards without a transparent auction process. The Comptroller and Auditor General (CAG) report revealed that the allocation of coal blocks led to significant losses to the public exchequer, similar to the 2G scandal. The scandal revolved around the fact that these coal blocks were allocated based on discretionary powers rather than through a competitive bidding process. Critics argued that this lack of transparency had resulted in undue benefits for private companies, many of whom were not even in the business of coal mining. As a result, the CAG estimated that the government had lost nearly 1.86 lakh crore in potential revenue.

While Dr. Singh was the prime minister during the coal allocation period, the allocation was carried out under the Ministry of Coal, which was headed by Shibu Soren, and later by Sriprakash Jaiswal. However, as the controversy grew, Dr. Singh came under pressure to respond. The political opposition accused him of turning a blind eye to the lack of due process and failure to take corrective action when the issue was first raised. The opposition parties, particularly the BJP, used the coal scam as a major rallying point to criticize the ruling government for corruption, mismanagement, and failure to implement reforms. Dr. Singh defended the government's actions, stating that the allocations were made with the intent to ensure the timely availability of coal for companies engaged in power generation, and that there was no personal benefit derived from these actions. Despite these defences, the coal scam had significant political ramifications. It was one of the main reasons for the decline in the popularity of the Congress party during Dr. Singh's second term as prime minister.

Political Fallout and Impact on Governance

Both the 2G spectrum scam and the coal allocation scandal were pivotal in shaping public perception of Dr. Singh's leadership. Although he was not directly involved in either of these scandals, they became associated with his tenure as prime minister. His leadership style, characterized by decisiveness and pragmatism, was criticized for being too passive when it came to addressing such issues. The perception that he allowed his ministers too much discretionary power or did not intervene when red flags were raised led to doubts about his effectiveness as a leader.

The political opposition, particularly from the BJP, accused Dr. Singh of being a puppet of party president Sonia Gandhi, and claimed that his government had become entrenched in corruption. The scandals also led to a loss of credibility among many of his allies in the UPA, weakening his position and affecting his ability to enact key reforms in his second term. In addition to the domestic political fallout, the scandals also attracted significant international media attention, further damaging India's reputation as an emerging economic power. The perception of a corrupt political system undermined investor confidence, leading to a temporary slowdown in FDI and a decline in India's global economic standing. Despite these challenges, Dr. Singh continued to defend his leadership decisions, and his government weathered the political storm. He continued to emphasize the importance of economic reforms and pursued policies that were designed to address the country's structural issues, even as the scandals unfolded. However, the controversies cast a long shadow over his legacy and complicated his attempts to push forward with an ambitious reform agenda.

Conclusion

The 2G scam and coal allocation issues were two of the most significant challenges Dr. Manmohan Singh faced during his tenure as prime minister. While he was not personally implicated in the corruption associated with these scandals, the controversy surrounding them had a lasting impact on his political reputation and leadership legacy. Critics argued that his government's failure to ensure transparency in these key areas undermined the economic reforms he had worked to implement, while supporters contended that he had done his best to manage complex governance challenges. Despite the political damage caused by these scandals, Dr. Singh's leadership ultimately proved resilient. His focus on economic reforms, his commitment to inclusive growth, and his ability to navigate difficult political waters ensured that his legacy remained a significant part of India's post-liberalization history. However, the controversies will continue to shape the public discourse surrounding his time in office, highlighting the challenges of governing a large, diverse democracy with competing interests and entrenched political systems.

REFERENCES

Gordon, S. (1995). *India's Rise to Power in the Twentieth Century and Beyond.* Macmillan Press Ltd.

Grégoire, F. & Mattoo, A. (2001). *India and ASEAN.* Manohar.

Harvey, D. (2005). *A Brief History of Neoliberalism.* Oxford University Press.

Held, D. (1999). *Global Transformations.* Stanford University Press.

Jain, T.R. & Ohri, V.K. (2010). *Indian Economic Development.* V.K. Publication.

Kapur, A. (2006). *India: From Regional to World Power.* Routledge.

Mann, P. (2000). *India's Foreign Policy in the Post-Cold War Era.* Harman Pub. House.

Mansingh, L. (1997). *Indian Foreign Policy.* Foreign Service Institute in association with Konark Publishers.

Ministry of Defence, India. (1990). *Annual Report 1989-90.* Ministry of Defence, Government of India.

Ministry of Finance, India. (1991). *Economic Survey 1990-91.* Economic Division, Ministry of Finance. indiabudget.gov.in

9

Tackling Global Recessions

Dr. Manmohan Singh's tenure as India's prime minister, especially during the global recession of 2008, was marked by his adept handling of the economic challenges that arose from the global financial crisis. His calm and composed leadership played a pivotal role in steering India through turbulent waters while safeguarding the nation's financial stability and economic growth. The 2008 crisis was a shock to the global system, leading to recessions in most advanced economies. Despite the global downturn, India's economy showed remarkable resilience, and much of this can be attributed to Dr. Singh's foresight, strategic decisions, and strong economic policies. India, like many other nations, experienced a slowdown as a result of reduced global demand, falling exports, and financial market disruptions.

The impact was felt particularly in sectors like manufacturing, services, and exports, as India's trading partners in the West experienced severe contractions in their economies. Yet, Dr. Singh's government reacted promptly to the crisis with a combination of fiscal and monetary policy interventions. Recognizing that India's economic growth could not be sustained in the face of global market contractions without effective counter-cyclical measures, his government launched a series of fiscal stimulus packages to invigorate domestic demand. One of the key responses to the global crisis was increased public expenditure, particularly in infrastructure. Recognizing the potential for infrastructure investment to not only provide immediate relief through job creation and demand generation but also to have long-term benefits for the economy, the government ramped up spending on projects related to roads, railways, ports, and energy.

This approach not only stimulated the economy in the short-term but also contributed to India's long-term growth potential, as these infrastructural investments improved the country's competitiveness and connectedness. Additionally, the Indian government took steps to enhance liquidity in the banking sector to ensure the continued functioning of financial institutions. The Reserve Bank of India (RBI), under Dr. Singh's guidance, implemented measures to inject liquidity into the system and lowered interest rates to encourage borrowing and investment. These steps ensured that the financial sector remained stable, despite the turmoil in global markets. Dr. Singh's careful approach to managing the banking sector helped avoid the widespread collapse of financial institutions that occurred in many advanced economies.

Table 9.1: Key Macroeconomic Indicators of India (2007—2011)

Year	GDP Growth Rate (%)	Inflation Rate (%)	Fiscal Deficit (% of GDP)	Forex Reserves (USD Billion)
2007	9.8	4.7	3.1	309
2008	3.9	9.1	5.9	252
2009	8.5	12.2	6.5	279
2010	10.3	9.5	4.8	297
2011	6.6	8.9	5.1	305

Another key element of India's success in managing the crisis was its relatively limited exposure to toxic financial assets, which had contributed to the collapse of financial institutions in the West. India's banking system was insulated from the risky subprime mortgage assets that caused the 2008 crisis in the United States. This precaution, along with the careful regulation and oversight of financial institutions, meant that India did not face the same level of instability in its financial markets as many Western nations. The strength of India's domestic banking system, along with a solid regulatory framework, allowed the country to weather the storm with fewer negative consequences.

Dr. Singh also implemented measures to bolster the economy through targeted social welfare programmes. His administration increased support for rural employment schemes such as the Mahatma Gandhi National Rural Employment Guarantee Act (MGNREGA), which ensured that people in rural areas had access to work, thereby sustaining domestic consumption levels. By focusing on rural development and ensuring that income continued to flow to the most vulnerable populations, Dr. Singh not only supported economic growth but also helped mitigate the social impact of the global recession. Dr. Singh's leadership during the crisis was characterized by pragmatism and a focus on economic stability. He was cautious but decisive, understanding that while immediate actions were necessary to address the economic slowdown, it was also important to maintain a steady focus on the long-term growth trajectory of the country.

His government avoided the temptation to take populist measures that might have provided short-term relief but would have harmed India's economic fundamentals in the long run. This balanced approach to policymaking further solidified Dr. Singh's reputation as a leader who prioritized economic stability and sustainable growth over short-term political gains. The global financial crisis also served as a reminder of the importance of strong economic governance and strategic economic diplomacy. India's robust macroeconomic policies, including fiscal discipline, inflation management, and a stable exchange rate, helped reassure global investors that the country was a safe place to invest, even in uncertain times. Dr. Singh's ability to maintain confidence in the Indian economy, both domestically and internationally, played a key role in ensuring that India did not experience the same depth of recession as many of its global counterparts.

As a result, India's economy grew at a relatively strong rate during and after the crisis compared to other large economies. Another vital aspect of Dr. Singh's leadership during this period was his capacity to communicate the government's strategy effectively to the public and the global community. In times of economic uncertainty, strong leadership communication is crucial in maintaining confidence in government policies. Dr. Singh's calm and measured communication reassured both domestic and international audiences that the government was fully aware of the economic challenges and was taking appropriate action to mitigate the effects of the crisis. His steady leadership ensured that India maintained its credibility as a growing economic power, even during one of the worst global recessions in history. While the global financial crisis posed significant challenges for India, Dr. Singh's leadership allowed the country to emerge relatively unscathed.

India's economic fundamentals remained strong, and the country continued to attract foreign investment during and after the crisis, albeit at a lower pace than before. India's relatively low dependence on exports to the West, combined with its growing domestic consumption and large population, allowed the country to rely more on its internal market to drive growth. This focus on domestic consumption, along with targeted stimulus measures, helped India recover faster than many other emerging economies. Dr. Singh's leadership during the global financial crisis reinforced his image as a steady and pragmatic economic leader. His ability to manage the Indian economy during one of the most tumultuous periods in recent history highlighted his economic acumen and his understanding of global markets.

His response to the crisis was not only effective in the short-term but also demonstrated his long-term vision for India's economic stability and growth. Ultimately, the 2008 global financial crisis served as a test for Dr. Singh's leadership, and he passed it with flying colours. The measures he implemented during this period laid the foundation for India's continued growth in the years that followed. His government's actions helped prevent a deeper recession in India, and the country was able to return to its growth trajectory more quickly than many other nations. Dr. Singh's handling of the crisis further cemented his legacy as a leader who could navigate complex economic challenges with skill and foresight.

▪ India During the 2008 Financial Crisis

During the 2008 financial crisis, India, like much of the global economy, faced severe economic challenges. However, due to its relatively insulated financial system and strong domestic consumption, India was able to navigate the crisis with less damage compared to other economies. Dr. Manmohan Singh's government took a range of policy measures to shield the Indian economy from the full effects of the crisis and ensure stability.

Fig. 9.1: Global GDP Growth Rate during the 2008 Financial Crisis (2007—2009).

Initial Impact of the Crisis on India

The global financial meltdown of 2008 originated primarily in the United States, triggered by the collapse of major financial institutions due to exposure to subprime mortgages. As the crisis spread, it led to global economic contraction, falling stock markets, and a dramatic reduction in international trade. India, with its robust growth story and burgeoning middle class, was not immune to these global shocks, though it was less vulnerable than many advanced economies due to its low exposure to toxic financial products. India faced a sharp slowdown in economic growth, with GDP growth dipping from a high of 9.3 per cent in 2007 to a low of around 6.7 per cent in 2008. Export sectors, particularly manufacturing and IT, were significantly impacted as demand from key markets like the US and Europe plummeted. Stock markets saw substantial losses, and there was a tightening of liquidity in the banking sector as global credit markets froze.

Policy Measures to Counter the Crisis

In response to the financial crisis, Dr. Singh's government, along with the RBI, implemented a series of stimulus measures aimed at mitigating the adverse effects of the crisis, boosting domestic demand, and maintaining the overall economic growth trajectory. These measures were broadly categorized into monetary policy, fiscal policy, and financial sector interventions.

Monetary Policy Adjustments

One of the key policy measures that India undertook was the easing of monetary policy by the RBI. The central bank significantly reduced interest rates in an attempt to encourage borrowing and stimulate investment. Repo rates, the rate at which the RBI lends to commercial banks, were cut sharply from 9 per cent to around 4.75 per cent by early 2009. This helped reduce the cost of credit, making it easier for businesses to borrow and continue operations despite global uncertainty. Additionally, the cash reserve ratio (CRR), which dictates the amount of cash that banks are required to keep with the RBI, was reduced to inject more liquidity into the banking system. This encouraged commercial banks to lend more and supported the overall functioning of the financial system.

Fiscal Stimulus Package

The government announced a fiscal stimulus package aimed at boosting demand and providing relief to various sectors of the economy. This package included direct government spending on infrastructure, tax cuts, and incentives for sectors such as automobiles, exports, and housing. The government increased public spending on infrastructure projects, such as roads, railways, and energy, to inject liquidity into the economy and create jobs. Tax relief was also provided, including a reduction in excise duties and service taxes. The corporate tax rate was slashed, giving businesses more financial flexibility to weather the downturn. Additionally, the government offered subsidies for sectors directly impacted by the slowdown, such as the export industry, to maintain their competitiveness in the global market. One of the key elements of the fiscal stimulus was the National Rural Employment Guarantee Act (NREGA), which was expanded and became a major tool in combating the slowdown. The programme aimed to provide guaranteed employment to rural households, particularly those that were hardest hit by the crisis, and generated substantial rural demand by increasing rural wages.

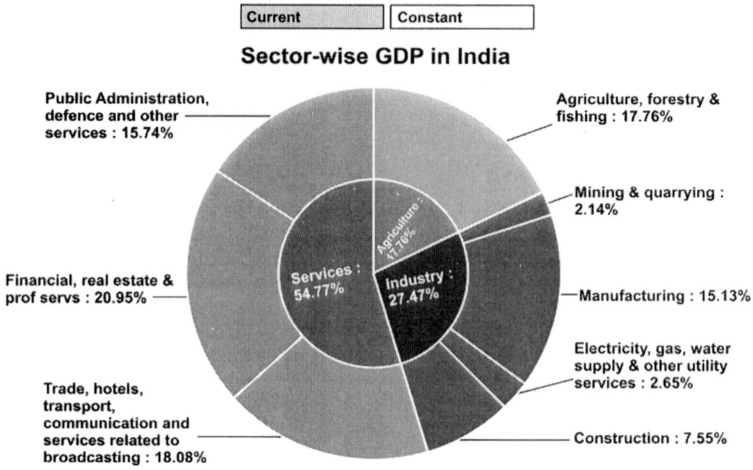

Fig. 9.2: Distribution of India's Stimulus Packages Across Key Economic Sectors.

Support to Financial Institutions

To ensure the stability of the financial system, the government and the RBI introduced several measures to support financial institutions. The government provided capital injections to public sector banks, ensuring that they had enough liquidity to continue lending and supporting businesses. The RBI also undertook measures to ensure liquidity in the banking system, including backstopping the money markets and increasing the lending limits for foreign exchange. In addition, the government expanded its guarantees for banks to boost confidence in the financial sector. It also created a special liquidity support programme to prevent the collapse of key financial institutions and protect depositors.

Ensuring Export Competitiveness

The export sector, which was significantly impacted by the crisis, received special attention from the government. The export promotion schemes were enhanced, with an emphasis on sectors such as textiles, engineering goods, and pharmaceuticals. The government introduced interest subsidies and refunds of taxes on exports to ensure that exporters could continue to stay competitive in the international market despite the global slowdown. In addition, the government negotiated trade agreements with key partners to maintain India's access to global markets. This helped to partially offset the contraction in demand from traditional Western markets.

The Success of the Policy Measures

India's policy measures played a crucial role in cushioning the economy from the worst effects of the financial crisis. Though growth slowed considerably, the Indian economy did not experience the kind of recession that plagued many advanced economies. In fact, India's GDP growth rebounded relatively quickly, rising to 8.5 per cent in 2010 as a result of the stimulus and ongoing structural reforms. The fiscal stimulus package injected critical demand into the economy, and the monetary policies of the RBI helped ensure sufficient liquidity. The expansion of the NREGA programme provided immediate relief to rural areas, where employment opportunities were scarce. The swift action to support the banking sector and ensure financial stability prevented a credit crunch, which could have exacerbated the crisis. India's export sector also recovered, helped by the government's quick interventions.

By 2009-10, India was able to maintain a competitive edge in several export industries, with exports rebounding as the global economy began to stabilize. The 2008 financial crisis was a significant event that tested the resilience of India's economy. Dr. Singh's government, with its well-timed policy responses, ensured that India was shielded from the worst effects of the crisis. Through a combination of monetary and fiscal measures, as well as targeted support for the banking system and export sectors, India was able to maintain economic stability and recover relatively quickly. While India was not immune to the global downturn, the effectiveness of these policies showcased the importance of proactive governance during a global economic crisis. The Indian economy not only survived the crisis but emerged stronger in many respects, with key sectors like banking and export industries benefiting from the reforms and interventions implemented in response to the financial turmoil.

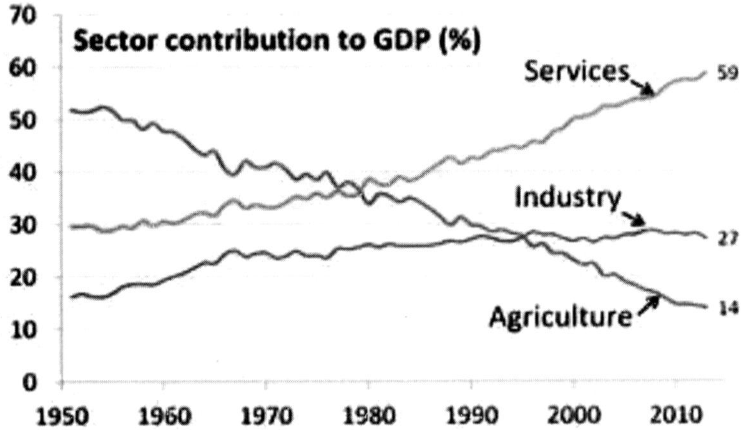

Fig. 9.3: India's GDP Growth Trend Pre- and Post-2008 Financial Crisis.

▪ Stimulus Packages and Fiscal Strategies

India's response to the 2008 financial crisis involved a combination of stimulus packages aimed at stabilizing the economy, boosting demand, and ensuring long-term growth. While the global financial crisis led to a sharp decline in economic activity worldwide, India adopted a proactive approach by rolling out a series of economic stimulus measures. These measures were designed to shield the economy from the worst impacts of the global downturn, revitalize growth, and address the immediate challenges posed by the slowdown. One of the central elements of the response to the crisis was a substantial increase in infrastructure spending, as it was considered one of the most effective ways to stimulate economic activity, create jobs, and lay the foundation for future growth. This strategy was complemented by demand creation policies, which aimed at spurring both private consumption and investment. The combination of these two strategies formed the backbone of India's crisis response, and their success in stabilizing the economy underscored the importance of government intervention during times of global economic stress.

Stimulus Packages: Overview and Goals

The Indian government, under the leadership of Prime Minister Dr. Manmohan Singh, unveiled several stimulus packages in the wake of the 2008 financial crisis. These packages were crafted to address the twin challenges of demand contraction and financial instability caused by the global recession. The first stimulus was announced in December 2008, with subsequent measures rolled out through early 2009. The overall goal was to counteract the slowdown in economic growth, safeguard jobs, and restore investor confidence. The stimulus packages were based on the assumption that India's domestic demand would need to be bolstered to offset the decline in external demand (especially exports). With global trade volumes shrinking, India's manufacturing and services sectors, particularly those dependent on external markets, were facing a significant downturn. To ensure that India did not slip into a recession, the government decided to focus on infrastructure spending as the primary tool for spurring demand.

Infrastructure Spending: A Core Element of the Stimulus

The government recognized that infrastructure was a key area where significant investment could have an immediate impact on economic activity. India's infrastructure deficit had been a bottleneck for economic growth for many years, and the financial crisis created an opportunity to address these deficiencies in a manner that would have short-term benefits and long-term growth potential.

By increasing public expenditure on infrastructure projects, the government hoped to not only generate immediate jobs but also improve the country's economic productivity in the future.

Key Infrastructure Sectors: Investments and Impact

The stimulus measures focused on critical infrastructure sectors that were poised to yield significant economic returns. Among the sectors that received the most attention were roads and highways, railways, power generation, urban infrastructure, and telecommunications. These sectors were strategically chosen because of their potential to create a multiplier effect on the economy—enhancing mobility, reducing costs, and stimulating demand in other sectors.

1. **Roads and Highways:** The development and upgrade of national highways and rural roads became a priority. The National Highways Development Project (NHDP) received a boost with increased funding for its expansion. This led to the construction of over 6,000 km of new highways and improved road infrastructure, which in turn facilitated the movement of goods and people, thereby reducing logistical costs. The improvement in road connectivity also enhanced access to markets, particularly for rural areas, and supported the broader economic growth by connecting previously isolated regions.
2. **Railways:** India's railway system, a critical backbone of its transport infrastructure, was another area where the government channelled funds. The aim was to modernize and expand the railway network to cope with the growing demand for freight transport and passenger movement. Projects to electrify railway tracks, enhance train frequencies, and introduce high-speed trains were

launched. These initiatives not only created jobs in construction and operations but also boosted the overall economic efficiency of the transport system.

3. **Power Generation:** One of the major constraints on India's economic growth has been the chronic power shortages that affected industries, services, and households. The stimulus packages directed funds toward power generation projects, particularly in renewable energy sources like solar and wind power, as well as in expanding thermal power plants. By enhancing the power supply, the government aimed to support industrial growth, boost productivity, and ensure a reliable supply of energy for future generations.
4. **Urban Infrastructure:** In addition to rural and transportation infrastructure, the government also focused on the improvement of urban infrastructure. With India's urban population growing rapidly, the demand for better public transportation systems, housing, water supply, and sanitation was immense. The government increased funding for metro systems in cities like Delhi, Bangalore, and Mumbai. These projects created jobs in construction and urban planning while improving overall urban livability and reducing congestion.
5. **Telecommunications:** The Indian government also invested in expanding the country's telecommunications infrastructure, particularly in rural areas. Expanding mobile networks and internet access to underserved regions helped improve communication, connectivity, and access to services like education and health care. In addition to boosting economic activities, this infrastructure also promoted digital inclusion and reduced the digital divide between urban and rural areas.

Demand Creation and Employment Generation

One of the central goals of the fiscal stimulus was to revitalize domestic demand. With the global economy in turmoil and external trade contracts, India needed to focus on internal demand to maintain economic momentum. To achieve this, the government implemented a combination of direct spending on welfare programmes, tax reductions, and subsidies aimed at stimulating consumption and investment.

Rural Employment: NREGA

The NREGA, which had been passed earlier, became a critical tool in the government's stimulus response. The NREGA guaranteed 100 days of paid employment annually to rural households. With additional funds allocated under the stimulus packages, the programme was expanded to provide jobs to millions of rural workers. By directly providing cash transfers to rural households, the government ensured that people in rural areas had money to spend on food, health care, and other essentials, thereby boosting demand.

Tax Cuts and Incentives

The government introduced excise duty cuts and tax relief to stimulate consumer demand. Tax cuts were applied across various sectors, including automobiles, consumer goods, and services, which helped reduce prices and made goods more affordable for the public.

The aim was to encourage spending and stimulate consumption in the economy. For businesses, corporate tax cuts were offered as incentives to promote investment. The government reduced corporate taxes and provided additional incentives for sectors like automobile manufacturing, exports, and construction, which were facing significant demand contraction.

Increased Public Spending on Welfare

In addition to NREGA, the government increased its spending on public health, education, and social welfare programmes. These expenditures played an important role in increasing purchasing power among the economically disadvantaged and helping to stabilize the economy. By targeting low-income populations, the government was able to create a self-sustaining demand for goods and services, which supported economic recovery.

Effectiveness of the Measures

India's stimulus packages and the focus on infrastructure and demand creation were highly effective in preventing a deeper recession. The immediate impact of the stimulus was visible in the increased industrial output, higher consumption levels, and job creation, particularly in the infrastructure sector. The measures helped maintain India's GDP growth rate during a period when most other economies were contracting. In the longer term, the infrastructure investments supported by the stimulus packages have continued to benefit India's economic growth. Improvements in transportation, energy, and telecommunications have enhanced the country's overall economic efficiency, productivity, and competitiveness.

In conclusion, India's stimulus measures, particularly in infrastructure spending and demand creation, played a crucial role in countering the economic impacts of the 2008 global financial crisis. These measures not only stabilized the economy in the short-term but also laid the groundwork for sustained growth in the future. The combination of government intervention, public spending, and tax incentives ensured that India remained on a path of positive growth while addressing critical structural issues in its economy. These steps were instrumental in ensuring that India emerged from the global financial crisis in a relatively strong position compared to many other countries.

Table 9.2: Breakdown of India's Stimulus Packages (2008-2009)

Sector	Allocation (INR Crore)
Infrastructure	1,00,000
Manufacturing	75,000
Exports	25,000
Social Welfare	50,000

• Lessons for Future Crises

India's response to the 2008 financial crisis provided valuable lessons in economic resilience and self-reliance, which are critical for managing future economic challenges. While the country's quick recovery demonstrated the effectiveness of timely government intervention and policy measures, the crisis underscored several key areas where India can build stronger foundations for future crises. Economic resilience refers to a nation's ability to withstand economic shocks, recover from them, and even grow in their aftermath.

Self-reliance, on the other hand, is the ability of a country to rely more on its own resources, capabilities, and strengths, rather than being overly dependent on external factors like global markets or foreign aid. The financial crisis of 2008 revealed that while India had a relatively insulated economy compared to many other nations, it was still vulnerable to external factors such as global economic slowdowns, fluctuations in commodity prices, and shifts in capital flows. However, the crisis response revealed crucial areas where India could focus its efforts to become more resilient and self-reliant in the future.

Diversification of the Economy

One of the most important lessons from the 2008 crisis was the need for economic diversification. Prior to the crisis, India had experienced robust growth, largely driven by the services sector, particularly IT and business outsourcing. However, the crisis led to a sharp reduction in global demand for these services, which in turn slowed growth. This exposed India's over-reliance on a few sectors, making the economy vulnerable to external shocks. In response to this vulnerability, India has been working towards diversifying its economic base by investing in sectors such as manufacturing, renewable energy, and agriculture. "Make in India" and "Atmanirbhar Bharat" (Self-Reliant India) initiatives are examples of strategies aimed at strengthening domestic industries and reducing dependence on imports. By promoting domestic manufacturing, particularly in electronics, defence, and pharmaceuticals, India aims to create a more balanced economy that is less susceptible to global disruptions.

Strengthening Financial Systems and Institutions

The 2008 crisis revealed weaknesses in global financial systems and the need for strong, well-regulated financial institutions to ensure that the economy can absorb shocks. While India's banking system was not as exposed to subprime mortgages as those in the US or Europe, the crisis still showed the vulnerabilities of India's financial sector, particularly in areas such as credit availability, capital adequacy, and non-performing assets (NPAs). Following the crisis, India took significant steps to reform its banking sector and increase its financial resilience. The government implemented measures to increase capital infusion into state-owned banks and improved the regulatory framework to ensure that they would remain strong in the event of another financial crisis. Additionally, the crisis highlighted the importance of strengthening capital markets, improving liquidity, and enhancing the efficiency of credit delivery systems.

In the future, India must continue to build on these reforms and adopt more sophisticated financial instruments and risk management practices. A stronger financial sector that is capable of withstanding global market fluctuations is a crucial pillar of economic resilience.

Boosting Domestic Consumption

The crisis also demonstrated the importance of nurturing domestic consumption as a pillar of economic growth. While external demand (exports) often drives the growth of emerging markets, India's focus on domestic consumption has allowed it to maintain steady growth even when global demand faltered. India's young population, combined with an expanding middle class, provides a solid foundation for domestic consumption to be a driver of growth during future crises. In future crises, India must focus on protecting and boosting consumer spending, especially in the lower-income groups, who are most vulnerable during economic downturns. This could be achieved through targeted social welfare programmes, such as direct cash transfers, food security measures, and policies that focus on job creation in high-employment sectors like agriculture, construction, and services.

Building Robust Supply Chains

The 2008 crisis also highlighted the risks of over-reliance on global supply chains, especially in times of global disruption. India's dependence on imports for critical goods such as crude oil, electronics, and industrial machinery became evident during the crisis. With disruptions in global supply chains, India experienced shortages of some essential products and saw prices rise sharply. The COVID-19 pandemic, which followed the 2008 crisis, further illustrated this vulnerability. To mitigate these risks, India has increasingly focused on building self-reliant supply chains, particularly in the manufacturing sector. The government's "Make in India" initiative is geared towards ensuring that critical goods are produced domestically and that India's supply chains are not dependent on external sources. India has also worked to diversify its import sources and negotiate better trade deals with multiple partners to reduce its exposure to global disruptions. In the future, it will be essential for India to continue strengthening its domestic manufacturing capabilities, especially in key sectors such as semiconductors, pharmaceuticals, agriculture, and energy. This will reduce India's dependence on imports and create a more resilient economy in the face of global challenges.

Importance of Technology and Innovation

The role of technology and innovation in enhancing economic resilience was another key lesson from the 2008 financial crisis. The rise of digital platforms, e-commerce, and fintech helped shield India's economy from some of the worst impacts of the global recession. The IT sector in particular played a crucial role in maintaining growth during the crisis, as it offered a source of foreign exchange and employment. In the future, India must focus on technological innovation and digitization as a means of building resilience. This involves promoting Research and Development (R&D) in cutting-edge technologies like artificial intelligence, renewable energy, and biotechnology. Digital inclusion, especially in rural areas, can also play a crucial role in building a more resilient economy. By investing in digital infrastructure and encouraging the growth of tech startups, India can ensure that it remains competitive on the global stage and less vulnerable to external shocks.

Sustaining Structural Reforms

Lastly, the crisis demonstrated the need for long-term structural reforms to build an economy that can withstand future shocks. India's continued focus on economic liberalization, regulatory reforms, and ease of doing business has played a key role in its recovery from the 2008 crisis. However, there is still much work to be done in areas such as labour market reforms, land acquisition processes, and fiscal consolidation. For future crises, India must continue its focus on structural reforms that enable the economy to be more flexible, competitive, and adaptable. This includes improving education systems, ensuring financial inclusion, and encouraging innovation.

A flexible labour market, business-friendly policies, and a modernized tax system will be essential for sustaining long-term growth and resilience. In conclusion, the 2008 financial crisis provided India with valuable lessons in economic resilience and self-reliance. The country's quick recovery demonstrated the effectiveness of timely government intervention, particularly in areas like infrastructure spending and domestic consumption. Moving forward, India must focus on economic diversification, strengthening its financial systems, building self-reliant supply chains, and fostering technological innovation. By continuing to implement structural reforms and focusing on long-term growth strategies, India can ensure that it is better equipped to handle future global economic crises and maintain a path toward sustainable and inclusive growth.

REFERENCES

archive.org

Banik, N. (2006). "How Promising is BIMSTEC?" *Economic and Political Weekly, 41*(51): 5264-68.

Chachavalpongpun, P. (2011). "Look East meets Look West: Indian-Southeast Asian Relations in Flux." *The International Spectator, 46*(2): 91-108. https://doi.org/10.1080/03932729.2011.576174

Nanda, P. (2003). *Re-discovering Asia: Evolution of India's Look East Policy*. Lancer Publishers & Distributors.

Nye, J.S. (1968). *International Regionalism*. Little Brown.

Raghavan, V. R. (Ed.). (2013). *Consequences of Long-term Conflicts in Northeast India*. Vij Books India.

Smith, A. (1909–1914). *Wealth of Nations* (ed. C.J. Bullock, Vol. X). P.F. Collier & Son.

Taneja, N. (2005). "Informal Trade in SAARC Region: Implications for Free Trade Agreement." In S. Soz, S.K. Sahni & R.N. Srivastava (Eds.), *Towards South Asian Economic Integration and Unity* (pp. 123-35). Foundation for Peace and Sustainable Development.

World Bank (1994). *India: Macroeconomics and Political Economy 1964-1991*. World Bank.

Yuan, J.D. (2006). *China-ASEAN Relations: Perspective, Prospects and Implications for U.S. Interests*. Strategic Studies Institute, U.S. Army War College.

10

Social Impact of Dr. Singh's Policies

Dr. Manmohan Singh, who served as the prime minister of India from 2004 to 2014, is often regarded as one of the most influential leaders in the history of modern India. With a background as an economist, Dr. Singh's tenure was largely defined by his efforts to continue India's economic liberalization and address the deep socio-economic challenges facing the country. As a pivotal figure behind the 1991 economic reforms, which opened India's economy to the world, he was instrumental in steering the nation through a period of significant global and domestic change. Dr. Singh's approach was shaped by a vision of inclusive development, where economic growth would not be just an elite benefit, but one that reached the poorest and most marginalized communities across India.

India, during Dr. Singh's leadership, was grappling with a multitude of challenges that stemmed from its colonial past, a rapidly expanding population, and the lingering effects of social inequality. While India had experienced economic growth since the early 1990s, vast disparities existed between the urban and rural sectors, the rich and the poor, and among various social groups. In this context, Dr. Singh's policies aimed to create a more equitable society through targeted interventions that focused on improving the lives of the disadvantaged. He often spoke about the need to harness India's demographic dividend, especially through improvements in health, education, infrastructure, and rural development.

Under Dr. Singh's leadership, the Indian government placed a strong emphasis on social welfare. Several flagship programmes were introduced or scaled up, such as the National Rural Employment Guarantee Act (NREGA), the Right to Education Act (RTE), the National Health Mission (NHM), and the Nirmal Bharat Abhiyan. These initiatives were designed to address the critical issues of poverty, unemployment, and underdevelopment, particularly in rural areas. In addition to these specific programmes, Dr. Singh's administration pursued broader macroeconomic reforms that were intended to promote economic stability and provide opportunities for all. Through policies aimed at reducing poverty, improving social infrastructure, and ensuring gender equality, Dr. Singh's government sought to pave the way for a more socially just and prosperous India.

Dr. Singh's social policies were rooted in the idea of "inclusive growth"—a development model that sought to ensure that the benefits of economic progress were felt not just by the urban elite but by the rural poor and other marginalized groups. His government's approach was based on the belief that economic growth and social justice should go hand in hand, as one could not exist without the other. As India continued its march toward becoming a global economic powerhouse, Dr. Singh sought to balance the demands of growth with the need for social equity. Despite the commendable intentions behind his policies, their implementation and long-term impact have been a subject of debate. Dr. Singh's social welfare programmes often faced criticism for their inefficiency, mismanagement, and lack of coordination between the central and state governments.

While some policies successfully lifted millions out of poverty and enhanced social services, others failed to meet expectations due to administrative challenges, corruption, and political opposition.

Moreover, the impact of these policies was not uniform, with certain regions and social groups benefiting more than others. In this regard, the social impact of Dr. Singh's policies can be seen as a complex mixture of achievements and limitations. The social landscape of India was deeply affected by Dr. Singh's policies. The Indian middle class expanded during his tenure, as millions of people moved out of poverty and into the formal economy. However, despite these advancements, inequality persisted, and the benefits of growth were not evenly distributed. His government's efforts to improve the lives of women, Scheduled Castes (SC), Scheduled Tribes (ST), and Other Backward Classes (OBCs) through affirmative action policies made significant strides, but social exclusion and discrimination continued to be pervasive challenges.

One of the most notable features of Dr. Singh's tenure was his focus on rural development. Recognizing that over 70 per cent of India's population lived in rural areas, the prime minister sought to address the developmental gap between rural and urban India. Initiatives such as the Mahatma Gandhi National Rural Employment Guarantee Act (MGNREGA) and the National Rural Livelihood Mission (NRLM) were designed to empower rural populations by providing employment, building infrastructure, and improving access to services. These programmes were intended to reduce migration to urban areas, stabilize rural communities, and create a more balanced development trajectory. Another area of focus was education and health. The Right to Education Act, which made education free and compulsory for children between the ages of 6 and 14, was a landmark achievement of Dr. Singh's government.

In the field of health care, the National Rural Health Mission worked to improve access to health services in underserved regions. However, while these initiatives expanded access to basic services, significant challenges in quality and availability of services remained, particularly in remote areas. Dr. Singh's tenure also marked a period of increased focus on gender equality. Several schemes aimed at empowering women, including the Beti Bachao

Beti Padhao Yojana and the Ujjwala Yojana, sought to improve access to education, health care, and economic opportunities for women, particularly in rural areas. These policies helped empower women economically, but cultural and societal barriers remained a challenge to achieving full gender equality. Despite the successes, Dr. Singh's government faced considerable challenges in policy implementation. Bureaucratic inefficiencies, political opposition, and corruption at various levels of government hampered the delivery of benefits to the intended populations.

Moreover, while Dr. Singh's policies aimed to achieve significant social transformation, they often fell short of addressing the underlying structural inequalities in Indian society. This chapter will explore the social impact of Dr. Singh's policies by delving into key areas such as economic reforms, rural development, health care, education, gender equality, and social justice. Each section will analyse the successes and challenges of these policies, drawing on data and examples to assess their overall effectiveness. The chapter will conclude with a reflection on Dr. Singh's legacy and the long-term social changes brought about by his tenure as prime minister. In conclusion, Dr. Singh's policies had a profound and lasting impact on the social fabric of India. While his government faced several obstacles in achieving its ambitious goals, it made significant strides in improving the lives of millions of Indians. The success of these policies, however, was tempered by challenges in implementation and the persistence of inequality. Dr. Singh's tenure serves as a reminder of the complexities of governing a diverse, rapidly developing nation like India and highlights the importance of balancing economic growth with social equity.

▪ Empowering Rural India

Rural India, constituting the majority of India's population, has historically faced numerous socio-economic challenges. With around 70 per cent of the Indian population residing in rural areas, much of the nation's economic activities, including agriculture, crafts, and small-scale industries, have been concentrated in these regions. Despite its crucial role in the national economy, rural India has long suffered from poverty, underemployment, inadequate infrastructure, lack of access to basic amenities, and poor governance.

While agriculture has remained the dominant occupation for rural India, it often provided insufficient returns, leaving millions dependent on seasonal incomes, periodic migration to urban centres, and informal labour markets. In this context, the importance of rural development and empowerment has become a central focus of India's socio-economic policies, particularly during the tenure of Dr. Manmohan Singh. One of the most significant steps taken by Dr. Singh's government was the introduction of the MGNREGA in 2005. This programme, regarded as one of the most ambitious and far-reaching rural development initiatives in India's history, aimed at providing guaranteed wage employment to rural households and helping them build essential infrastructure. Its ultimate goal was to uplift the socio-economic conditions of rural India by offering both employment opportunities and long-term rural development through infrastructure projects.

MGNREGA: The Foundations of Rural Employment and Infrastructure

The MGNREGA, now renamed the Mahatma Gandhi National Rural Employment Guarantee Scheme (MGNREGS), was designed to provide 100 days of guaranteed wage employment annually to every rural household whose adult members are willing to engage in manual labour at minimum wages. The programme's primary objectives were to reduce rural poverty, enhance rural infrastructure, and promote social equity, especially for vulnerable groups like women, SC, ST, and landless labourers.

The Role of Employment Guarantee in Rural India

Prior to the introduction of MGNREGA, many rural households

were forced to seek seasonal and low-paying labour or migrate to cities in search of employment. Many of them were stuck in the cycle of poverty, unable to break free due to the irregularity of work and underemployment. By guaranteeing employment, MGNREGA provided a much-needed safety net for the rural poor, offering financial security and an escape from the traditional patterns of migration and exploitation in informal labour markets. It helped to reduce seasonal unemployment and gave rural workers more control over their livelihoods. The work under the scheme was focused on creating public infrastructure—such as rural roads, water conservation structures, irrigation systems, drainage systems, afforestation, and land development. This not only offered immediate employment but also contributed to long-term rural development by creating lasting assets that improved the quality of life in these areas.

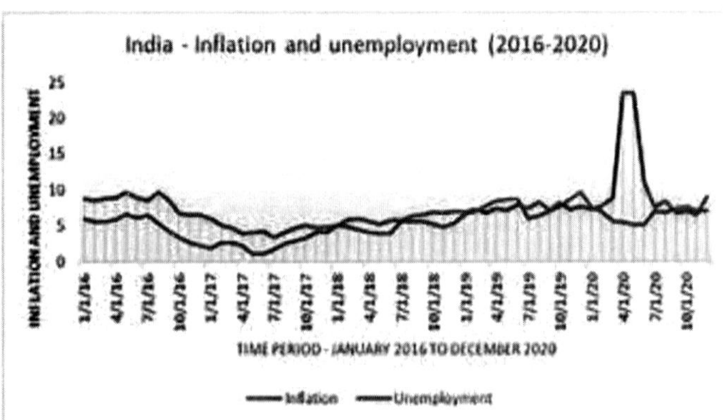

Fig. 10.1: Impact of the Recession on Employment Levels in India (2016-20)

For instance, the development of rural roads improved connectivity, making it easier for rural communities to access markets, education, health care, and government services. Likewise, the construction of water conservation structures such as check dams, water harvesting pits, and ponds helped farmers mitigate the effects of water scarcity and improved agricultural productivity. These small yet significant infrastructure projects contributed to the broader objective of improving rural resilience and sustainability, especially in areas prone to natural calamities like floods or droughts.

Gender Equality and Empowerment Through MGNREGA

One of the unique features of MGNREGA was its focus on empowering women in rural India. The programme offered significant opportunities for women, especially in remote rural areas, where gender discrimination often limits women's access to the formal labour market. Under MGNREGA, women could participate in manual labour and earn wages equal to men, which was a significant step toward gender equality in rural economies. The programme's impact on women was multidimensional. It empowered rural women economically by providing them with income independent of family earnings, which in turn enhanced their social standing within the household and community. Additionally, women's involvement in these activities contributed to the overall economic development of their households, allowing them to invest in education, health care, and nutrition, which are key drivers of social change. Moreover, by ensuring that one-third of the participants in the programme were women, MGNREGA aimed to provide gender equity in rural employment.

In many rural areas, women traditionally undertook household chores and caregiving responsibilities, but MGNREGA offered them a formal opportunity to engage in paid labour, thus improving their economic independence and empowering them within their communities.

Long-term Economic Impact and Poverty Reduction

The most significant impact of MGNREGA has been its contribution to poverty reduction in rural India. By providing regular employment and ensuring income security, it enabled rural households to meet their basic needs, such as food, health care, and education. This had a profound effect on economic well-being and helped lift many families out of the clutches of poverty. According to various studies and reports, MGNREGA's success in reducing rural poverty has been particularly evident in states such as Rajasthan, Bihar, Uttar Pradesh, and Madhya Pradesh, where the programme was widely implemented. The programme has also played a crucial role in improving access to education for children in rural households. With the provision of guaranteed wages, many parents were able to send their children to school rather than forcing them into child labour or keeping them at home due to financial constraints. In this way, MGNREGA helped to break the intergenerational cycle of poverty and foster social development in rural areas.

Rural Infrastructure: Building the Foundation for Sustainable Growth

In addition to providing direct employment to rural workers, MGNREGA's focus on infrastructure development has been one of its most significant contributions to rural India. The creation of infrastructure assets such as rural roads, irrigation systems, and water conservation structures has played a pivotal role in enhancing rural productivity and facilitating market access for rural farmers. For example, the construction of roads under MGNREGA has enabled farmers to transport their goods to local markets, which has reduced the time and cost associated with transportation and improved the sale price of their produce. The focus on irrigation and water conservation under MGNREGA has been especially important for agriculture, which remains the backbone of the rural economy. By providing access to water for irrigation, MGNREGA helped improve crop yields, increase agricultural sustainability, and mitigate the risks posed by climate change and water scarcity. In some areas, the construction of small check dams and rainwater harvesting systems allowed farmers to retain water during dry seasons, thus improving agricultural productivity in the long-term.

Challenges and Implementation Issues

While MGNREGA has been widely hailed as a revolutionary programme, it has not been without its challenges. One of the primary issues faced by the programme has been implementation inefficiencies at the ground level. Despite the scheme's ambitious objectives, local-level corruption, delays in wage payments, poor monitoring, and lack of transparency in fund allocation have hampered the programme's full potential in some areas. In some regions, funds meant for workers were misappropriated, or the wages were delayed, leading to frustration among workers and diminishing the programme's impact. Another concern was that the focus of MGNREGA remained heavily on manual labour. While the programme provided crucial short-term employment, it did not adequately address the long-term need for skilled labour and sustainable employment in rural India.

Critics argued that there was insufficient focus on skills training or the creation of higher-paying jobs, which could have helped uplift rural workers from basic labour to more sustainable, skill-based employment. Furthermore, some scholars and policymakers have questioned the programme's ability to promote sustainable development. While the infrastructure projects funded by MGNREGA had short-term benefits, there was concern about their long-term utility and maintenance. In some cases, poor planning and lack of coordination between various government agencies led to the construction of inadequate or poorly designed infrastructure that failed to deliver lasting benefits.

Complementary Initiatives for Rural Empowerment

In addition to MGNREGA, Dr. Manmohan Singh's government also rolled out several other rural development programmes aimed at addressing the multidimensional challenges faced by rural India. These complementary programmes were designed to provide broader solutions for poverty alleviation, livelihood creation, and rural welfare. For example, the NRLM, also known as Aajeevika, was aimed at promoting self-employment and enhancing the livelihoods of rural poor families, especially women. Through this initiative, rural households were provided with credit, skills training, and access to various livelihood options like agriculture-based enterprises, animal husbandry, and handicrafts. Furthermore, the Pradhan Mantri Gram Sadak Yojana (PMGSY), launched in 2000, aimed at improving rural connectivity by constructing all-weather roads to link remote villages to larger towns and cities. This, along with rural electrification programmes, significantly improved access to markets, education, and health care, further contributing to rural empowerment.

Financial Inclusion and Empowerment

A key aspect of rural empowerment during Dr. Singh's tenure was the focus on financial inclusion. Through the Pradhan Mantri Jan Dhan Yojana (PMJDY), the government aimed at providing bank accounts to every household in rural India, enabling them to access financial services such as savings, credit, insurance, and pensions. Financial inclusion is seen as a critical enabler of rural empowerment, as it ensures that rural households have access to the tools necessary for economic growth and security. The empowerment of rural India through initiatives such as MGNREGA and other rural development programmes has had a transformative impact on the socio-economic landscape of the country.

These programmes not only provided immediate relief to the rural poor by offering guaranteed employment but also helped to build the foundation for long-term rural development by improving infrastructure, access to services, and economic opportunities. Despite challenges in implementation and areas that require further focus, these initiatives have laid the groundwork for sustainable rural growth and empowerment, helping millions in rural India escape the cycle of poverty and build better lives for themselves and their families. The success of MGNREGA and complementary rural development programmes in empowering rural India reflects the importance of inclusive economic policies that prioritize sustainable livelihoods, gender equality, and social inclusion. As India continues its path toward modernization, ensuring the continued empowerment of rural India remains central to its development agenda.

▪ Infrastructure Development

Infrastructure plays a crucial role in the overall development of any nation, especially in a vast and diverse country like India, where a large portion of the population still resides in rural areas. Effective infrastructure is essential for economic growth, social development, and the equitable distribution of resources. In the context of rural India, infrastructure development has been a pivotal aspect of both economic progress and social welfare, especially since the early 2000s when various government initiatives aimed to connect rural and urban India more effectively. Among the most significant areas of infrastructure development in India have been roads, electricity, and urban-rural connectivity. These three pillars are fundamental in enhancing the livelihoods of rural populations, reducing poverty, fostering economic opportunities, and bridging the urban-rural divide. By improving access to markets, education, health care, and government services, infrastructure development is central to enabling long-term growth in rural areas.

Roads: Enhancing Connectivity and Market Access

One of the most important elements of infrastructure development in rural India has been the focus on road construction. Access to well-built, all-weather roads is vital for linking rural areas to urban centres, where there is better access to economic opportunities, services, and markets. Rural roads are crucial not only for economic integration but also for enhancing social equity, as they make it easier for rural populations to access essential services such as healthcare and education. The PMGSY, launched in 2000, was a significant initiative aimed at improving rural roads. The scheme's primary objective was to provide all-weather roads to connect rural habitations to main roads and urban centres.

By improving rural road infrastructure, PMGSY contributed to economic growth by enabling farmers and small entrepreneurs to transport goods more efficiently, reducing transportation costs, and increasing the potential market for agricultural products and crafts. Improved road connectivity also facilitates better social mobility. Rural residents can now access markets more easily, sell products at competitive prices, and make informed decisions based on market conditions. Moreover, better roads improve access to health care and education, as people can travel to urban areas for specialized treatments or better schools. Rural tourism has also benefited from improved roads, with easier access to tourist destinations in rural regions helping create local employment and promoting regional development.

Electricity: Powering Rural Development

Electricity plays a critical role in ensuring economic development and quality of life. Reliable and affordable electricity supply is essential for businesses, education, health care, and livelihoods. Historically, rural India has faced challenges related to inadequate electricity supply and unequal distribution, which has often hindered its growth potential. In response to these challenges, the Indian government launched the Deen Dayal Upadhyaya Gram Jyoti Yojana (DDUGJY) in 2015, aimed at providing 24×7 electricity to rural areas. The goal was to improve the availability and reliability of electricity by expanding the grid and upgrading the existing infrastructure. This initiative sought to address long-standing issues like erratic power supply, high transmission losses, and low electrification rates in remote villages. Electricity has a multifaceted impact on rural communities. For farmers, the reliable supply of electricity is crucial for irrigation systems and agriculture.

It powers water pumps for irrigation, making farming less dependent on rain and helping improve crop yields. Cold storage facilities and processing units that rely on electricity can enhance the shelf life of agricultural produce, reduce wastage, and improve farmers' income. Moreover, electricity supports educational opportunities. With the availability of power, rural students can benefit from digital learning tools, e-books, and other online educational resources, which can bridge the educational gap between urban and rural areas. Electricity also supports rural industries, enabling small-scale manufacturing, craft production, and entrepreneurial ventures that contribute to local employment and economic growth. In addition, the electrification of rural areas improves the quality of life by providing access to essential services like clean drinking water, health care, and reliable lighting, which can reduce dependency on traditional, often hazardous, forms of energy like kerosene lamps or firewood.

Urban-Rural Connectivity: Bridging the Divide

Urban-rural connectivity refers to the physical, economic, and social links between urban and rural areas. Strengthening this connectivity is crucial for improving economic opportunities, access to services, and social welfare. Urban-rural connectivity is not just about physical infrastructure like roads and railways but also includes digital connectivity, economic integration, and access to government schemes. India's rural areas have long faced isolation from the mainstream economy due to poor infrastructure, particularly in remote and underserved regions. The government recognized that better urban-rural connectivity was essential to reducing the disparity between cities and villages. Various initiatives, such as PMGSY, DDUGJY, and the National Optical Fiber Network (NOFN), have focused on improving infrastructure to create stronger links between urban and rural India.

Improved road networks, especially through initiatives like PMGSY, not only reduce transportation costs but also facilitate better social integration. By connecting rural populations to urban markets, the availability of goods and services in remote areas is increased, and consumers benefit from a broader range of products. Rural farmers, artisans, and small-scale industries can access larger markets, leading to better pricing, better value for their products, and economic stability. Beyond physical infrastructure, digital connectivity has become increasingly important. The NOFN, launched by the government in 2011, sought to connect rural India to high-speed Internet. This connectivity facilitates access to a wide array of services, including e-government, digital education, health-care consultations, online financial services, and agriculture-related information.

The expansion of digital infrastructure has helped bridge the information gap between urban and rural areas, enabling rural communities to be more informed and self-reliant.

Synergies between Roads, Electricity, and Urban-Rural Connectivity

The synergy between roads, electricity, and urban-rural connectivity is essential for holistic rural development. Improving rural roads enhances the effectiveness of electricity supply by making it easier to install and maintain power lines in rural areas. Similarly, electrifying rural areas contributes to better access to digital infrastructure, as it enables Internet services to reach even the most remote locations. This integrated approach is evident in government initiatives that promote comprehensive rural development. For example, the Pradhan Mantri Awas Yojana (PMAY) and PMGSY work in tandem to build both physical infrastructure (roads, housing) and provide electricity to rural areas, thereby improving living conditions and creating a sustainable foundation for economic development. These projects not only provide tangible benefits in the form of better housing, roads, and energy but also contribute to broader objectives such as health care, education, and employment generation.

Challenges and the Road Ahead

Despite significant progress, the development of infrastructure in rural India still faces numerous challenges. Geographical isolation, funding constraints, bureaucratic inefficiencies, and maintenance issues remain barriers to progress. The sheer scale of the task—improving infrastructure for millions of rural residents across diverse terrains and regions—is daunting, and often progress is slower than desired. One of the biggest challenges lies in the maintenance of the infrastructure once it is built. In many instances, rural roads, irrigation systems, and other infrastructure have fallen into disrepair due to insufficient maintenance budgets or lack of community involvement.

Similarly, electricity supply remains unreliable in certain regions, especially during peak demand seasons. Another challenge lies in ensuring that urban-rural connectivity is not just about access to physical infrastructure but also about creating inclusive growth opportunities for rural populations. Many rural areas still suffer from a lack of access to education, health care, and employment opportunities, despite improvements in physical infrastructure. The development of roads, electricity, and urban-rural connectivity has been central to India's rural transformation. Programmes like PMGSY, DDUGJY, and NOFN have significantly improved the infrastructure landscape in rural areas, promoting economic growth, enhancing livelihoods, and bridging the rural-urban divide.

As the government continues to focus on these areas, there is immense potential for sustainable rural development, especially when infrastructure projects are paired with economic empowerment, skills training, and entrepreneurship development. In conclusion, the road ahead for India's rural infrastructure development lies in overcoming challenges related to implementation, maintenance, and inclusive growth. By improving connectivity, electricity access, and market access, India can empower its rural communities and ensure that they have the tools necessary to thrive in a rapidly developing economy.

• Financial Inclusion

Financial inclusion remains one of the most important drivers of sustainable development. In India, a country with one of the largest rural populations in the world, the expansion of banking services to underserved areas has become a pivotal policy goal. The absence of access to financial services in rural areas, such as savings accounts, credit, insurance, and pensions, has long been a barrier to socio-economic growth. In India, where a significant percentage of the population lives in rural regions, financial exclusion often limits opportunities, prevents economic participation, and perpetuates poverty. Therefore, ensuring that even the most marginalized populations have access to banking services is key to unlocking the potential for sustainable development.

The Need for Financial Inclusion

Financial inclusion serves as the bedrock for promoting economic empowerment and reducing poverty, particularly in rural areas. Lack of access to banking services means individuals cannot access credit, insurance, or savings accounts, thus stifling entrepreneurship, limiting growth opportunities, and leaving individuals vulnerable to economic shocks. Historically, rural India has been marked by a heavy dependence on informal financial sources such as moneylenders and local traders, which often come with exploitative interest rates and unfavourable terms. As a result, many rural populations have been economically disenfranchized. Additionally, for rural households, limited access to formal credit and savings systems often means being unable to invest in business opportunities, secure education for children, or meet health-related expenses. Access to formal financial products such as insurance, credit facilities, and government subsidies can significantly improve an individual's or community's resilience to economic challenges, offering a safer and more reliable alternative to informal financial networks.

Women, in particular, benefit greatly from financial inclusion, as it empowers them to contribute to household income and become more financially independent, offering them greater opportunities for social and economic mobility. Given the challenges that rural populations face in accessing financial services, addressing financial inclusion is not merely a matter of improving access to banking, but also about transforming the very nature of how finance and banking services reach and serve rural communities. Creating a financial ecosystem where services are accessible, affordable, and relevant to the needs of low-income households and communities is key to driving sustainable economic development.

Government Initiatives for Financial Inclusion

The Indian government has launched several initiatives to address the gaps in financial inclusion, specifically targeting rural and underserved populations. By modernizing the banking sector, providing financial literacy, and increasing the accessibility of banking services, the government has laid the foundation for a more inclusive financial system. These initiatives focus on leveraging technology, increasing access to financial products, and expanding the outreach of banking services to rural areas.

- **Pradhan Mantri Jan Dhan Yojana (PMJDY):** One of the most significant policy initiatives aimed at financial inclusion is the PMJDY, launched in 2014. The programme's core objective is to provide universal access to banking services by opening zero-balance savings accounts for the unbanked, especially in rural areas. Under PMJDY, individuals are not only provided with a savings account but also have access to other services such as insurance, overdraft facilities, and pension schemes. The scheme also connects Aadhaar numbers to bank accounts, facilitating Direct Benefit Transfers (DBT) for various government subsidies and schemes. This integration of bank accounts with Aadhaar and mobile phones has significantly reduced the incidence of leakages and fraud in government benefit distribution. Since its inception, PMJDY has been hailed as a success, with over 450 million accounts being opened as of 2021. This massive expansion of banking access has made a considerable impact in rural areas, where the reach of financial institutions was previously limited. By targeting those most in need of financial services, PMJDY has helped reduce exclusion, improve access to social benefits, and boost economic security for millions of Indians.

- **Financial Literacy and Digital Banking:** The expansion of digital banking has played an instrumental role in promoting financial inclusion in rural areas. With the growing penetration of smartphones and the Internet, mobile banking has emerged as a cost-effective solution for extending financial services to underserved areas. The government has actively promoted digital banking through initiatives such as M-Governance, and mobile wallets. Mobile banking has made it possible for people in remote areas to access essential services such as fund transfers, bill payments, and loan applications without having to visit physical bank branches.

The Pradhan Mantri Gramin Digital Saksharta Abhiyan (PMGDISHA), launched in 2017, is a programme designed to improve digital literacy across rural India. The initiative aims to digitally empower citizens, particularly in rural areas, and enable them to participate in the digital economy. By promoting financial literacy and educating people on the use of mobile wallets and Internet banking, PMGDISHA ensures that digital tools are used effectively for financial transactions. Moreover, Self-Help Groups (SHGs) have played a major role in financial inclusion by providing credit, savings, and insurance to low-income households, especially for women. These groups allow members to pool their savings and lend to each other, creating access to capital for small-scale businesses or individual needs. The SHGs model has proven successful in promoting social cohesion and financial independence in rural areas.

- **Microfinance Institutions (MFIs):** Microfinance institutions (MFIs) have been crucial in addressing the credit gap in rural areas. These institutions provide small, unsecured loans to individuals, particularly women and small-scale entrepreneurs, who may not have access to traditional banking loans due to the lack of collateral or credit histories. MFIs use a group lending model, where groups of borrowers come together to vouch for one another's creditworthiness. This model has proven to be effective in enabling rural populations to secure small loans for business ventures, agriculture, or emergency expenses.

The Role of Commercial and Regional Rural Banks (RRBs)

India's commercial banks, along with RRBs, have been at the forefront of promoting financial inclusion. RRBs, established in 1976, have been tasked with providing banking services to rural areas and have made considerable progress in extending access to credit, savings accounts, and insurance to low-income households.

These banks, unlike large commercial banks, operate with a focus on rural customers and often provide loans for agricultural purposes or support for small businesses. Commercial banks, especially public sector banks, have been active participants in expanding financial access in rural areas. Over the years, many public sector banks have increased their rural network of branches and ATMs to serve customers who may otherwise have to travel long distances to access banking services. The banking correspondent model has further strengthened this push by deploying agents to perform basic banking services on behalf of banks, making banking more accessible for rural populations.

• Challenges to Financial Inclusion

Despite the progress made through various initiatives, India still faces several challenges when it comes to financial inclusion in rural areas.

Geographical and Technological Barriers

India's vast and often difficult-to-reach rural areas remain a significant hurdle to financial inclusion. While cities and towns have benefited from widespread access to digital banking, remote villages still struggle with poor infrastructure, lack of Internet connectivity, and inadequate road networks. These challenges hinder the growth of banking services in rural areas, and solutions to these problems are necessary to ensure that financial services reach every corner of the country. Digital banking, while effective, also faces technological barriers, particularly in rural areas with low Internet penetration and poor mobile network coverage. Even though the smartphone revolution has reached rural India, low literacy rates and technological illiteracy continue to limit the adoption of mobile banking and digital financial tools in certain areas.

Financial Literacy and Awareness

Low levels of financial literacy continue to be a major obstacle to widespread adoption of formal financial services. Many rural individuals are not fully aware of the benefits of savings accounts, insurance, or access to credit, and often mistrust the formal banking system. Financial education programmes are crucial to bridging this gap and encouraging people to adopt banking services.

Cultural and Behavioural Barriers

In many rural communities, there exists a strong reliance on informal lending networks, which often offer quick access to credit, albeit with higher interest rates. This cultural reliance on informal systems poses a significant challenge to convincing rural populations to switch to formal banking, even if the terms are more favourable. Changing long-established financial behaviours and mindsets requires sustained effort through education, trust-building, and outreach programmes.

▪ The Road Ahead

Looking forward, the path to full financial inclusion in India involves several key steps:

- **Enhancing Digital Infrastructure:** Continued investment in digital infrastructure and Internet connectivity in rural areas will be crucial for extending financial services.
- **Tailored Financial Products:** There is a need to develop more tailored financial products for rural populations, especially in sectors like agriculture, fisheries, and small businesses.
- **Improved Financial Literacy:** Financial literacy programmes need to be expanded to ensure that people in rural areas are aware of the full range of financial products available to them.
- **Support for Financial Institutions:** Continued support for institutions such as microfinance and SHGs will help provide access to credit for underserved populations.

Conclusion

Financial inclusion is not just about providing access to banking services; it is about creating an ecosystem where individuals in rural India can participate in the broader economy, improve their livelihoods, and achieve financial security. Through a combination of government initiatives, the expansion of digital banking, and the strengthening of local financial institutions, India has made remarkable strides toward ensuring that its rural population is no longer excluded from the formal financial system. However, continued efforts are needed to address remaining barriers and ensure that financial inclusion reaches every individual, regardless of their geographical location, socio-economic status, or literacy levels.

The future of India's rural economy depends on this inclusive approach, which will not only foster economic growth but also contribute to greater social equality.

REFERENCES

Asian Relations (1948). *Report of the Proceedings and Documentation of the First Asian Relations Conference,* New Delhi, March 1947. Asian Relations Organization.

Bhattacharya, B.B. (1992). *India's Economic Crises: Debt Burden and Specialisation.* Delhi: B.R. Publishing Corporation.

Ghosh, M. (2013). *Liberalization, Growth and Regional Disparities in India.* Springer, India.

Gordon, S. (1995). "India and Southeast Asia: A Renaissance in Relations?" In S. Gordon & S. Henningham (Eds.), *India Looks East: An Emerging Power and Its Asia-Pacific Neighbours* (pp. 207-29). Australian National University.

______(1995). *India's Rise to Power in the Twentieth Century and Beyond.* Macmillan Press Ltd.

Grare, F. & Mattoo, A. (2001). *India and ASEAN.* Manohar.

Haokip, T. (2011). "India's Look East Policy: Its Evolution and Approach." *South Asian Survey, 18*(2): 239-57. https://doi.org/10.1177/0971523113513368

Harshe, R. (1999). "South Asian Regional Co-operation: Problems and Prospects." *Economic and Political Weekly, 44*(19): 1100-1105.

Harvey, D. (2005). *A Brief History of Neoliberalism.* Oxford University Press.

Jaffrelot, C. (2003). "India's Look East Policy: An Asianist Strategy in Perspective." *India Review, 2*(2): 35-68.

11

Challenges During His Tenure

Dr. Manmohan Singh's tenure as India's prime minister, from 2004 to 2014, was marked by complex challenges that not only tested his leadership abilities but also shaped the trajectory of India's political and economic landscape for years to come. Singh, an economist by training and known for his technocratic approach, inherited an India that was increasingly becoming an important player on the global stage, but also one fraught with deep-rooted political, economic, and social challenges. While his tenure is often remembered for the remarkable economic growth India experienced during the 2000s, it was also a time of significant internal strife and external pressures that demanded tough decisions and at times, compromises. One of the most pressing challenges Dr. Singh faced was managing a coalition government, which often acted as a double-edged sword.

Leading the United Progressive Alliance (UPA), a coalition of more than a dozen parties with divergent ideologies and priorities, Singh was forced to navigate the intricacies of coalition dynamics. Maintaining a stable political front required constant balancing of competing interests, often leading to delays in decision making and policy paralysis. For instance, the inability to push through critical reforms in areas like labour laws, land acquisition, and retail trade liberalization was a result of constant friction between the various parties within the coalition, with the Left parties being particularly vocal in their opposition to market-oriented reforms.

Singh's leadership was put to the test as he had to constantly juggle the needs of coalition partners, regional parties, and factions within his own party, the Indian National Congress (INC). Dr. Singh's tenure was also marred by a series of corruption scandals that severely dented the public's trust in the government. The 2G spectrum scam, one of the largest corruption scandals in India's history, became a focal point of political opposition. The alleged irregularities in the allocation of spectrum licences resulted in the loss of billions of dollars to the exchequer, according to some estimates, and led to widespread outrage. Singh, despite being known for his integrity, found it challenging to distance himself from the scandal as it involved several members of his cabinet.

Table 11.1: India's Export and Import Trends During the Recession

Year	Exports (USD Billion)	Imports (USD Billion)
2007	155	235
2008	175	300
2009	165	257
2010	220	350
2011	302	412

The political fallout from this scandal was compounded by the coal allocation scam, where allegations of illegal coal mine allotments to private companies under the UPA government led to public indignation and demands for accountability. The opposition, led by the Bharatiya Janata Party (BJP), seized on these scandals to launch a vigorous campaign against Singh and his government, calling it the most corrupt in Indian history. Despite Singh's own clean image, the scandals eroded the credibility of his leadership and diverted attention from the government's successes. Economic challenges also loomed large during Singh's second term, particularly in the form of rising inflation and a burgeoning fiscal deficit.

While India's economy had grown at an impressive rate of 8-9 per cent annually during the early years of the twenty-first century, the global financial crisis of 2008 shook the foundations of the world economy, including India's. Although India was relatively insulated from the immediate effects of the crisis due to its limited exposure to global financial markets, the ripple effects were felt through declining export demand, slower foreign direct investment (FDI), and capital outflows. Singh's government responded with a series of stimulus packages designed to counter the slowdown. These measures included increased public spending on infrastructure, rural development programmes, and fiscal stimuli aimed at boosting domestic consumption. However, the measures had limited success in curbing inflation, which remained high, particularly in food prices, leading to public discontent.

The government's failure to contain inflation became one of the major criticisms of Singh's leadership, particularly as food prices, especially for essential items like onions and pulses, soared to alarming levels. The issue of inflation was not the only challenge on the economic front. Singh's government faced increasing pressure to tackle the growing fiscal deficit, which had ballooned as a result of the stimulus packages and rising expenditure. While economic growth remained robust in the years immediately following the global financial crisis, fiscal prudence was a constant concern. Singh's government grappled with the task of managing the deficit while ensuring that the growth momentum was not lost. This became particularly challenging as the government faced demands for increased public spending on social welfare programmes, including the National Rural Employment Guarantee Act (NREGA) and the Food Security Bill, both of which were central to Singh's vision of inclusive growth.

Singh's focus on these social welfare programmes was part of his broader agenda to address the socio-economic inequalities that were exacerbated by the country's rapid economic growth.

However, the increased fiscal burden of these programmes led to mounting concerns about the long-term sustainability of India's public finances. Another significant challenge faced by Dr. Singh's government was the slow pace of infrastructure development. Despite the impressive economic growth during the early 2000s, India's infrastructure remained inadequate to meet the demands of a rapidly growing economy. The country's road network, power generation capacity, and urban-rural connectivity were woefully insufficient, limiting the ability of industries to expand and for rural areas to benefit from economic growth. In particular, power shortages became a major bottleneck to industrial growth, and delays in the construction of key infrastructure projects led to frustrations among businesses and citizens alike.

Singh's government made significant efforts to address these gaps, with initiatives such as the National Highways Development Project (NHDP) and the Jawaharlal Nehru National Urban Renewal Mission (JNNURM). However, these projects faced delays due to bureaucratic red tape, land acquisition challenges, and a lack of coordination between central and state governments. The slow pace of infrastructure development became a constant challenge to Singh's vision of India as an emerging global economic power. On the foreign policy front, Dr. Singh's leadership was similarly tested by a complex global environment. India's rise as an economic power brought with it both opportunities and challenges. Singh sought to balance India's economic interests with its growing diplomatic influence, particularly in the areas of trade and investment.

India's relationship with the United States became a key focus during Singh's tenure, particularly with the signing of the Indo-US nuclear deal in 2008. While the deal was hailed as a landmark achievement that would improve India's energy security and enhance its global standing, it also faced considerable opposition domestically, with political parties accusing the government of compromising India's sovereignty for the sake of strategic ties with the US. Singh's leadership in navigating the nuclear deal was emblematic of the broader challenges he faced in balancing domestic concerns with international aspirations. Dr. Singh's government was also engaged in strengthening India's relations with other emerging economies, particularly through forums like the BRICS (Brazil, Russia, India, China, South Africa) and G20. Singh's advocacy for multilateralism and greater economic cooperation among developing nations was a key feature of India's foreign policy during his tenure.

He worked to strengthen India's trade relations with countries in Africa, Asia, and Latin America, and sought to position India as a leader of the global South. However, balancing India's aspirations for global leadership with the domestic realities of poverty and inequality presented a persistent challenge. Throughout his tenure, Dr. Singh's leadership was characterized by his calm demeanour, pragmatism, and commitment to long-term growth. However, the myriad challenges he faced, from managing a fractious coalition government to dealing with corruption scandals, political opposition, and global economic pressures, meant that his government was constantly under scrutiny. Despite his successes in driving India's economic growth, the challenges he encountered left a complicated legacy. Dr. Singh's tenure, therefore, represents a period of significant transformation for India, but also one marked by missed opportunities, political turbulence, and an often-difficult struggle to reconcile the ambitions of a growing global power with the realities of domestic governance.

▪ Navigating Political Opposition

Navigating political opposition during Dr. Manmohan Singh's tenure as prime minister was a critical challenge that shaped the policy decisions of his government. A key aspect of this opposition revolved around resistance to economic liberalization, which had been a central theme of India's economic reforms since the early 1990s. Dr. Singh, a strong proponent of market-driven policies, faced significant opposition from both within his government's coalition and from various political factions outside it, particularly those with left-wing ideologies. Economic liberalization in India had begun in earnest in 1991 under the leadership of then-Finance Minister Dr. Manmohan Singh, when the country was forced to adopt structural reforms in response to a balance of payments crisis. These reforms included trade liberalization, reducing import tariffs, privatization of state-owned enterprises, and encouraging foreign direct investment (FDI).

By the time Dr. Singh became prime minister in 2004, the reform process had already set the country on a path of rapid economic growth. However, the implementation of deeper reforms faced fierce opposition, especially from political parties and interest groups who believed that liberalization disproportionately benefited the wealthy and neglected the country's marginalized communities. A significant portion of the resistance came from left-wing parties, particularly the Communist Party of India (CPI) and the Communist Party of India (Marxist) (CPI-M), who were staunchly against liberalization policies. These parties had been influential coalition partners in the United Progressive Alliance (UPA), Dr. Singh's governing coalition, and their opposition to economic reforms posed a constant challenge.

They viewed the liberalization agenda as inherently capitalist and believed it would lead to the widening of inequality, unemployment, and exploitation of the working class. The Left's resistance was not only ideological but also deeply rooted in concerns over the impact of privatization, foreign investment, and deregulation on India's public sector and labour market. The Left parties pushed for policies that favoured state control and protectionism, which directly conflicted with Dr. Singh's vision of a market-driven economy. The challenge was particularly evident when Dr. Singh's government attempted to introduce new reforms such as the introduction of FDI in the retail sector. The proposal to allow global retail giants like Walmart and Carrefour to enter India faced vehement opposition from not just left-wing parties but also from sections of the Congress party, regional parties, and traders' associations who feared it would harm small businesses and lead to job losses.

Despite his own convictions about the need for opening up the retail sector to global competition, Dr. Singh was forced to backtrack on several occasions due to the strong political pushback. This was emblematic of the broader challenge he faced in advancing economic liberalization while maintaining political support from a diverse coalition of parties with differing views on economic policy. In addition to left-wing parties, the opposition parties, particularly the Bharatiya Janata Party (BJP), also capitalized on the discontent surrounding economic reforms to target Dr. Singh's government. The BJP frequently accused the UPA government of being "pro-business" and "anti-poor", arguing that liberalization had failed to deliver benefits to India's rural population and the underprivileged sections of society. The opposition painted the economic reforms as a betrayal of the Congress party's traditional support base, particularly in rural and agricultural constituencies.

During this period, concerns about the growing rural-urban divide and the agrarian distress were widely discussed, with critics arguing that liberalization had failed to address the pressing needs of India's vast rural population. The opposition parties often used these arguments to garner support from rural voters, who felt neglected by the economic policies of the central government. Dr. Manmohan Singh's tenure as prime minister of India was marked by a strong commitment to continuing the economic liberalization policies that had begun in 1991. However, this commitment did not come without substantial political opposition, especially from parties and groups that were ideologically opposed to the free-market reforms. The most significant resistance came from Left-wing parties, regional political groups, and certain sections of the Congress party itself, who expressed concerns over the social and economic impacts of liberalization.

Resistance from Left-Wing Parties

The CPI and the CPI-M were vocal opponents of the liberalization policies pursued by Dr. Singh's government. These parties, which were part of the UPA, the coalition government led by the Congress party, believed that economic liberalization represented a capitalist shift that would disproportionately benefit the rich, exacerbate inequality, and lead to the exploitation of workers. The Left's ideology emphasized the need for state control of key sectors of the economy, particularly in industries like energy, transportation, and infrastructure, as well as in banking and agriculture.

One of the most notable instances of this resistance was the Left's opposition to the proposed introduction of FDI in the retail sector. The Left, along with various other political groups and trade unions, argued that allowing multinational corporations like Walmart and Carrefour to set up retail chains in India would devastate small businesses and hurt the livelihoods of millions of small shopkeepers and traders. This led to strong political protests and public opposition, which forced Dr. Singh's government to backtrack on its decision, illustrating the difficulties he faced in implementing his economic vision within the political realities of a coalition government.

Challenges from the Congress Party and Regional Parties

In addition to the Left, resistance to economic liberalization also came from within the Congress party and its regional allies. The Congress party, which had traditionally been seen as the champion of state-led development, was divided on the issue of liberalization. While Dr. Singh was a staunch advocate of market-driven reforms, many Congress members, particularly those with ties to labour unions and state-owned enterprises, were hesitant to embrace the full extent of liberalization. These internal divisions often resulted in policy compromises and delays in the implementation of key reforms, particularly in sectors like banking, energy, and retail. Regional parties, too, played a crucial role in shaping the policy landscape. Many regional leaders feared that liberalization would lead to the erosion of their political power, as it could shift economic activities away from the state and central government-controlled sectors. These parties often used their influence in the coalition to block or delay certain reforms, demanding greater compensation or safeguards for their constituents before supporting liberalization measures. For example, when the government proposed the privatization of state-owned enterprises, regional parties raised concerns about the impact on local employment and the distribution of wealth, further complicating the reform agenda.

Opposition from the Bharatiya Janata Party (BJP)

The BJP, the main opposition party, also capitalized on the growing discontent over economic liberalization to undermine Dr. Singh's government. The BJP frequently accused the UPA government of being overly "pro-business" and of neglecting the interests of the rural poor. The party used the issues of agrarian distress, unemployment, and the rural-urban divide to attack the government's economic policies.

The BJP's critique focused on the fact that the benefits of liberalization were not being felt equally across the country, especially in rural areas where poverty, unemployment, and agricultural distress remained significant challenges. During the 2009 general elections, the BJP made economic liberalization a key issue, arguing that it had failed to create sufficient jobs or improve the lives of the country's vast rural population. By highlighting the growing wealth inequality and the perceived neglect of agriculture, the BJP sought to rally support among rural voters, who were frustrated by the slow pace of change and the challenges brought on by globalization.

Public Protests and Strikes

In addition to formal political opposition, there was also significant public protest against the economic reforms of the Dr. Singh's government. Trade unions, farmer groups, and civil society organizations organized widespread strikes and protests against privatization, foreign investments, and reductions in government subsidies. These protests were often coordinated by Left-wing groups but also involved a broad coalition of social and political actors who were sceptical of the benefits of liberalization. Workers in public sector industries, in particular, were concerned about job security as privatization efforts began to accelerate. Farmer groups, already facing challenges due to the decline in agricultural productivity and rising input costs, feared that liberalization would lead to increased corporate control over agriculture, further exacerbating their economic hardships. These protests not only created political challenges for Dr. Singh's government but also led to public distrust of the liberalization agenda.

Impact of Global Economic Crisis (2008)

The global financial crisis of 2008 further intensified opposition to Dr. Singh's economic policies. Although India was one of the few major economies to avoid a severe recession, the crisis led to a slowdown in growth and an increase in unemployment and inflation. The opposition parties seized upon the crisis to argue that the government's focus on liberalization had failed to provide the resilience needed to weather global economic shocks. They pointed to the crisis as evidence that the Indian economy was overly dependent on foreign markets and external factors, a situation that had been worsened by the government's policies of trade liberalization and deregulation. The opposition also accused the government of not doing enough to protect the most vulnerable sections of society during the crisis. With the economy slowing down and inflation rising, many people, particularly in rural areas, were feeling the pressure.

The criticism was compounded by reports of corruption and mismanagement in the government, including scandals related to 2G spectrum allocation and coal mining, which further damaged Dr. Singh's political credibility. Navigating the political opposition to economic liberalization was one of the defining challenges of Dr. Manmohan Singh's tenure as prime minister. While he remained steadfast in his belief that liberalization was essential for India's economic progress, the political realities of a coalition government made it difficult to implement reforms without facing significant resistance. The opposition from Left-wing parties, regional groups, and the BJP forced Dr. Singh to constantly balance his economic vision with the demands of his political allies. Despite these challenges, his government was able to push through a number of significant reforms that helped to modernize India's economy and strengthen its position on the global stage. However, the resistance to liberalization also highlighted the tensions between market-oriented policies and the social and political realities of a developing country like India.

▪ Dealing with Controversies

Dr. Manmohan Singh's tenure as India's prime minister, from 2004 to 2014, was a period marked by sweeping reforms, economic growth, and increased global stature. However, it was also a time when his leadership style and governance came under heavy scrutiny. Critics questioned his ability to manage the political complexities of the Indian system, often portraying him as a figurehead rather than a decisive leader. While he was widely praised for his intellect and economic acumen, his handling of several controversies and governance challenges during his tenure became a focal point of political discourse in India.

The "Silent" Leader: Perceptions of Passivity

One of the central criticisms directed at Dr. Singh was his perceived passivity and reluctance to engage actively in the political battles that often characterize Indian politics. As a technocrat, he was focused on economic growth and development but was seen as lacking the political instincts and aggression required to navigate India's complex and sometimes turbulent political environment. His leadership style was often compared to that of his predecessors, who were known for their strong personalities and hands-on involvement in both governance and political manoeuvring. Dr. Singh's approach to leadership was seen as one of consensus-building rather than confrontation. His manner was calm and measured, and his decision making was generally rooted in careful deliberation.

While this made him a highly respected economist and policymaker, it also led to criticisms from those who believed that he was too passive in his leadership of the country. In a system where bold political moves often result in quick rewards or punishments, his measured approach sometimes made him appear indecisive or disengaged from the day-to-day politics of governance. This perception was exacerbated by his relationship with the Congress party, which often viewed him as a less assertive leader compared to previous party stalwarts like Indira Gandhi and Rajiv Gandhi. Critics argued that while Dr. Singh was undeniably competent in economic affairs, he lacked the political will to confront opposition within his own party, the coalition government, or even within his cabinet. This passivity was perceived as a major weakness in the face of growing challenges, both political and economic.

Political Compromise and Coalition Dynamics

Dr. Singh's tenure as prime minister was also heavily influenced by the nature of the coalition government he led. The UPA, which he headed, was a coalition of multiple parties with differing ideologies and interests. In such a scenario, political compromise became a necessity, but it also contributed to governance challenges. The necessity to balance competing interests within the coalition often meant that Dr. Singh had to make concessions that were not always in line with his personal beliefs or economic policies. This balancing act created a political environment where Dr. Singh's leadership was often questioned. Critics argued that the need to appease coalition partners led to a situation where he was unable to assert his vision effectively.

For example, during the second term of the UPA government (2009-14), the coalition was plagued by internal disagreements and frequent resignations, particularly over issues such as the nuclear deal with the United States and the implementation of key economic reforms. Many viewed these challenges as indicative of Dr. Singh's inability to firmly control the political dynamics of the coalition. In addition, the UPA's reliance on the support of regional parties, which were sometimes at odds with national interests, contributed to a sense of instability in governance. While Dr. Singh was known for his ability to build consensus, critics believed that this very quality was exploited by political actors seeking to push their own agendas, often at the expense of the country's long-term interests. The inability to deliver on key reforms due to coalition pressures left Dr. Singh vulnerable to attacks from both the opposition and factions within his own party.

Scandals and Corruption Allegations

Another major controversy that defined Dr. Singh's tenure was the series of corruption scandals that plagued the UPA government, particularly during its second term. The most notable of these scandals was the 2G spectrum scam, in which senior politicians and officials were accused of allocating telecom licences at below-market prices, leading to massive losses to the public exchequer. The 2G scandal dominated the political discourse for much of 2010 and was seen as a major blow to Dr. Singh's credibility as a leader committed to good governance. Dr. Singh's handling of the 2G scam was widely criticized. While he consistently denied any personal involvement or knowledge of the corrupt practices, his critics argued that as the head of the government, he had a responsibility to oversee the actions of his ministers and ensure that such malpractices did not occur under his watch.

The lack of a firm response to the scandal led to accusations that he was either unaware of the irregularities or, worse, complicit in allowing them to occur. In either case, Dr. Singh's image as an incorruptible leader was severely damaged. The 2G scam was followed by the coal allocation scam, another instance of alleged corruption involving the improper allocation of coal mining licences to private companies. The scandal raised questions about the government's lack of transparency and accountability in its dealings with major corporate entities. Despite Dr. Singh's insistence that he was committed to fighting corruption, his government's handling of these scandals was widely seen as inadequate. The perception that his leadership had allowed corruption to flourish eroded public trust in his administration and provided ample ammunition for the opposition to attack the UPA government.

Economic Policy and Governance Challenges

While Dr. Singh's economic policies were widely praised, particularly his role in steering India through the global financial crisis of 2008, there were significant challenges on the domestic front. One of the key criticisms of his governance was his failure to deliver on key economic reforms, particularly in areas such as labour laws, land acquisition, and the introduction of the Goods and Services Tax (GST). These reforms, which were considered critical to India's continued economic growth, faced considerable resistance from political factions and interest groups, and Dr. Singh's inability to push them through contributed to the sense that his leadership was ineffective in addressing India's long-term structural issues. Dr. Singh's failure to secure consensus on these important reforms was partly due to the fragmented nature of India's political system, where state governments and regional parties held considerable sway.

The political gridlock that ensued made it difficult for the central government to enact legislation, and Dr. Singh was frequently criticized for not taking a more proactive role in breaking the deadlock. This was particularly evident in the second term of the UPA, when the government struggled to implement key reforms that had been promised during the 2009 election campaign. In addition, the Indian economy itself faced several challenges during Dr. Singh's second term. While India had experienced strong growth in the years following the economic reforms of the 1990s, the global economic slowdown, rising inflation, and a deteriorating fiscal situation made it difficult for the government to maintain its earlier momentum. Critics argued that Dr. Singh, as the chief architect of India's economic reforms, had failed to adapt his policies to the changing global environment and to address the emerging domestic challenges. While his government did take steps to tackle inflation and fiscal deficits, the measures were often seen as too little, too late.

The Leadership Dilemma: Balancing Technocracy and Political Reality

At the heart of many of the controversies surrounding Dr. Singh's leadership was a fundamental dilemma: the tension between technocratic governance and the political realities of Indian democracy. As a technocrat, Dr. Singh brought a wealth of economic knowledge and expertise to the office of prime minister, but as a politician, he was often seen as unable to reconcile his economic vision with the political imperatives of governance in a democratic, coalition-based system. His focus on long-term economic growth and stability often clashed with the immediate demands of populist politics. While Dr. Singh was committed to the idea of inclusive growth and poverty alleviation, he faced significant pressure from his coalition partners to adopt policies that would provide immediate benefits to specific constituencies, often at the expense of long-term economic health.

In such a scenario, Dr. Singh's technocratic approach, which prioritized sound economic policy over short-term political gains, was not always in line with the expectations of the political class, which often relied on populist measures to win elections and maintain political relevance. This disconnects between economic vision and political necessity contributed to Dr. Singh's struggles as a leader. While he maintained a reputation as a man of integrity and intellect, his ability to translate that into effective political leadership was often questioned. The criticism of his leadership style thus reflected the broader challenges of governing a country as diverse and complex as India, where balancing economic reforms with the demands of a coalition government and a vibrant democracy requires not just knowledge but also political skill.

Conclusion

In conclusion, while Dr. Manmohan Singh's tenure was defined by significant achievements in economic policy and international diplomacy, it was also marred by controversies related to governance and leadership. The criticisms of his leadership style—characterized as passive and overly cautious—were compounded by the political realities of coalition politics, corruption scandals, and an inability to push through crucial reforms. Despite these challenges, Dr. Singh's legacy as an economic reformer remains largely intact, but the controversies surrounding his leadership and governance will continue to be a part of his political history.

▪ Defending His Vision

Dr. Manmohan Singh, one of India's most respected economists and a central figure in the country's economic transformation, faced substantial criticism over the years regarding his economic philosophy and leadership approach. His tenure, especially during the implementation of sweeping economic reforms, attracted both praise and strong opposition. While many hailed his vision of liberalization, market-driven growth, and global integration, his critics often portrayed these very policies as detrimental to India's sovereignty, social fabric, and long-term sustainability. Dr. Singh's unwavering defence of his economic philosophy, however, was grounded in his firm belief in market principles, fiscal discipline, and global cooperation, which he saw as essential for India's continued progress and prosperity.

Economic Liberalization and Market-Driven Growth

One of the most significant criticisms levelled against Dr. Singh's economic philosophy was his strong advocacy for economic liberalization and market-driven growth. In the early 1990s, when India faced a severe balance of payments crisis, Dr. Singh, then the finance minister, took bold steps to open up the Indian economy, dismantling the Licence Raj system that had previously controlled and restricted industrial growth. The move towards economic liberalization and globalization was met with strong opposition, particularly from those who believed that it would erode India's sovereignty and exacerbate inequalities.

Dr. Singh consistently defended this vision, explaining that India's long-term economic success was deeply linked to global integration. He argued that economic liberalization was not about abandoning the state's role in the economy, but rather about ensuring that the country could effectively compete in the global market, attract foreign investment, and achieve higher levels of growth. His perspective was that India's earlier protectionist policies had stifled innovation, entrepreneurship, and competitiveness, and that liberalization was necessary to unleash the potential of the Indian economy. In his defence, Dr. Singh repeatedly emphasized that the liberalization policies were aimed at improving the standard of living for all Indians, particularly by creating jobs and fostering a competitive environment. He acknowledged that the transition to a market economy posed challenges but maintained that the eventual benefits, such as higher GDP growth, increased FDI, and greater access to global technology, would outweigh these challenges. Dr. Singh often referred to the rapid economic growth witnessed in India after the 1991 reforms as evidence of the success of liberalization.

Inclusive Growth and Poverty Alleviation

While Dr. Singh's economic vision was rooted in market reforms, he never lost sight of the need for inclusive growth, poverty alleviation, and addressing social disparities. Critics of his policies often argued that liberalization led to rising inequality and marginalized rural and disadvantaged sections of society. They contended that the growth driven by foreign investment and industrialization primarily benefited urban areas and affluent groups, leaving behind a large segment of the population. Dr. Singh, however, consistently rebutted these claims by asserting that growth, when managed effectively, could serve as a powerful tool for poverty alleviation.

His defence of inclusive growth was articulated through the implementation of programmes designed to directly benefit the rural poor and vulnerable populations. For instance, during his tenure as prime minister, the UPA government introduced the MGNREGA, which provided guaranteed wage employment to rural households. Dr. Singh argued that such initiatives, combined with market-led growth, were essential to bridging the urban-rural divide and ensuring that the benefits of economic progress were more widely distributed. Dr. Singh's vision was one where growth and equity went hand in hand, with economic policies tailored to address the specific needs of the rural and economically disadvantaged.

He defended the idea that the focus should be on creating opportunities for all, rather than merely focusing on wealth redistribution. In his view, economic growth would generate the necessary resources to fund social programmes and uplift marginalized groups, allowing for a gradual reduction in poverty.

Globalization and Foreign Relations

Another area of criticism for Dr. Singh's economic philosophy was his firm belief in globalization and India's integration into the world economy. Critics argued that India's increased reliance on foreign trade and investment made the country vulnerable to global economic fluctuations and reduced its economic sovereignty. They contended that globalization, while benefiting a few sectors, led to the undermining of India's indigenous industries and a growing dependence on multinational corporations. Dr. Singh, however, staunchly defended globalization, arguing that India's economic growth and global standing were closely linked to its engagement in the global market.

He believed that India could not afford to remain isolated from the rest of the world, especially in an era of technological advances and shifting geopolitical dynamics. In his view, India's integration into the global economy was essential not just for economic growth, but for enhancing its political and strategic influence on the world stage. Dr. Singh's advocacy for globalization was particularly evident in his handling of India's foreign relations. His government worked tirelessly to strengthen ties with major global powers, including the United States, European Union, and countries in Asia. A notable achievement was the Indo-US nuclear deal in 2008, which lifted India's restrictions on nuclear trade and opened the door for greater collaboration with Western countries. While this deal attracted criticism from nationalist groups, Dr. Singh defended it as a strategic necessity that would bolster India's energy security and global standing.

Fiscal Discipline and Governance

Dr. Singh's critics also targeted his economic philosophy

for its emphasis on fiscal discipline and the prioritization of macroeconomic stability. In their view, the focus on maintaining low fiscal deficits and controlling inflation came at the expense of crucial social welfare programmes. Critics argued that fiscal austerity measures, especially during times of crisis, disproportionately impacted the poor, who depended on government assistance for basic needs such as food, health care, and education.

In response, Dr. Singh consistently argued that fiscal discipline was a prerequisite for long-term sustainable growth. He explained that high fiscal deficits and rising public debt posed a serious risk to India's financial stability and could lead to higher inflation and interest rates, which would ultimately hurt the very people critics sought to protect. For Dr. Singh, the goal was to strike a balance between economic growth, social welfare, and fiscal health. While acknowledging that austerity measures might be painful in the short-term, he believed they were necessary to create the fiscal space for future investments in infrastructure, education, and health care—key components of his vision for India's development.

Criticism of Technocratic Leadership

One of the most consistent criticisms of Dr. Singh was his technocratic approach to governance, which often led to charges that he was more focused on economic principles than the practical realities of Indian politics. His critics contended that while his economic policies were sound from a technical perspective, they were out of touch with the political and social realities of India. They argued that India's diverse and complex society required more than just economic expertise—it needed a leader who could unite different political factions, navigate populist pressures, and engage with the masses. Dr. Singh, however, defended his technocratic approach, stating that his economic philosophy was driven by a commitment to long-term development and the well-being of future generations, rather than short-term political gains.

He maintained that India needed a leader who could think beyond the immediate electoral cycles and make decisions that would benefit the country in the decades to come. His philosophy was rooted in the belief that sound economic policies, though often unpopular in the short-term, would eventually lead to better living standards, reduced poverty, and a stronger nation. Dr. Singh was also adamant that India's economic growth and reforms should be guided by objective economic principles rather than political expediency. He believed that his technocratic background allowed him to make decisions based on rationality and data, without being swayed by populist pressures or political considerations. This approach, while effective in many areas, led to a disconnect with certain sections of the population, who viewed him as aloof or disconnected from their day-to-day struggles.

Defence of Social Programmes and Reforms

Throughout his tenure, Dr. Singh defended his government's commitment to social welfare and poverty alleviation. While he prioritized economic reforms and growth, he argued that these were not mutually exclusive with social goals.

For instance, the introduction of the MGNREGA, the Right to Information (RTI) Act, and the Right to Education (RTE) Act were all key aspects of his administration's broader vision of inclusive growth. Dr. Singh firmly believed that economic growth could not be meaningful unless it addressed the basic needs of the population. His defence of these social programmes centred on their potential to empower the most vulnerable sections of society and ensure that the fruits of India's economic growth were widely shared. Critics, however, argued that these programmes were often poorly implemented and susceptible to corruption. Dr. Singh acknowledged these challenges but maintained that social welfare programmes were an essential component of India's development model, offering protection to the marginalized while ensuring their participation in the economic mainstream.

In conclusion, Dr. Manmohan Singh's response to the criticism of his economic philosophy was characterized by a steadfast belief in liberalization, globalization, fiscal discipline, and inclusive growth. He defended his vision of India's economic future by arguing that the country needed to embrace market-driven reforms and integration into the global economy in order to secure long-term prosperity. While his critics were vocal in pointing out the social and political costs of such policies, Dr. Singh remained committed to the idea that economic growth, when managed with equity and foresight, would benefit all sections of Indian society. His leadership, marked by technocratic precision and a long-term outlook, faced numerous challenges but laid the foundation for India's transformation into a global economic power.

REFERENCES

Held, D. (1999). *Global Transformations*. Stanford University Press.

Jain, T.R. & Ohri, V.K. (2010). *Indian Economic Development*. V.K. Publication.

Kapur, A. (2006). *India: From Regional to World Power*. Routledge.

Mann, P. (2000). *India's Foreign Policy in the Post-Cold War Era*. Harman Pub. House.

Mansingh, L. (1997). *Indian Foreign Policy*. Foreign Service Institute in association with Konark Publishers.

Ministry of Defence, India (1990). *Annual Report 1989-90*. Ministry of Defence, Government of India.

Ministry of Finance (1991). *Economic Survey 1990-91*. Economic Division, Ministry of Finance, India.

Nanda, P. (2003). *Rediscovering Asia: Evolution of India's Look East Policy*. Lancer Publishers & Distributors.

Nye, J.S. (1968). *International Regionalism*. Little Brown.

Raghavan, V.R. (Ed.). (2013). *Consequences of Long-term Conflicts in North-east India*. Vij Books, India.

Smith, A. (1909–1914). *Wealth of Nations* (C.J. Bullock, Ed., Vol. X). The Harvard Classics. P.F. Collier & Son.

Taneja, N. (2005). "Informal Trade in SAARC Region: Implication for Free Trade Agreement." In S. Soz, S.K. Sahni & R.N. Srivastara (Eds.), *Towards South Asian Economic Integration and Unity*. Foundation for Peace and Sustainable Development.

12

Legacy in Economic Policy

Dr. Manmohan Singh's tenure as finance minister and prime minister of India left an indelible mark on the country's economic trajectory. His policies were instrumental in transforming India's economic landscape from a largely state-controlled, inward-looking system to one that embraced liberalization, globalization, and market reforms. His economic philosophy was rooted in the belief that India's future lay in opening up its economy, integrating more closely with the global marketplace, and fostering growth through private enterprise. This shift came at a crucial juncture in India's history when the country faced a severe balance of payments crisis in 1991, with foreign exchange reserves at critically low levels, inflation soaring, and economic growth stagnating.

In response to this crisis, Dr. Singh, then serving as the finance minister under Prime Minister P.V. Narasimha Rao, introduced a series of far-reaching economic reforms aimed at liberalizing the Indian economy. These included the devaluation of the Indian rupee, the reduction of trade barriers, deregulation of key industries, and the opening up of several sectors to foreign direct investment (FDI). These reforms, known as the "New Economic Policy" of 1991, marked the beginning of a new era for India. The country moved away from the restrictive economic model of the past, characterized by the "Licence Raj" and extensive government control over business and industry, toward a market-driven, open economy. The initial effects of these reforms were positive. India's GDP growth accelerated, foreign exchange reserves stabilized, and inflation was brought under control.

Over the years, the country experienced sustained economic growth, and it became one of the world's fastest-growing major economies. Dr. Singh's role in navigating India through this period of economic transition is widely acknowledged as a defining moment in the country's economic history. The liberalization policies he championed laid the foundation for India's integration into the global economy, providing access to new markets, technology, and investment. These changes also spurred industrial growth, particularly in sectors such as information technology and telecommunications, which became key drivers of the country's economic expansion. In addition to his economic reforms, Dr. Singh's vision for India included a commitment to inclusive growth.

While he championed market-driven reforms, he also recognized the importance of addressing the social challenges facing India, particularly poverty and inequality. His government introduced several social welfare programmes aimed at improving the lives of the country's poor and marginalized populations. One of the most notable of these was the Mahatma Gandhi National Rural Employment Guarantee Act (MGNREGA), which provided employment to rural households and aimed to alleviate rural poverty. Other initiatives, such as the Right to Information (RTI) Act and the National Rural Health Mission (NRHM), were designed to improve governance, transparency, and access to basic services for India's rural population. Dr. Singh's approach to governance was also characterized by fiscal prudence. Throughout his tenure, he emphasized the importance of maintaining macroeconomic stability, controlling inflation, and reducing fiscal deficits.

This commitment to sound fiscal management was evident in the way his government handled India's finances during periods of rapid growth. Even when faced with external shocks, such as the

2008 global financial crisis, Dr. Singh's government took decisive action to shield the Indian economy from the worst effects of the crisis. His administration implemented a series of stimulus packages and fiscal measures aimed at boosting infrastructure spending and demand creation, which helped India weather the storm better than many other economies. However, despite these successes, Dr. Singh's legacy is not without its criticisms. Some argue that the benefits of liberalization were unevenly distributed, with the urban middle class and large corporations benefiting more than the rural poor and smaller businesses. While India's economic growth surged, the country's inequality also increased, with large sections of the population still living in poverty, especially in rural areas.

Furthermore, Dr. Singh's economic policies were often seen as overly technocratic, with critics arguing that he failed to effectively navigate the political challenges of coalition governance. His leadership style, while seen as pragmatic and focused on long-term goals, was also criticized for being too passive and lacking the political acumen to manage controversies and internal party dynamics. Dr. Singh's government also faced significant challenges in terms of corruption scandals, such as the 2G spectrum scam and the coal allocation scam, which marred his administration's reputation. While Dr. Singh was not directly implicated in these scandals, his government's slow response to addressing these issues led to questions about his leadership and accountability. These controversies overshadowed some of the significant achievements of his economic policies and created an image of a leader who was unable or unwilling to confront corruption within his administration.

Despite these criticisms, Dr. Singh's contributions to India's economic growth and development cannot be overlooked. His role in transforming India into an open, market-oriented economy, his commitment to inclusive growth, and his efforts to maintain fiscal discipline all contributed to India's rise as a global economic power. Under his leadership, India became one of the world's largest economies, with a growing middle class, increasing foreign investment, and a strong presence in global trade and finance. Dr. Singh's economic legacy is also evident in the continued success of India's information technology (IT) sector, which he championed as a key driver of the country's economic future.

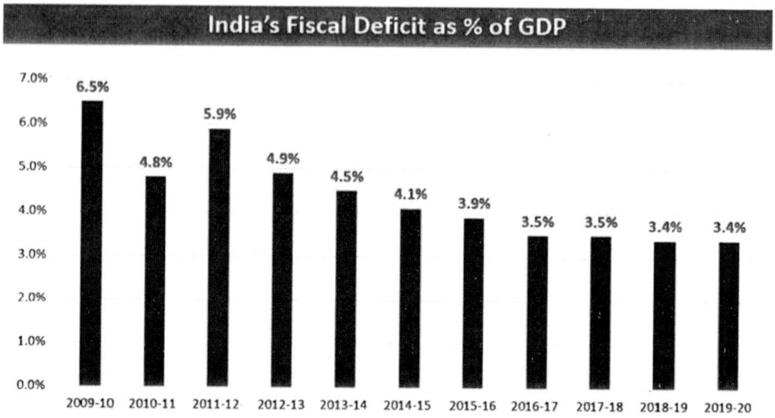

Fig. 12.1: India's Fiscal Deficit Levels before and after the 2008 Recession.

His policies helped create an environment conducive to the growth of the IT industry, leading to the emergence of India as a global IT outsourcing hub. The Software Technology Parks of India (STPI) and the regulatory reforms he implemented played a crucial role in fostering the growth of this sector, which continues to be one of the main contributors to India's exports and employment. In the realm of global economic diplomacy, Dr. Singh's legacy is equally important. As prime minister, he took a leading role in shaping India's foreign economic policy, advocating for trade liberalization, debt relief for developing countries, and India's integration into global economic institutions. His government's efforts to secure the Indo-US nuclear deal in 2008 were a significant step in strengthening India's global standing and strategic partnerships, particularly with the United States.

While Dr. Singh's policies have been credited with transforming India's economy, his legacy remains a subject of debate. His economic reforms were undeniably successful in many respects, but they also led to some unintended consequences, including rising inequality and concerns about the social impact of globalization. Furthermore, his leadership style and his ability to navigate political challenges have been questioned, particularly in light of the scandals that tarnished his government's image. In conclusion, Dr. Manmohan Singh's legacy in economic policy is complex and multifaceted. His reforms helped shape India's modern economy, opening it up to global markets, fostering growth, and positioning the country as a major economic power. At the same time, his tenure was not without its challenges, both in terms of economic inequality and political controversies. Nonetheless, Dr. Singh's contributions to India's economic development and his vision for the country's future will remain a significant part of India's economic history. His legacy will continue to influence economic policy in India, as the country seeks to balance growth with equity, navigate new global challenges, and address the social and economic issues that remain at the heart of India's development story.

■ Evaluation of His Reforms

Dr. Manmohan Singh's economic reforms, which began in 1991 and continued throughout his tenure as finance minister and later as prime minister, marked a critical juncture in India's growth trajectory. The reforms reshaped the Indian economy, shifting it from a largely state-controlled, protectionist model to a more liberalized, market-oriented one. These reforms were fundamental in steering India towards high growth rates, creating a robust economic foundation, and integrating India into the global economy. The subsequent changes had lasting effects on various sectors and played a major role in India's economic success in the twenty-first century. The first and most noticeable impact of Dr. Singh's reforms was the dramatic shift in India's growth trajectory. At the time of the 1991 balance of payments crisis, India was experiencing severe economic challenges: stagnant growth, high inflation, burgeoning fiscal deficits, and a dwindling foreign exchange reserve. The initial reforms, including trade liberalization, devaluation of the Indian rupee, reduction of import tariffs, and the encouragement of FDI, were essential in stabilizing the economy. These measures were crucial in building investor confidence, fostering industrial expansion, and providing the foundation for India's economic revival.

Sustained Economic Growth

Following the reforms, India experienced a surge in its GDP growth rate. Prior to 1991, India's economy grew at an average rate of around 3.5 per cent per year, often referred to as the "Hindu rate of growth". After the reforms, however, the growth rate consistently improved, and by the mid-1990s, India's economy was expanding at an average rate of around 6 per cent. By the early 2000s, India's GDP growth rate reached an impressive 8-9 per cent annually, which continued throughout the decade. This was a remarkable turnaround, driven by the liberalization policies that opened India's markets to global competition and investment. The introduction of market-oriented policies created a more conducive environment for private sector participation, which accelerated industrial growth. The opening of the economy led to an increase in exports, the influx of foreign capital, and the entry of multinational corporations into the Indian market. These factors helped diversify the industrial base and allowed India to move up the value chain in terms of manufacturing and services.

Boost to Services Sector

One of the most significant drivers of India's economic growth post-reforms was the rapid expansion of the services sector, particularly information technology (IT) and business process outsourcing (BPO). Dr. Singh's liberalization policies, particularly those focusing on technology and telecommunications, helped India become a global hub for IT and outsourcing services. The establishment of STPI and the deregulation of the telecommunications industry helped India develop a competitive IT sector that became a cornerstone of the country's economy. This sector alone contributed significantly to India's GDP growth, with Indian IT companies such as Infosys, Wipro, and Tata Consultancy Services (TCS) becoming major players on the global stage. IT and BPO exports saw exponential growth, contributing not only to economic expansion but also to job creation, particularly for young, educated Indians. The growth in the IT sector further reinforced the importance of skilled human capital in driving economic progress, aligning with Dr. Singh's emphasis on education and human resource development.

Foreign Direct Investment (FDI) and Export Growth

The liberalization of India's trade policies and the reduction of restrictions on foreign investments played a key role in the country's economic transformation. FDI inflows increased significantly after the reforms, as global investors saw India as a promising market.

Between 1991 and the early 2000s, India attracted large-scale investments in various sectors, including telecommunications, automobiles, pharmaceuticals, and retail. This FDI inflow helped increase industrial productivity, improve infrastructure, and create jobs. Additionally, the removal of trade barriers and the simplification of export procedures led to a substantial increase in India's exports. Sectors such as textiles, pharmaceuticals, and engineering goods benefited from greater access to international markets. By integrating India more fully into the global economy, Dr. Singh's reforms set the stage for the country to become a significant player in global trade.

Agricultural Growth and Rural Impact

While the services and industrial sectors flourished, the agricultural sector experienced more mixed outcomes. One of the key concerns after the 1991 reforms was the failure to focus adequately on agriculture, which remained a large part of India's economy, particularly for rural populations. Agricultural growth stagnated for a considerable period after the liberalization, as the emphasis was placed on industrial and services growth. The reduced government involvement in agriculture and the lack of investment in rural infrastructure created a gap in rural development, leading to unequal benefits from the reforms. However, Dr. Singh's later policies did attempt to address this imbalance. Under his leadership, the government launched rural development schemes, including the Mahatma Gandhi National Rural Employment Guarantee Act (MGNREGA), which aimed to provide guaranteed employment to rural households and improve rural infrastructure. Despite these initiatives, the rural-urban divide persisted, and agricultural productivity did not grow at the pace needed to match the rapid expansion of other sectors.

Financial Sector Reforms

Dr. Singh's tenure also witnessed significant financial sector reforms that modernized India's banking and financial system. Under his leadership, the banking sector was strengthened with the introduction of measures such as prudential regulations, improved capitalization of public sector banks, and the adoption of market-based interest rates. These reforms helped stabilize the financial system, reduced the risk of financial crises, and increased the efficiency of credit markets. Furthermore, the liberalization of India's financial markets encouraged the growth of capital markets, facilitating the entry of foreign institutional investors and providing Indian firms with access to more diverse sources of capital. This expansion of the financial sector, combined with the growth in the services sector, contributed to increased economic activity and overall growth.

Long-term Structural Changes

While the immediate impact of Dr. Singh's reforms was highly positive, their long-term effects have been mixed. The structural changes implemented during his tenure, particularly those that liberalized trade and investment policies, set India on a path of sustained economic growth. The opening up of the economy encouraged domestic industries to become more competitive and spurred the growth of new sectors such as IT and pharmaceuticals. However, the economic reforms also exposed India's weaknesses in certain areas, such as infrastructure, health care, and education. These gaps hindered the ability of the broader population to benefit equally from the growth. Dr. Singh's inability to enact further reforms in critical sectors, such as labour and agriculture, left some of the structural issues unresolved, resulting in slower improvements in rural areas and certain marginalized communities.

In conclusion, the evaluation of Dr. Manmohan Singh's economic reforms reveals their transformative impact on India's growth trajectory. The policies he implemented shifted India's economic focus from a closed, protectionist model to a more open, market-driven economy. These reforms led to sustained growth, particularly in the services and industrial sectors, and positioned India as a global economic player. However, the benefits of these reforms were not evenly distributed, and challenges such as rural stagnation and income inequality remained persistent issues. Despite these challenges, Dr. Singh's reforms were critical in setting the foundation for India's emergence as one of the world's fastest-growing economies. His legacy in economic policy is one of both success and ongoing challenges, as India continues to navigate the complexities of a rapidly evolving global economy.

• Influence on Subsequent Policies

Dr. Manmohan Singh's economic reforms, which laid the groundwork for India's transformation into a fast-growing economy, had a profound influence on subsequent policies. Even after his tenure as finance minister and later as prime minister, his vision and the economic framework he established continued to guide India's economic policy decisions. Successive governments, irrespective of their political affiliations, largely maintained the trajectory of economic liberalization that Dr. Singh had championed, albeit with certain adjustments in response to changing domestic and international circumstances.

Legacy of Economic Liberalization

Dr. Singh's most significant contribution to India's economic policy was the liberalization of the economy in 1991. His reforms, which included reducing trade barriers, deregulating key sectors, and encouraging FDI, were foundational in India's transition from a closed, state-dominated economy to a more open, market-oriented one. This liberalization strategy formed the basis of India's economic policies for decades. Following his tenure as finance minister, successive governments, including those led by both the Bharatiya Janata Party (BJP) and the Indian National Congress (INC), largely adhered to the principles of economic liberalization. Even when there were slight deviations, such as protective measures for specific sectors or changes in tax policy, the overall direction of India's economic policy remained consistent with Dr. Singh's reforms. For example, the BJP-led government in the early 2000s continued to promote economic growth through the encouragement of FDI, trade liberalization, and the adoption of technology-driven growth strategies, all of which were part of Dr. Singh's original vision.

Consolidation of Fiscal Policies

Dr. Singh's fiscal policies, which emphasized reducing fiscal deficits and controlling inflation, also had a lasting impact. Throughout his tenure as finance minister, Dr. Singh made significant strides in curbing fiscal deficits, which were seen as a major obstacle to India's long-term growth. He implemented a series of measures, including reducing subsidies and improving tax collections, which helped stabilize the economy. After his term, the focus on fiscal discipline continued under successive governments. The introduction of the Fiscal Responsibility and Budget Management (FRBM) Act in 2003, which set targets for reducing fiscal deficits, was a direct result of Dr. Singh's emphasis on sound fiscal management. Successive governments continued to prioritize fiscal consolidation, even as they made efforts to expand social welfare programmes and improve public services.

Focus on Infrastructure and Connectivity

Infrastructure development was another key pillar of Dr. Singh's economic policy. He recognized that robust infrastructure was essential to sustaining India's economic growth, and he worked towards improving roads, ports, airports, and telecommunications. His government also promoted the creation of Special Economic Zones (SEZs) to attract foreign investment and boost industrial development.

The subsequent governments continued to prioritize infrastructure development, with the Narendra Modi-led government focusing heavily on infrastructure projects such as the "Bharatmala" highway programme, "Sagarmala" for port modernization, and the development of smart cities. These initiatives built upon the foundation laid by Dr. Singh, with an emphasis on improving connectivity between rural and urban areas and enhancing India's integration into global supply chains.

Financial Sector Reforms and Inclusion

Dr. Singh's reforms to the financial sector, which focused on modernizing banking regulations and promoting financial inclusion, were crucial in expanding access to banking services and improving financial stability. Under his leadership, steps were taken to recapitalize public sector banks, improve banking infrastructure, and facilitate access to credit. Successive governments have continued to emphasize financial inclusion. The launch of schemes like the Pradhan Mantri Jan Dhan Yojana (PMJDY) in 2014, which aimed to provide banking services to every household, and the introduction of the Goods and Services Tax (GST) in 2017, which streamlined the taxation system, were further extensions of the financial sector reforms that Dr. Singh initiated. Additionally, the focus on digital financial services and mobile banking, seen in initiatives such as the Digital India campaign, can be seen as a natural progression of the financial reforms Dr. Singh championed.

Trade Liberalization and Globalization

India's trade policy, which was dramatically transformed by Dr. Singh's 1991 reforms, continued to evolve in the years following his tenure. Dr. Singh's liberalization policies were critical in making India an active participant in the global economy, and his approach to trade and globalization set the tone for future trade agreements and negotiations. The post-1991 period saw India enter into several bilateral and multilateral trade agreements, including with the ASEAN nations and the World Trade Organization (WTO). Dr. Singh's influence can be seen in the continued focus on reducing trade barriers, promoting exports, and enhancing India's participation in global value chains. Successive governments have adhered to these principles, including in negotiations for free trade agreements and regional cooperation initiatives.

Technological Advancement and Innovation

Dr. Singh's economic reforms also placed a strong emphasis on technology and innovation, which led to the emergence of India as a global leader in information technology (IT) and software services. The IT boom of the late 1990s and early 2000s was a direct result of the policy environment created by Dr. Singh's government.

Under successive governments, technology and innovation have continued to be a focus area. The rise of India's IT sector and its dominance in global software exports became one of the key components of India's economic narrative. The government's policies in the years following Dr. Singh's tenure also placed a significant emphasis on technology, from the "Digital India" initiative to the promotion of innovation-driven entrepreneurship and the startup ecosystem.

Social Welfare and Inclusivity

One of the key criticisms of Dr. Singh's reforms was their limited focus on addressing inequality and promoting inclusive growth. While his reforms spurred growth, they did not adequately address issues such as poverty, unemployment, and rural-urban disparities. As a result, there was growing pressure to ensure that the benefits of economic growth were shared more equitably across society. Subsequent governments, particularly under the leadership of Prime Minister Manmohan Singh's successor, Prime Minister Narendra Modi, sought to address these issues by implementing social welfare schemes aimed at empowering the poor and marginalized communities. Programmes such as MGNREGA (Mahatma Gandhi National Rural Employment Guarantee Act), which guaranteed rural employment, and the Swachh Bharat Abhiyan, aimed at improving sanitation, were direct responses to the need for inclusive growth. These programmes, while not always aligned with Dr. Singh's market-oriented approach, reflected the ongoing effort to build on his reforms by addressing social inequities.

Conclusion

In conclusion, Dr. Manmohan Singh's economic reforms were instrumental in shaping the future of India's economy, and their influence on subsequent policies is undeniable. His emphasis on liberalization, fiscal discipline, infrastructure development, financial inclusion, and trade liberalization laid the foundation for India's transformation into a global economic power. Successive governments, regardless of their political leanings, have largely adhered to the core principles of Dr. Singh's reforms, with modifications and adjustments to reflect changing circumstances and emerging challenges. Dr. Singh's legacy in economic policy remains one of continuity, guiding India through a new era of economic growth, integration into the global economy, and ongoing efforts towards inclusive development.

▪ Long-term Impacts

The long-term impacts of Dr. Manmohan Singh's economic reforms are evident in various aspects of India's economic landscape, particularly in terms of poverty reduction and the expansion of the middle class. The liberalization measures of the early 1990s, which facilitated trade, FDI, and the development of key sectors such as IT and manufacturing, triggered significant shifts in the economy. These shifts not only fuelled economic growth but also played a critical role in improving the living standards of millions of Indians, contributing to the reduction of poverty and the growth of the middle class.

Poverty Reduction

One of the most significant outcomes of Dr. Singh's economic reforms was the reduction in poverty levels in India. The economic liberalization policies unleashed a wave of growth that created job opportunities, improved access to goods and services, and enhanced incomes for many, particularly in urban areas. The expansion of industries such as information technology, services, and manufacturing helped absorb large numbers of labour, creating millions of new jobs. This economic expansion allowed the government to increase investments in social welfare programmes and poverty alleviation initiatives. A major catalyst in the reduction of poverty was the acceleration of GDP growth that followed liberalization.

India's annual GDP growth rate increased significantly during the 1990s and 2000s, reaching an average of 7-8 per cent annually, a level that was unprecedented in the country's history. This high growth rate directly translated into better economic prospects for the population. The boom in sectors such as IT, services, and construction allowed individuals, especially in urban and peri-urban areas, to experience increased wages and enhanced access to resources like health care, education, and housing. Additionally, government programmes that sought to address rural poverty, such as the National Rural Employment Guarantee Act (NREGA), began to play a more prominent role after the reforms. Although NREGA was implemented after Dr. Singh's tenure, the groundwork for such programmes had been laid by his policies, which focused on providing a framework for rural empowerment. These policies not only sought to provide employment but also aimed to break the cycle of rural poverty by improving access to public services.

Middle-Class Expansion

Another major long-term impact of Dr. Singh's economic reforms was the dramatic expansion of India's middle class.

As economic growth surged, so did the purchasing power and income levels of a significant portion of the population. The growth of the middle class in India was driven by several factors, including rising wages, increasing employment opportunities, access to credit, and growing access to consumer goods. The opening up of the Indian economy created new job opportunities, particularly in the urban sectors, which fuelled demand for goods and services and stimulated consumption. The rise of sectors like IT and telecommunications provided well-paying jobs that attracted millions of young Indians. By the 2000s, India's IT sector had become one of the largest in the world, and many skilled workers, particularly from middle-class backgrounds, experienced upward mobility. The export-oriented nature of the IT and business process outsourcing (BPO) sectors also helped India tap into global markets, further boosting incomes.

In addition to employment in emerging sectors, the reforms also allowed for a more competitive business environment, leading to the creation of new enterprises and industries. With the liberalization of trade, increased foreign investment, and the reduction of trade barriers, India's private sector saw a surge in growth. Many individuals, particularly in cities, had access to new and diverse goods and services, from automobiles to luxury items, expanding their consumption patterns and contributing to the rise of the middle class. Moreover, the expansion of the middle class in India was also driven by improvements in education and health care. Policies that increased public investment in these sectors, alongside growing private sector participation, allowed many individuals to access better education and health care services, raising their living standards and economic mobility. As the middle class grew, it created a substantial demand for housing, consumer products, and services, further stimulating economic growth.

Regional Disparities

While the reduction in poverty and the growth of the middle class were widespread, the impacts of Dr. Singh's economic reforms were not uniform across all regions of India. Some states, particularly those with better infrastructure, access to education, and higher levels of industrialization, benefited more from liberalization than others. States like Maharashtra, Gujarat, and Tamil Nadu saw the highest growth in income levels and the expansion of their middle class. Conversely, many less-developed states, especially in the northern and eastern parts of India, lagged in terms of economic progress, and poverty reduction was slower. This disparity was compounded by differences in state policies, local governance, and the pace of infrastructure development. However, the overall trend across India was positive, as even the relatively poorer regions began to see improvements in living standards, albeit at a slower pace than the more developed states.

The Role of Technology in Poverty Reduction and Middle-Class Growth

Technology played a pivotal role in the long-term impacts of Dr. Singh's reforms on poverty reduction and middle-class expansion. The IT revolution, which was spurred by the liberalization policies, not only provided India with a competitive edge in the global economy but also created vast opportunities for millions of individuals. The growth of digital technology, including mobile phones and the Internet, facilitated access to information, financial services, and markets, benefiting both rural and urban populations. In particular, the expansion of digital financial services and mobile banking helped provide access to banking and financial products for millions of previously unbanked individuals. This was a key factor in poverty reduction, as it allowed underserved populations to save money, access credit, and participate in the formal economy. The availability of low-cost mobile phones and the internet further enabled rural populations to connect with urban markets, find employment, and access educational resources, thus contributing to both poverty reduction and the growth of the middle class.

Globalization and Its Impact on India's Growth

The liberalization of the Indian economy under Dr. Singh set the stage for deeper integration into the global economy. India's exports grew rapidly, especially in sectors like IT, textiles, pharmaceuticals, and services. This increase in exports created more jobs, which in turn helped raise incomes and reduce poverty. Furthermore, the influx of foreign investment helped modernize industries, enhance infrastructure, and create more economic opportunities, contributing to the broader expansion of the middle class. The rise of globalization also meant that India became more attractive to multinational companies seeking new markets and lower labour costs. The arrival of foreign companies brought with it a range of new job opportunities, particularly in urban areas, where demand for skilled labour skyrocketed. This phenomenon not only benefited urban professionals but also provided economic opportunities to individuals from less developed areas who moved to cities in search of work.

Conclusion

In conclusion, the long-term impacts of Dr. Manmohan Singh's economic reforms on poverty reduction and middle-class expansion were profound. The liberalization policies he introduced in 1991 set in motion a series of changes that led to sustained economic growth, job creation, and rising incomes, which contributed significantly to the reduction of poverty in India. At the same time, the expansion of the middle class, spurred by rising wages, access to credit, and improvements in infrastructure, helped fuel further economic growth and development. While regional disparities remained a challenge, the overall trajectory of poverty reduction and middle-class expansion in India has been one of significant progress. The lasting impact of Dr. Singh's reforms continues to shape India's economic future, providing a foundation for continued growth and prosperity.

REFERENCES

Banik, N. (2006). "How Promising is BIMSTEC?" *Economic and Political Weekly*, *41*(51): 5264-68.

Chachavalpongpun, P. (2011). "Look East Meets Look West: Indian-Southeast Asian Relations in Flux." *The International Spectator*, *46*(2): 91-108. https://doi.org/10.1080/03932729.2011.576174

Haokip, T. (2011). "India's Look East Policy: Its Evolution and Approach." *South Asian Survey*, *18*(2): 239-57. https://doi.org/10.1177/0971523113513368

Harshe, R. (1999). "South Asian Regional Co-Operation: Problems and Prospects." *Economic and Political Weekly*, *44*(19): 1100-1105.

Jaffrelot, C. (2003). "India's Look East Policy: An Asianist Strategy in Perspective." *India Review*, *2*(2): 35-68.

Malik, J.M. (1991). "India's Response to the Gulf Crisis: Implications for Indian Foreign Policy." *Asian Survey*, *31*(9): 847-61. https://doi.org/10.1525/as.1991.31.9.00p0092d

Mohapatra, B. (2014). "India's Look East Policy and Development of North Eastern India: Priorities and Prospects." *Search*, *3*(1): 65-70.

Munro, R.H. (1993). "The Loser: India in the Nineties." *The National Interest*, *33*: 62-63.

Naidu, G.V.C. (1996). "India and Southeast Asia." *World Focus*, *17*(10-12): 82-84.

Nayar, B. R. (1998). "Political Structure and India's Economic Reforms of the 1990s." *Pacific Affairs*, *71*(3): 337-60. https://doi.org/10.2307/2761414

Saikia, H. (2010). "Look East Policy: Southeast Asian Economic Integration of India." *Applied Economic Journal*, *17*(2): 1-11.

World Bank. (1994). *India: Macroeconomics and Political Economy 1964-1991*. World Bank.

Yuan, J.D. (2006). *China-ASEAN Relations: Perspective, Prospects and Implications for U.S. Interests*. Strategic Studies Institute, U.S. Army War College.

13

Contributions to Global Economic Leadership

Dr. Manmohan Singh's contributions to global economic leadership are central to his legacy as a statesman and economist. His tenure as finance minister during the early 1990s, and later as prime minister of India, coincided with a transformative period for the global economy. He not only shaped India's economic future but also played a pivotal role in positioning India as an influential player in the global economic landscape. His economic policies, diplomatic efforts, and leadership on international economic forums cemented his status as a global economic leader. One of the most significant contributions of Dr. Singh was his role in the economic liberalization of India, which was a turning point not just for the country, but for the world. When India opened its markets in the early 1990s, it was seen as a major shift from a protectionist, state-controlled economy to one that embraced free-market principles.

This shift had far-reaching implications, not only for India's growth trajectory but for its role in global trade and investment flows. Dr. Singh, a firm believer in the power of liberalization and globalization, was instrumental in this shift, championing reforms that integrated India into the global economy. India's economic reforms, which were led by Dr. Singh, marked a departure from the country's previous policies of economic self-sufficiency. By opening up to foreign investment, cutting tariffs, and promoting privatization, Dr. Singh set the stage for India to become an economic powerhouse. His belief in the power of globalization, free markets, and deregulation resonated with international investors and institutions, making India an attractive destination for foreign capital and trade.

On the international stage, Dr. Singh represented India with an unwavering commitment to the principles of global economic cooperation. His role in international organizations, such as the World Trade Organization (WTO), the International Monetary Fund (IMF), and the Group of Twenty (G20), was crucial in advocating for the interests of developing economies and ensuring that India had a voice in global economic governance. Dr. Singh's diplomatic finesse, combined with his understanding of economics, made him a respected figure in these international forums. In addition to his work at the WTO and IMF, Dr. Singh was also instrumental in strengthening India's relations with key global economic powers. He played a crucial role in shaping India's foreign policy and its economic engagements, particularly with countries like the United States, Japan, and the European Union.

Table 13.1: G20 Commitments Made by India During the Crisis

Summit	Commitment
Washington (2008)	Support global financial regulation reforms
London (2009)	Increase financial aid to developing nations
Pittsburgh (2009)	Promote sustainable global recovery measures

His focus on multilateralism and his advocacy for the development of global trade frameworks benefited both India and the broader developing world. A defining feature of Dr. Singh's global economic leadership was his emphasis on the importance of sustainable development and inclusive growth. He recognized that economic growth should not come at the expense of social welfare or environmental sustainability. His leadership in pushing for these principles on the global stage was instrumental in shaping the global discourse around development. Dr. Singh also worked tirelessly to promote India's role as a leader in the global south, advocating for the interests of developing countries in international negotiations.

Dr. Singh's leadership extended beyond economics and trade. He played a key role in shaping India's position on climate change, advocating for policies that balanced economic growth with environmental responsibility. His participation in international climate change negotiations, particularly during his tenure as prime minister, highlighted India's emerging role as a global leader on environmental issues. His economic policies, which prioritized sustainable growth, set a precedent for other emerging economies seeking to balance development with environmental stewardship. Moreover, Dr. Singh was a key architect of India's nuclear diplomacy, working to secure the landmark India-US nuclear deal in 2008.

This deal, which provided India with access to nuclear technology and fuel for its civilian energy needs, was a testament to Dr. Singh's ability to navigate complex geopolitical issues and secure India's strategic interests on the global stage. The deal also reflected India's growing stature as a global power, and Dr. Singh's leadership was critical in achieving this breakthrough. Dr. Singh's advocacy for multilateralism and his consistent efforts to strengthen India's role in global institutions helped to increase India's influence in the global economic order. His tenure coincided with a period of global economic challenges, including the 2008 financial crisis, and he was instrumental in shaping India's response to these challenges. Under his leadership, India weathered the global financial storm more effectively than many other countries, largely due to the strong economic fundamentals built during the early years of liberalization.

His economic policies, which focused on inclusive growth, poverty reduction, and sustainable development, resonated with the broader international community. Dr. Singh's approach to economic policy was both pragmatic and forward-looking, and his ability to articulate India's economic vision in international forums made him a respected figure in global economic circles. His leadership helped position India as a key player in the global economy, and his legacy continues to shape India's economic policy and its role in global governance today. Dr. Singh's tenure as prime minister also marked a significant period of economic engagement with India's immediate neighbours, particularly in South Asia. His leadership in promoting regional economic cooperation through initiatives like the South Asian Free Trade Area (SAFTA) and his advocacy for greater economic integration in the region helped strengthen India's position as a leader in South Asia.

His commitment to fostering peace and economic cooperation in the region laid the foundation for stronger economic ties and greater stability in South Asia. Dr. Singh's global economic leadership was also characterized by his consistent advocacy for trade liberalization and the reduction of trade barriers. He was a strong proponent of free trade agreements and worked tirelessly to secure deals that benefited India and the global economy. His leadership in advancing trade liberalization not only helped to position India as a key player in global trade but also contributed to the overall growth of the global economy. Dr. Singh's emphasis on open markets and his belief in the transformative power of trade were central to his economic vision and his approach to global economic leadership.

In conclusion, Dr. Manmohan Singh's contributions to global economic leadership were profound and far-reaching. His role in liberalizing India's economy, advocating for global trade liberalization, and promoting sustainable development placed him at the forefront of global economic policymaking. His leadership on the international stage, particularly in organizations like the WTO, IMF, and G20, helped to elevate India's stature as a global economic power. Dr. Singh's vision of inclusive growth, his emphasis on multilateralism, and his ability to navigate complex global challenges have left a lasting legacy in the world of global economic leadership. Through his work, Dr. Singh not only shaped

India's economic future but also contributed to the development of a more inclusive, sustainable, and interconnected global economy.

▪ Role in G20, BRICS, and WTO

Dr. Manmohan Singh's tenure as the prime minister of India saw India's growing prominence in the global economic arena. His leadership in multilateral forums such as the G20, BRICS, and the WTO played a significant role in shaping the global economic order, especially in the context of the evolving global power structure. His strong advocacy for multilateralism—the idea that global challenges require collective action and solutions—was a key feature of India's foreign economic policy under his leadership. Dr. Singh's vision of multilateralism was rooted in his belief that global economic issues, such as financial crises, trade imbalances, and development challenges, could not be addressed by any single nation acting in isolation. Instead, these issues required collective action from a wide array of nations, particularly the developing countries. Through his involvement in the G20, BRICS, and the WTO, Dr. Singh pushed for reforms in global economic governance, aimed at ensuring a more inclusive, equitable system that would allow developing nations like India to play a more prominent role in shaping global economic policies.

Role in G20

The G20, a forum that brings together the world's major economies, became increasingly relevant in the post-2008 global financial crisis period. Dr. Singh, as a key member of the G20, advocated for reforms in global financial institutions and a cooperative approach to tackle the effects of the financial crisis. Under his leadership, India became an influential voice in urging for a reform of the global financial architecture to better represent emerging economies. Dr. Singh played a pivotal role in pushing for policies that advocated for global financial stability, as well as the promotion of trade liberalization and inclusive growth.

One of Dr. Singh's key contributions to the G20 discussions was his push for reducing protectionist policies, which he saw as detrimental to global economic recovery. He called for a more equitable global economic system that acknowledged the needs of developing nations. His advocacy focused not only on restoring economic growth but also on addressing issues such as poverty alleviation and sustainable development. By doing so, Dr. Singh reinforced India's role as a key player in global economic governance, while also highlighting the importance of inclusive development on the global stage.

Role in BRICS

The BRICS countries—Brazil, Russia, India, China, and South Africa—represented a collective voice of emerging economies in global forums. Under Dr. Singh's leadership, India became an active participant in BRICS, working towards strengthening economic cooperation among these countries. Dr. Singh viewed BRICS as an essential counterbalance to the traditional Western-dominated economic structures and institutions. As a member of BRICS, Dr. Singh advocated for reforms in the IMF and World Bank, emphasizing that these institutions needed to reflect the changing global economic realities. Dr. Singh's focus on multilateralism in BRICS revolved around promoting South-South cooperation, which would allow emerging economies to engage in mutually beneficial partnerships.

He also emphasized the importance of shared development goals among BRICS countries, particularly in areas such as infrastructure development, trade cooperation, and financial stability. Under his leadership, India played a central role in fostering closer economic ties within BRICS, thereby strengthening the group's influence in shaping global economic policies. Furthermore, Dr. Singh championed the idea that BRICS should not just be an economic forum but should also contribute to global peace and stability. His leadership helped ensure that BRICS maintained its focus on inclusive development, addressing poverty, and global inequality, while strengthening its economic footprint. The BRICS grouping under his guidance was a platform for emerging economies to advocate for a reform of global governance structures, making sure that the voices of developing countries were amplified on the global stage.

Fig. 13.1: Dr. Manmohan Singh Advocating for Emerging Markets during the BRICS Summit.

Role in WTO

Dr. Singh's engagement with the WTO was equally important in advocating for multilateralism. India, under his leadership, emphasized the importance of a fair and inclusive trade system. Dr. Singh's key focus at the WTO was to ensure that the interests of developing nations were adequately represented in trade negotiations, especially in areas such as agriculture, services, and intellectual property. His efforts to push for trade liberalization within the framework of the WTO were aligned with India's long-term goal of promoting inclusive economic growth and poverty reduction through global trade.

At the WTO, Dr. Singh worked to secure better market access for India's agricultural products and services, while also advocating for the reduction of developed country subsidies that disproportionately affected developing nations. His leadership emphasized that trade negotiations should not only prioritize market access but should also consider the developmental needs of emerging economies. Dr. Singh also stressed the need for reforms in the WTO's decision making process, arguing that the organization should be more inclusive of developing nations' concerns. He advocated for a system where trade rules were not just set by a few dominant economies but were reflective of the needs of a more diverse range of countries. In this context, Dr. Singh's leadership at the WTO was pivotal in positioning India as a vocal advocate for the reform of international trade rules that would benefit developing countries.

Dr. Manmohan Singh's active role in global multilateral platforms such as the G20, BRICS, and WTO cemented his legacy as an advocate for multilateralism. His leadership in these forums reflected his belief in the importance of global cooperation to address the pressing challenges facing the world economy. Through his advocacy, Dr. Singh pushed for reforms in global economic governance, ensuring that the voices of emerging economies, particularly India, were heard in shaping global economic policies. His efforts helped promote inclusive growth, global trade liberalization, and poverty alleviation, while also ensuring that the concerns of developing nations were adequately addressed. Ultimately, Dr. Singh's leadership in these multilateral institutions enhanced India's standing in the global economic order and contributed to a more equitable global system, particularly in the face of emerging challenges.

▪ India's Position as an Emerging Power

Dr. Manmohan Singh's tenure as finance minister and later as prime minister played a crucial role in positioning India as an emerging power within the global economy. His leadership allowed India to rise as a significant force in the Global South, with its economic transformation setting the stage for a larger role in international affairs. The country's shift from a protectionist, state-controlled economy to an open market-driven system was instrumental in reshaping India's position in the world. India's emergence as an economic leader in the Global South was marked by several key policy decisions. Dr. Singh's commitment to liberalization and economic reforms, initiated in the early 1990s, laid the foundation for the country's accelerated growth.

By embracing globalization, reducing trade barriers, and increasing foreign direct investment (FDI), India became a magnet for investment and a key player in the global supply chain. The government's emphasis on creating a robust manufacturing sector, coupled with strides in the information technology (IT) and service industries, further enhanced India's standing as an economic powerhouse in the developing world. Moreover, Dr. Singh's advocacy for multilateralism, especially through his involvement in global forums like the G20, BRICS, and the WTO, gave India a prominent platform to represent the interests of developing nations. At the WTO, he championed the causes of the Global South, particularly in terms of trade rules that favoured poorer countries, agricultural subsidies, and intellectual property issues. Similarly, India's role in BRICS (Brazil, Russia, India, China, and South Africa) allowed it to position itself alongside other rapidly developing nations, asserting the importance of a more inclusive global economic order.

India's participation in the G20 further solidified its status as a global economic leader. As part of the group of the world's largest economies, India helped shape discussions around global economic stability, financial reforms, and climate change. Dr. Singh was a key advocate for policies that emphasized financial regulation, promoting global economic recovery post-2008 financial crisis, and addressing global imbalances. India's growing economic power and leadership in such forums allowed the country to wield influence on issues like climate change, trade, and financial regulation, positioning itself as a voice for the Global South in broader international economic discussions. Dr. Singh's leadership also centred on creating a favourable business environment within India, which helped integrate the country into the global economy.

Reforms aimed at improving ease of doing business, coupled with efforts to strengthen infrastructure, were designed to ensure that India's growth was sustainable and could contribute meaningfully to global development. Furthermore, India's growing middle class, its large consumer market, and its technological prowess, especially in software and IT services, made it an attractive destination for international companies seeking new markets and opportunities for investment. In sum, Dr. Singh's policies and initiatives helped position India not just as an economic success story but as a prominent emerging power in the Global South. By leveraging economic reforms, multilateral engagement, and global leadership, he ensured that India would play a critical role in the twenty-first century global economy, shaping the future of the developing world on the global stage.

Economic Leadership in the Global South

Dr. Manmohan Singh's leadership played a crucial role in positioning India as a major emerging economic power, particularly within the context of the Global South. Throughout his tenure as finance minister and later as prime minister, Dr. Singh's visionary policies and strategic reforms propelled India to the forefront of international economic discussions, ensuring the country's rise as an influential player in the global economic landscape. His efforts to transform India's economy from a largely protectionist, state-controlled model to one more aligned with free-market principles were foundational to India's emergence as an economic leader among developing nations. India's transformation during Dr. Singh's leadership was propelled by landmark reforms initiated in the early 1990s.

These reforms, which included the liberalization of the economy, reduction of trade barriers, encouragement of FDI, and privatization of state-owned enterprises, facilitated India's integration into the global economy. India's embrace of globalization allowed it to leverage the forces of the global marketplace, attracting international investments and expanding its role in the global supply chain. The liberalization of trade policies enabled India to tap into foreign markets, while at the same time, increasing competition and efficiency in domestic industries, fostering sustainable economic growth.

Advocacy for Multilateralism and India's Role in Global Economic Forums

Dr. Singh's leadership also marked a significant shift in India's foreign economic policy. He was a staunch advocate for multilateralism, striving to enhance India's influence in global economic and political forums such as the G20, BRICS, and the WTO. Through his active participation in these institutions, India was able to represent the interests of the Global South, calling for more equitable global economic governance that took into account the developmental needs of emerging economies. Dr. Singh played a pivotal role in representing the interests of developing nations at the WTO, focusing on issues such as agricultural subsidies, fair trade practices, and intellectual property rights. India, under his leadership, advocated for reforms that would allow developing countries to have a more significant say in shaping global trade rules, arguing that the existing trade framework disproportionately benefited wealthier nations.

In the context of BRICS, Dr. Singh's efforts solidified India's role as a central figure among emerging economies. The BRICS nations collectively aimed to create a more balanced global economic order that better reflected the needs of the developing world. India, through its participation in BRICS, emphasized the importance of sustainable development, financial regulation, and infrastructure investment in emerging markets, pushing for policies that could uplift the Global South as a whole. Similarly, India's role in the G20 further cemented its economic leadership. As part of the group of the world's largest economies, India was instrumental in discussions surrounding global economic stability, financial reforms, and issues like climate change. Dr. Singh's leadership in the G20 allowed India to advocate for global financial stability, promote inclusive economic growth, and push for a more equitable international financial system.

His efforts were especially vital in addressing the aftermath of the 2008 global financial crisis, where India's voice was key in advocating for economic policies that ensured recovery for emerging markets and developing economies.

Fig. 13.2: Road and Urban Development Projects Boosted by Stimulus Spending.

Economic Reforms and Integration into the Global Economy

Dr. Singh's focus on reforming India's domestic business environment was also a key factor in India's position as an emerging economic power. Recognizing that infrastructure and regulatory reforms were necessary for sustained economic growth, Dr. Singh worked to improve India's infrastructure, banking systems, and investment climate. Through initiatives like the creation of Special Economic Zones (SEZs) and improvements in ease of doing business, India became an increasingly attractive destination for foreign investment. India's expanding middle class, large consumer market, and growing technological capabilities also contributed to its rise as an economic leader in the Global South. The IT sector, in particular, became one of the key drivers of India's economic growth. India's prowess in software and IT services made it a hub for global outsourcing, while the country's burgeoning startup ecosystem began to attract attention from global investors. These sectors played a crucial role in boosting India's economic profile on the international stage. Moreover, Dr. Singh's policies laid the foundation for a more globally integrated economy, encouraging trade and investment flows that further bolstered India's economic standing.

The country's increased participation in global trade, coupled with its growing consumer base and burgeoning technological capabilities, enabled it to exert greater influence over international economic policies and global financial governance. Through a combination of strategic economic reforms, active participation in multilateral forums, and a focus on domestic growth, Dr. Manmohan Singh was instrumental in positioning India as an emerging economic power. Under his leadership, India transitioned from an economy plagued by stagnation and protectionism to one that was globally connected and increasingly influential in shaping global economic trends. His advocacy for multilateralism and his focus on enhancing India's role in the Global South ensured that India would be a key player in global economic governance, representing the interests of developing nations and pushing for a more inclusive and balanced global economic order. India's rise as an economic leader in the Global South during Dr. Singh's tenure continues to shape its role in the world today.

▪ Dr. Singh's Vision for Global Integration

Dr. Manmohan Singh's approach to globalization, particularly during his tenure as India's finance minister in the 1990s and as prime minister, reflected his deep understanding of both the opportunities and challenges that global economic integration presented. He sought to ensure that India's engagement with the global economy was strategic, with an eye on both short-term benefits and long-term sustainability. His careful navigation through the complex dynamics of economic liberalization and integration provided a roadmap for India's successful transition into the global economic arena, while still focusing on its domestic priorities. Dr. Singh's emphasis on balancing national interests with global aspirations was rooted in his experience as an economist with a global perspective.

Having spent significant time at international organizations such as the IMF and World Bank, he understood the economic forces shaping the world. However, he also recognized that India, with its vast and diverse population, could not afford to pursue the same path as other developing countries. Instead, he championed a model of globalization that prioritized India's unique economic structure, its need for inclusive growth, and its aspirations to maintain cultural and political autonomy. One of the key aspects of Dr. Singh's vision was ensuring that India's domestic policies were aligned with the realities of global economic integration. He recognized that India's economic success in a globalized world would depend on its ability to effectively participate in international trade, attract foreign investment, and enhance its competitive advantage in global markets.

At the same time, he understood the necessity of implementing reforms that would stimulate job creation, provide access to resources, and promote social welfare.

Fig. 13.3: Dr. Manmohan Singh at the G20 Summit Discussing Strategies for Global Recovery.

This dual focus on economic growth and social inclusion was central to Dr. Singh's understanding of global integration. The economic reforms of the 1990s, which Dr. Singh was instrumental in shaping, paved the way for India to engage with the world more proactively. The opening up of markets, liberalization of foreign investment policies, and removal of trade barriers were all components of his strategy to bring India closer to the global economy. However, Dr. Singh was keenly aware that the benefits of these reforms needed to be evenly distributed across the population. The pro-poor growth policies, aimed at improving access to education, health care, and employment opportunities, were critical to ensuring that the poorest and most vulnerable communities were not excluded from the economic benefits of globalization. Dr. Singh's commitment to balancing national interests with global integration was evident in his strategic leadership within multilateral institutions like the WTO and the G20. He used these platforms to advocate for a more inclusive global economic system that would be more favourable to developing countries. His advocacy for multilateralism was not just about ensuring that India had a seat at the table, but also about creating opportunities for other developing nations to have their voices heard.

Under his leadership, India played a central role in shaping the global economic order by advocating for reforms that would benefit the Global South and ensure a more balanced distribution of economic power and wealth. At the WTO, Dr. Singh was a strong advocate for the interests of developing countries, particularly in the areas of agriculture, trade subsidies, and market access. His efforts to secure favourable trade agreements for India helped position the country as a rising global economic player. Similarly, his work in the G20 and BRICS forums showcased his vision for a new global economic order in which emerging economies could exert greater influence and have a stronger role in shaping international policies. This was an essential component of Dr. Singh's broader vision for India as an emerging power in the global economy.

While Dr. Singh's approach to globalization emphasized economic liberalization and market integration, it was never at the expense of India's sovereignty or cultural values. His leadership was marked by a careful balancing act between embracing the opportunities of the global economy and safeguarding India's independence. This nuanced approach helped India maintain its identity while becoming a key player in the global economic landscape. Dr. Singh's efforts to reform India's economy in line with global trends were also guided by his belief in creating a welfare state that could ensure equitable growth, social security, and poverty reduction. Dr. Singh's legacy in global integration can be seen in India's continued growth as an economic power. His reforms in the 1990s laid the foundation for India to become one of the world's fastest-growing economies.

India's growing influence on the global stage, particularly within the BRICS bloc and the G20, is a testament to the vision he set in motion. India has emerged as a leader in global economic governance, playing a critical role in shaping trade policies, contributing to global financial stability, and offering an alternative voice to the dominant economic powers of the West. Another crucial aspect of Dr. Singh's legacy in global integration is his commitment to addressing global inequalities. Throughout his career, Dr. Singh championed the cause of developing nations, ensuring that their economic needs were not sidelined by more powerful countries. His role at the WTO, as well as his leadership in global forums like the G20, allowed him to challenge the conventional wisdom of economic globalization and ensure that the voices of the Global South were heard. Dr. Singh's advocacy for fair trade practices, debt relief, and poverty reduction initiatives demonstrated his belief that global integration should not be a one-sided affair, but should involve cooperation and mutual benefit for all nations.

Dr. Singh's role as an economic statesman was not just about navigating global economic currents, but also about ensuring that India's integration into the world economy was sustainable and inclusive. His approach to globalization sought to address the concerns of India's rural populations, who were often left behind in the rush towards economic liberalization. His government's focus on rural development, poverty alleviation, and social welfare programmes was designed to complement the benefits of globalization by ensuring that the poorest communities had access to the opportunities created by economic growth. In conclusion, Dr. Manmohan Singh's vision for global integration was both pragmatic and forward-thinking. He understood that globalization could bring both opportunities and challenges, and he sought to create an environment in which India could thrive while protecting its national interests. His leadership in multilateral forums, his advocacy for inclusive growth, and his commitment to creating a more balanced global economic system have left a lasting impact on India's position in the world. As India continues to navigate the complexities of the global economy, Dr. Singh's legacy of balancing national interests with global engagement remains a guiding principle for policymakers today.

Balancing Globalization with National Interests

Dr. Manmohan Singh's tenure as India's finance minister and later as prime minister was characterized by his strong belief in the need for India to be deeply integrated into the global economy. His approach to globalization was not simply about embracing the forces of global markets; it was also about finding ways to ensure that these forces could be harnessed in a way that would benefit India while safeguarding its national interests. Dr. Singh's vision for global integration was shaped by the recognition that India's economic growth was increasingly interlinked with global trends, and for India to realize its full potential, it had to become an active participant in the global economic system. However, he also understood that globalization posed challenges to India's existing social and economic structures, and therefore it was essential to manage this integration carefully, striking a balance between participating in the global economy and protecting the interests of its citizens, especially the poorer sections of society.

Economic Reforms and Global Integration

One of the key aspects of Dr. Singh's approach to globalization was his commitment to economic reforms that could strengthen India's position in the global economic system. When India embarked on its liberalization journey in the early 1990s, Dr. Singh, as the architect of the reforms, was acutely aware of the need to balance the country's economic aspirations with the realities of its domestic challenges. He recognized that economic liberalization, including the reduction of trade barriers, encouragement of foreign investment, and privatization of state-owned enterprises, would open India up to the global market. However, these reforms also had to be implemented in a way that did not undermine the country's socio-economic goals, particularly poverty alleviation and inclusive growth. Dr. Singh's vision was clear: India could not afford to remain isolated from the global economy, but neither could it allow the full force of globalization to destabilize its domestic priorities. He advocated for an open economy that embraced international trade and investment but emphasized that the government's role in providing basic welfare services, supporting key industries, and ensuring social safety nets was essential in mitigating any adverse effects of globalization on vulnerable segments of the population.

Multilateralism and Global Governance

As a proponent of multilateralism, Dr. Singh believed that global integration should not be driven solely by the dictates of the most powerful economies, but should involve collective efforts from all nations, especially developing countries like India. His vision for global economic integration included a strong focus on global governance, ensuring that institutions such as the WTO, the IMF, and the World Bank worked towards a more inclusive, fair, and balanced global economic order. India's participation in multilateral institutions was an integral part of Dr. Singh's strategy for global integration.

He recognized the importance of strengthening India's voice in these forums and used platforms such as the G20, BRICS, and the WTO to advocate for policies that favoured the Global South. Under his leadership, India pushed for reforms that would give developing nations a greater say in global trade rules and ensure that international financial systems did not disproportionately favour wealthier countries. Dr. Singh's advocacy for multilateralism also extended to India's foreign policy. By championing a rules-based international order, he sought to ensure that India could engage with the world on its own terms, protecting its economic and geopolitical interests while fostering stronger ties with both developed and developing countries. India's strategic partnerships with key global players, as well as its deepening engagement in regional cooperation frameworks, were central to Dr. Singh's vision of global integration.

Domestic Considerations and the Need for a Pragmatic Approach

While Dr. Singh was an ardent supporter of globalization, he also believed that India's unique socio-economic challenges required a pragmatic approach. He understood that globalization could bring tremendous economic benefits but also posed risks, particularly in terms of increased inequality and the potential for social unrest. Thus, he was committed to ensuring that India's participation in the global economy would not come at the expense of its social and economic stability. Dr. Singh was keen on ensuring that the benefits of globalization were shared widely across Indian society. He believed that the Indian government had a responsibility to create policies that would ensure the most vulnerable populations were not left behind.

Programmes aimed at rural development, poverty alleviation, and inclusive growth were integral to his vision of global integration. These initiatives were designed to ensure that the fruits of economic growth were not concentrated in a few sectors or regions but were spread more evenly across the country, particularly in rural and underdeveloped areas. At the same time, Dr. Singh emphasized the need for a robust regulatory framework that would protect India's interests in a rapidly changing global environment. He was aware of the risks that unregulated global markets posed to developing economies, particularly in the financial sector. Under his leadership, India gradually liberalized its economy but also strengthened its regulatory institutions to ensure that the benefits of globalization could be harnessed without exposing the economy to excessive risks.

India's Role in the Global Economy

Dr. Singh's vision of global integration was rooted in the idea that India should be a leading voice in shaping the future of the global economy. He saw India not just as a participant in global economic affairs, but as a leader among developing nations, advocating for policies that could lift millions out of poverty and create a more equitable global economic system. Dr. Singh's leadership in the global arena also sought to redefine India's role in global economic governance. Through his advocacy for multilateral institutions, his leadership in the G20, BRICS, and other international organizations, India emerged as a champion of economic reforms that benefited not only itself but also other developing nations.

Dr. Singh's approach to global integration was not just about embracing global markets but also ensuring that India could influence the direction of global economic policies to better serve the interests of developing countries. Dr. Manmohan Singh's vision for global integration was characterized by a careful balance between embracing the opportunities presented by globalization and protecting the national interests of India. His belief in multilateralism, domestic economic reforms, and inclusive growth ensured that India could fully participate in the global economy while safeguarding the interests of its citizens. Under his leadership, India became an important player in global economic governance, advocating for a more equitable global economic system and positioning itself as a leader in the Global South. Dr. Singh's pragmatic and visionary approach to globalization continues to shape India's economic policies today, as the country seeks to navigate the complexities of an increasingly interconnected global economy.

▪ Indo-US Civil Nuclear Deal: A Milestone in Economic Diplomacy

The Indo-US Civil Nuclear Deal, officially known as the "India-United States Civil Nuclear Agreement", signed in 2008, stands as one of the most pivotal moments in the history of India's foreign policy and economic diplomacy. This landmark agreement not only altered India's trajectory in the global energy sector but also reshaped the geopolitical landscape of Asia, redefining India's role in global nuclear diplomacy. It was a monumental achievement for Dr. Manmohan Singh's government, as it exemplified his skill in balancing India's domestic priorities with its international obligations. The deal, which allowed India to access civilian nuclear technology from the United States and other nuclear-capable countries, was seen as a turning point that secured India's energy future, strengthened Indo-US ties, and contributed to India's emergence as a major global player in the twenty-first century.

The Background and Context of the Deal

India's nuclear journey had always been fraught with complexities. Following its first successful nuclear test in 1974, India found itself at odds with the global nuclear non-proliferation regime, primarily represented by the Nuclear Non-Proliferation Treaty (NPT). India's refusal to sign the NPT, which it viewed as discriminatory, placed it in a unique position as a nuclear-armed state outside the formal framework of nuclear governance. As a result, India faced significant diplomatic and economic sanctions from the international community, limiting its access to advanced nuclear technology, which hindered its capacity to meet the growing demands for energy in its rapidly developing economy.

The need for a new energy paradigm became increasingly evident in the early 2000s, when India's burgeoning economy led to an escalating demand for energy resources. Conventional sources of energy, such as coal and oil, were not sufficient to meet the country's needs, and the environmental and health consequences of reliance on fossil fuels were becoming a pressing concern. Nuclear power, with its potential for providing large-scale, clean energy, emerged as a critical solution. However, India's nuclear isolation and lack of access to global nuclear markets hindered its ambitions to expand its nuclear energy sector. In this context, Dr. Singh, a seasoned economist with deep knowledge of global affairs, saw the Indo-US Civil Nuclear Deal as an opportunity to modernize India's energy infrastructure while simultaneously strengthening its position in the global order. His decision to pursue this deal marked a significant shift in India's foreign policy, from self-reliance to greater global integration, and showcased his pragmatism in navigating complex international negotiations.

Negotiating the Indo-US Civil Nuclear Deal

The negotiations leading up to the signing of the Indo-US Civil Nuclear Deal were long and complicated, requiring strategic diplomacy on multiple fronts. The deal was driven by India's need for energy security and the United States' interest in improving its bilateral relations with India, a growing economic power and strategic ally in the region. The relationship between India and the US had evolved over the years, with increasing cooperation in various sectors, including defence, trade, and technology. However, the nuclear issue remained a contentious point, as the US had traditionally adhered to a policy of non-proliferation that was at odds with India's nuclear ambitions.

Dr. Singh's government embarked on a series of diplomatic engagements with the US, emphasizing India's need for civilian nuclear technology to address its energy challenges. The negotiations were difficult, as they involved navigating both domestic and international opposition. At home, the deal faced criticism from various quarters, including political parties, environmental groups, and Left-wing allies in the coalition government, who viewed the agreement as a compromise on India's sovereignty and autonomy in defence and foreign policy. Internationally, the deal had to be reconciled with the global nuclear non-proliferation regime, which was hesitant to reward India's nuclear status without adherence to the NPT.

Despite these challenges, Dr. Singh's leadership and diplomatic acumen were instrumental in securing the deal. One of the key aspects of the agreement was the waiver granted by the Nuclear Suppliers Group (NSG), which allowed India to access nuclear technology without requiring it to sign the NPT. This was a breakthrough for India, as it opened up global markets for nuclear technology, which had previously been inaccessible. Dr. Singh's government also ensured that India's strategic autonomy was preserved by negotiating safeguards that allowed India to continue its nuclear weapons programme while engaging in civilian nuclear cooperation. The deal required extensive negotiations with the US Congress, which had to approve the agreement. Dr. Singh's political acumen was on full display as he managed to secure bipartisan support for the deal, despite significant opposition from some quarters. The US Congress ultimately passed the agreement, and in 2008, the deal was signed, marking a historic moment in Indo-US relations.

Economic Implications of the Deal

The Indo-US Civil Nuclear Deal had profound economic implications for India, particularly in terms of energy security, industrial growth, and access to advanced technology. For India, the agreement opened the doors to the international civilian nuclear market, allowing it to import nuclear fuel and technology from countries such as the US, Russia, and France. This access was crucial for expanding India's nuclear power capacity, which was seen as a key component of the country's energy future. Nuclear power generation is a clean, efficient, and reliable source of energy, making it an attractive option for a country like India, which faces severe challenges related to air pollution, carbon emissions, and the depletion of natural resources.

The deal allowed India to diversify its energy mix and reduce its dependence on fossil fuels, which in turn contributed to the nation's efforts to mitigate climate change and meet its international environmental commitments. The deal also had significant economic ripple effects, as it led to the development of a robust nuclear industry in India. It created new opportunities for FDI in the nuclear sector and opened up avenues for technological collaboration with leading global nuclear powers. India's growing nuclear infrastructure attracted investment in related sectors such as research and development, manufacturing, and nuclear safety, providing a boost to the Indian economy.

Moreover, the deal facilitated greater cooperation between India and the US in sectors beyond nuclear energy, including defence, technology, and trade. The strengthening of bilateral ties opened new opportunities for Indian businesses to access the global market, particularly in high-tech industries. The economic benefits of the deal were not confined to the energy sector alone, but also contributed to India's broader economic development goals.

Strategic and Geopolitical Significance

Beyond the economic benefits, the Indo-US Civil Nuclear Deal had significant strategic and geopolitical implications for both India and the US. The deal was a clear signal of India's growing stature on the global stage and its willingness to engage with major powers on terms that preserved its sovereignty and autonomy. For the US, the agreement represented a strategic move to strengthen its relationship with India, a key partner in the Indo-Pacific region, especially in light of China's rise as a global power. The deal cemented India's status as a major global player in the nuclear arena, and it provided a platform for India to advocate for reforms in global nuclear governance.

By securing access to nuclear technology while maintaining its nuclear weapons programme, India set a precedent for other countries outside the NPT framework, signalling that it could engage in global non-proliferation efforts while preserving its national security interests. The Indo-US Civil Nuclear Deal also played a crucial role in shaping India's regional security dynamics.

With improved relations with the US, India was better positioned to counterbalance China's growing influence in Asia. The deal paved the way for increased defence and strategic cooperation between India and the US, strengthening India's defence capabilities and its role in regional security.

Domestic and International Reactions

While the Indo-US Civil Nuclear Deal was hailed as a major diplomatic triumph, it was also met with considerable opposition both domestically and internationally. In India, the deal faced criticism from various political parties, particularly the Left, which was concerned about India's growing alignment with the US. There were fears that the deal would constrain India's strategic autonomy and make it vulnerable to external pressures on issues such as foreign policy and defence. The Left parties, which were part of the coalition government at the time, opposed the deal, leading to the collapse of the coalition and Dr. Singh's decision to seek a vote of confidence in parliament.

Despite the opposition, Dr. Singh's government managed to survive the vote, which underscored the political support for the deal within India's ruling coalition. Internationally, the deal raised concerns among some countries, particularly those in the non-proliferation community. Critics argued that the deal could undermine the global non-proliferation regime and set a dangerous precedent for other countries seeking to bypass the NPT. However, Dr. Singh's government successfully argued that India's unique circumstances—its status as a responsible nuclear power and its commitment to non-proliferation—made the deal justifiable. Ultimately, the deal's success was a testament to India's diplomatic prowess and its ability to navigate complex international negotiations.

Conclusion

The Indo-US Civil Nuclear Deal stands as a landmark achievement in India's foreign policy and economic diplomacy. It represented a bold step in securing India's energy future, strengthening its global standing, and enhancing its strategic partnership with the US. The deal's economic implications were profound, offering India access to clean and reliable energy sources, while its geopolitical significance was equally transformative, enhancing India's role in global nuclear governance and regional security. Dr. Singh's leadership, strategic foresight, and diplomatic acumen played a critical role in the success of the deal, making it one of the defining moments of his tenure as prime minister.

• Pioneering India's Participation in the G20 and Global Economic Governance

India's active participation in the G20 represents a significant evolution in its role within global economic governance. The G20, which comprises the world's major economies, both developed and developing, serves as an essential forum for addressing global economic challenges, coordinating international policy responses, and fostering multilateral cooperation. Dr. Manmohan Singh, as prime minister of India from 2004 to 2014, played a pivotal role in shaping India's approach to the G20, positioning the country as a key player in the global economic order. Under his leadership, India's participation in the G20 became a cornerstone of its foreign policy and economic strategy, reflecting both the country's growing economic clout and its aspirations to contribute to a more inclusive, balanced, and sustainable global economic system.

India's Initial Engagement with the G20

India's engagement with the G20 began in the aftermath of the 2008 global financial crisis, which exposed the vulnerabilities of the global financial system and underscored the need for a coordinated global response to economic instability. The G20, which had originally been established as a meeting of finance ministers and central bank governors in 1999 to address issues related to international financial stability, was elevated to a leaders' summit in 2008 in response to the severity of the crisis. This shift marked the G20's transformation into the premier forum for addressing global economic issues at the level of heads of state and government. Dr. Singh's leadership came at a crucial time, as the global economy faced its worst recession since the Great Depression of the 1930s. The crisis revealed the limitations of existing global governance structures, particularly the IMF, the World Bank, and the WTO, in dealing with the scale and interconnectedness of the crisis.

India, which had weathered the crisis relatively well due to its strong domestic economic fundamentals, saw an opportunity to play a more prominent role in global economic decision making. As a representative of the Global South, India was keen to ensure that the voices of developing countries, which were often marginalized in global forums, were heard and considered in the formulation of solutions to the crisis. Dr. Singh's participation in the G20 was characterized by a clear vision: to ensure that the global response to the crisis took into account the needs and aspirations of emerging economies and developing countries. India's emphasis on inclusive growth, financial stability, and sustainable development became central themes in its approach to G20 discussions, and Dr. Singh's leadership in the forum reflected these priorities. India's engagement with the G20 also allowed it to push for reform of international financial institutions, with a focus on making them more representative of the emerging economies that were increasingly driving global growth.

India's Vision for a More Inclusive Global Economic System

At the heart of India's approach to the G20 under Dr. Singh's leadership was the belief that the global economic system needed to be more inclusive, equitable, and sustainable. India's rapidly growing economy, coupled with its large and diverse population, provided it with a unique perspective on the challenges faced by both developing and developed countries. Dr. Singh consistently advocated for policies that would ensure that the benefits of global economic growth were widely shared and that the most vulnerable economies were not left behind.

One of the key themes that India emphasized in the G20 discussions was the need for more balanced global growth. In the wake of the financial crisis, many advanced economies turned to protectionist measures and trade barriers as a means of protecting their industries and jobs. India, however, called for the promotion of open and free trade, arguing that global growth could only be sustained if trade barriers were dismantled and developing countries had access to the global market. Dr. Singh's government also pushed for the reform of the international financial architecture, which had been designed in the aftermath of Second World War and was seen by many as outdated and not reflective of the current global economic reality. India argued that the IMF, World Bank, and other international institutions should have greater representation from emerging economies, which now accounted for a significant portion of global economic activity.

In addition to advocating for financial and trade reforms, India also called for a greater focus on sustainable development in the G20's agenda. Dr. Singh recognized that the global economy could not thrive in the long-term if it continued to ignore the environmental and social dimensions of growth. He pushed for the inclusion of climate change, environmental sustainability, and social equity as integral components of global economic governance. Under his leadership, India made it clear that any solution to the global economic crisis must also address the challenges posed by environmental degradation and rising inequality, which threatened long-term economic stability.

Dr. Singh's Role in the Global Financial Crisis

The 2008 financial crisis provided India with a unique opportunity to assert itself as a leader in global economic governance. While many advanced economies were grappling with deep recessions, India's economy remained relatively insulated from the worst effects of the crisis, largely due to its domestic-driven growth model and relatively limited exposure to global financial markets. India's resilience during the crisis gave Dr. Singh a strong platform to argue for the need for a new approach to global economic management—one that took into account the realities of an increasingly multipolar world. Dr. Singh's leadership during the crisis was marked by his emphasis on coordinated global action. At the 2009 G20 summit in London, India played a key role in advocating for fiscal stimulus packages, increased financial assistance to developing countries, and the establishment of new regulatory frameworks to prevent future financial crises.

India also called for the reform of global financial institutions, including the IMF and the World Bank, to make them more representative of the changing global economic landscape. Dr. Singh's advocacy for these reforms resonated with other emerging economies, many of which were experiencing rapid growth but were not adequately represented in the decision making processes of global institutions. One of the key outcomes of the G20 summit in London was the agreement to expand the IMF's resources and to reform the governance structure of the IMF and World Bank. These reforms were seen as a victory for emerging economies, including India, and represented a step toward making the global financial system more inclusive and reflective of the new economic realities. India's leadership in pushing for these reforms was a testament to Dr. Singh's vision of a more equitable global economic system, where developing countries had a greater say in the decisions that affected their economies.

India's Role in Shaping the Post-Crisis Global Economic Order

Dr. Singh's leadership in the G20 was not limited to responding to the immediate aftermath of the financial crisis. He also focused on shaping the long-term direction of global economic governance. India's growing economic influence gave Dr. Singh the leverage to push for structural reforms in international financial institutions, trade policy, and climate change agreements. One of the key areas where India sought to exert influence was in the reform of the global financial architecture. Dr. Singh's government called for the creation of a more representative and accountable system of global governance, one that took into account the rise of emerging economies and the need for a more balanced distribution of power. This vision was reflected in India's call for greater voting rights for emerging economies in the IMF and World Bank, as well as its support for expanding the membership of the G20 to include additional emerging economies.

India also played a key role in shaping the G20's agenda on climate change and sustainable development. Dr. Singh was a strong advocate for including environmental sustainability as a central pillar of global economic governance, arguing that economic growth and environmental protection were not mutually exclusive but rather mutually reinforcing. India's position on climate change was informed by its own developmental needs and its commitment to addressing poverty and inequality. Dr. Singh's government sought to ensure that climate policies did not disproportionately burden developing countries, which had contributed the least to global emissions but were most vulnerable to the impacts of climate change.

India's Strategic Vision in the G20

Dr. Singh's participation in the G20 was not just about economic governance—it was also about positioning India as a global leader in a rapidly changing world. As India's economic and strategic influence grew, Dr. Singh recognized the importance of strengthening India's diplomatic relationships with key players in the G20, including the US, China, the European Union, and other emerging economies. India's participation in the G20 allowed it to forge closer ties with these countries and to advocate for policies that would benefit both India and the global community. India's engagement with the G20 also reflected Dr. Singh's broader vision of multilateralism and the importance of working within global frameworks to address common challenges.

Whether it was promoting economic growth, tackling climate change, or advancing global trade, Dr. Singh emphasized the need for cooperation and collaboration among nations. India's leadership in the G20 under his guidance helped to enhance its reputation as a responsible global power and a champion of the interests of developing countries. India's participation in the G20 under Dr. Manmohan Singh's leadership marked a transformative period in the country's role in global economic governance. Through strategic diplomacy, advocacy for reform, and a commitment to inclusive growth, India asserted itself as a key player in shaping the post-crisis global economic order. Dr. Singh's vision for a more inclusive, balanced, and sustainable global economy resonated across the G20, and his leadership in the forum helped to secure India's place at the table of the world's most influential economic powers. As India continues to grow as a global economic force, Dr. Singh's contributions to the G20 and global economic governance will remain a defining aspect of India's foreign policy legacy.

▪ Advocacy for Developing Countries: Strengthening the Voice of the Global South

Dr. Manmohan Singh's tenure as prime minister of India was characterized by his steadfast advocacy for the interests of developing countries, particularly those in the Global South. As a leader who was acutely aware of the disparities that exist in global economic governance, Dr. Singh sought to amplify the voices of the Global South, ensuring that their concerns were taken seriously in international forums and negotiations. Through his diplomatic initiatives and strategic leadership, Dr. Singh contributed to reshaping global economic structures, with a focus on equitable development, poverty reduction, and greater representation for developing nations in global decision making bodies.

The Global South refers to the group of countries that are often characterized by lower levels of industrialization, lower Human Development Index (HDI) rankings, and less-developed infrastructure. These countries, which make up the majority of the world's population, have historically been marginalized in global economic governance, where policies often favour the developed countries of the Global North. Dr. Singh's vision was to promote a more inclusive, fair, and balanced global system—one that recognized the challenges faced by the Global South and provided them with greater opportunities for growth and development.

Advocating for Reform of Global Institutions

One of the key aspects of Dr. Singh's advocacy for the Global South was his push for reforms in international financial and economic institutions. Organizations such as the IMF, the World Bank, and the WTO have long been dominated by developed countries, with policies that often did not reflect the needs and realities of developing nations. Dr. Singh recognized the need to reform these institutions to make them more representative and responsive to the challenges of developing countries. Under Dr. Singh's leadership, India took a prominent role in advocating for changes to the governance structures of these institutions. India's position was clear: developing countries needed a greater say in decisions that affected their economies, and the global financial architecture should be more inclusive, transparent, and accountable.

Dr. Singh pushed for reforms in the IMF, including a greater voting share for emerging economies, and argued that the institution's policies should be aligned with the realities of the modern global economy. This stance was especially significant in the context of the 2008 global financial crisis, which disproportionately affected developing countries and exposed the vulnerabilities of the existing global economic framework. India's efforts to reform the World Bank also centred around making it more responsive to the development needs of poor and middle-income countries. Dr. Singh believed that the World Bank should prioritize issues such as poverty reduction, education, and health care, and he sought to ensure that its funding mechanisms would support projects that would directly benefit the most vulnerable populations in developing countries. At the WTO, India argued for a fairer global trade system that would provide greater market access to developing countries, remove trade barriers, and eliminate subsidies that disproportionately benefited developed nations.

Through his active participation in these discussions, Dr. Singh succeeded in pushing for more inclusive decision making processes. India's influence within these institutions grew, and the country's advocacy helped to secure key reforms, including changes to voting power within the IMF and commitments to prioritize development in the policies of the World Bank.

Promoting South-South Cooperation

In addition to advocating for reforms within existing global institutions, Dr. Singh also placed a significant emphasis on strengthening South-South cooperation. South-South cooperation refers to the collaboration between developing countries to address shared challenges, such as poverty, climate change, and economic inequality. Dr. Singh recognized that developing countries could benefit from pooling their resources, sharing knowledge, and collaborating on initiatives that addressed their common concerns. One of the most notable initiatives during Dr. Singh's tenure was India's leadership in the Group of 77 (G77), a coalition of developing nations that aims to promote the economic and political interests of the Global South. As a prominent member of the

G77, India advocated for policies that would empower developing countries and foster greater cooperation among them.

Dr. Singh also supported initiatives that would increase trade between developing countries, reduce dependency on developed nations, and promote collective bargaining on global issues such as climate change and trade. India's commitment to South-South cooperation was also evident in its role in various regional and multilateral organizations, such as the Non-Aligned Movement (NAM), BRICS (Brazil, Russia, India, China, and South Africa), and the African Union. Dr. Singh worked to strengthen India's ties with countries in Africa, Latin America, and Asia, recognizing that the collective strength of the Global South was essential in advocating for global reforms and in addressing development challenges. Through these initiatives, Dr. Singh sought to empower developing countries to take a more active role in global governance, ensuring that their voices were heard and their interests were represented in international negotiations.

Addressing Climate Change and Sustainable Development

One of the most pressing challenges facing the Global South is the issue of climate change. Developing countries are the most vulnerable to the effects of climate change, yet they are often the least responsible for the environmental degradation that causes it. Dr. Singh consistently emphasized that climate change was not only an environmental issue but also an economic and social issue that required urgent action.

India, under Dr. Singh's leadership, played a leading role in advocating for a fair and equitable approach to climate change negotiations. At international forums such as the United Nations Framework Convention on Climate Change (UNFCCC), India argued that developed countries, which were historically responsible for the majority of global emissions, should take the lead in reducing their carbon footprints. At the same time, Dr. Singh advocated for the principle of "common but differentiated responsibilities", which acknowledged that developing countries should not be expected to make the same level of commitments as developed countries in the fight against climate change.

Dr. Singh's government also worked to ensure that developing countries had access to the resources and technologies needed to mitigate and adapt to climate change. He advocated for financial assistance from developed countries to support climate change projects in the Global South and for technology transfer that would help developing nations build sustainable infrastructure without compromising their development goals. India's stance on climate change was based on the recognition that the challenges of development and environmental sustainability could not be seen in isolation, and that solutions needed to be tailored to the unique circumstances of the Global South.

Strengthening the Voice of Developing Countries in Global Trade

Global trade has long been an area where the interests of developing countries have been sidelined in favour of the developed world. The Doha Round of trade negotiations, which began in 2001 under the auspices of the WTO, aimed to address the imbalances in the global trading system by focusing on issues important to developing countries, such as agricultural subsidies, market access, and intellectual property rights. However, the Doha Round has been plagued by deadlock, with developed countries often unwilling to make concessions that would benefit developing nations.

Dr. Singh's government played a central role in advocating for the interests of developing countries in global trade negotiations. India consistently pushed for reforms that would eliminate trade barriers, provide better access to markets, and remove agricultural subsidies that disproportionately benefited developed nations. Dr. Singh argued that global trade rules should reflect the realities of developing countries and promote policies that would foster sustainable development. At the same time, India worked to strengthen regional trade agreements with other developing countries, such as the South Asian Free Trade Area (SAFTA) and the India-ASEAN Free Trade Agreement, to promote intra-regional trade and reduce dependency on developed markets. These efforts were designed to create a more balanced global trade system that would empower developing countries and provide them with greater opportunities for economic growth.

Conclusion

Dr. Manmohan Singh's advocacy for the Global South was a defining feature of his leadership, both domestically and internationally. Through his efforts to reform global institutions, promote South-South cooperation, and address the challenges faced by developing countries, Dr. Singh strengthened the voice of the Global South in global economic governance. His leadership helped to shift the global economic paradigm, making it more inclusive, equitable, and responsive to the needs of developing nations. Dr. Singh's emphasis on a fairer global order, one that took into account the realities of poverty, inequality, and environmental degradation, continues to resonate in the global discussions on economic development, climate change, and trade. His legacy as an advocate for the Global South remains an enduring testament to his vision of a world where the interests of all nations, particularly those in the Global South, are respected and considered in the decisions that shape the future of the global community.

REFERENCES

Anand, V. (2013). *India's Look East Policy Gains Momentum.* Institute for Transnational Studies.

Banik, N. (2006). "How Promising is BIMSTEC?" *Economic and Political Weekly, 41*(51): 5264-68.

Baruah, S. (2004). "Between South and Southeast Asia: Northeast India and Look East policy." *Ceniseas Paper, 4.* Centre for Northeast India South and Southeast Asia Studies.

Chachavalpongpun, P. (2011). "Look East meets Look West: Indian-Southeast Asian relations in flux." *The International Spectator, 46*(2): 91-108. https://doi.org/10.1080/03932729.2011.576174

Haokip, T. (2011). "India's Look East Policy: Its Evolution and Approach." *South Asian Survey, 18*(2): 239-57. https://doi.org/10.1177/0971523113513368

Harshe, R. (1999). "South Asian Regional Co-operation: Problems and Prospects." *Economic and Political Weekly, 44*(19): 1100-1105.

Lahiri, I. (2013). "Evolution and Rationale of India's Look East Policy with Special Reference to BIMSTEC". *UGC-CAS-1*. Department of International Relations, Jadavpur University.

Muni, S.D. (2011). "India's 'Look East' Policy: The Strategic Dimension." *ISAS Working Paper 121*. Institute of South Asian Studies, National University of Singapore.

Singh, M. (2004). PM's Address at the Inauguration of New Capital Complex of Assam.

_____(2006). PM's Speech at the Asian Corporate Conference, "Driving Global Business: India's New Priorities, Asia's New Realities."

Sreedhar. (1994). *Security Situation in Southern Asia*. Strategic.

Zhang, D. (2006). "India Looks East: Strategies and Impact." *AUSAID Working Paper*.

14

Reflections and Tributes

The section titled "Reflections and Tributes" stands as a fitting conclusion to the life and legacy of Dr. Manmohan Singh, one of India's most distinguished economists and political figures. His life and career embody an extraordinary journey of intellectual rigour, political foresight, and an unwavering commitment to India's development, both at home and on the global stage. This section seeks to reflect upon the monumental impact that Dr. Singh has had on India's economic transformation, its place in the world, and the lives of millions of its citizens. Additionally, it examines the numerous tributes paid to him from various quarters of society, politics, and academia, offering a panoramic view of how his leadership has shaped the trajectory of India's development and how his contributions will be remembered for generations to come.

Dr. Singh's tenure as India's finance minister in the 1990s, followed by his role as prime minister from 2004 to 2014, is often seen as a defining period in the nation's economic history. The economic reforms he spearheaded in the 1990s reshaped the Indian economy from a closed, state-controlled system to a more open and market-driven economy. His leadership was instrumental in charting India's course through a complex set of economic challenges, from balancing the needs of a growing economy with the demands of a globalized world, to ensuring that the benefits of economic growth reached the most vulnerable sections of society. The process of reflection on Dr. Singh's contributions involves a deeper understanding of the intellectual, moral, and practical underpinnings of his policies.

His economic philosophy, often described as one rooted in the belief of balanced, sustainable, and inclusive growth, has shaped many of the key policies that defined his tenure in office. Whether it was his advocacy for liberalization and globalization or his commitment to reducing poverty and increasing social welfare, Dr. Singh's leadership and decisions were always marked by a rare combination of vision and pragmatism. His policies were not mere reactions to external circumstances, but the products of a deep, nuanced understanding of India's position in the global economic order and the long-term requirements of its socio-economic development.

Dr. Singh's ability to articulate and implement economic reforms, while simultaneously navigating the turbulent political waters of coalition politics, left an indelible mark on India's governance model. His tenure in office was often characterized by a sense of quiet confidence and a preference for long-term policy decisions over short-term political gains. This approach, although at times controversial, helped create an economic foundation that propelled India towards becoming one of the fastest-growing economies in the world. In reflecting on his leadership, one must also consider the challenges Dr. Singh faced during his tenure, particularly in navigating political opposition, handling controversies, and managing economic crises. His tenure was not without its difficulties, and while his policies were revolutionary, their implementation was often met with resistance from various political factions, including both the opposition and sections of his own party.

Nonetheless, Dr. Singh remained steadfast in his commitment to the long-term goals he had set for India. His ability to maintain a steady course despite political turbulence is one of the hallmarks of his leadership. Tributes to Dr. Singh have come from various quarters, acknowledging his transformative role in India's rise on the global stage. Politicians, economists, academics, and global leaders have all lauded his contributions to India's economic resurgence. Internationally, he is recognized not just for his role in economic reforms, but also for his diplomatic skills and his leadership in global institutions such as the United Nations, the World Trade Organization (WTO), the G20, and BRICS. His advocacy for multilateralism, his work on climate change, and his leadership in securing India's position in the global economic order have been widely praised.

In India, tributes to Dr. Singh have highlighted his role in making India an economic powerhouse and a major player in global trade and politics. His tenure as prime minister witnessed a period of unprecedented economic growth, even amidst global economic downturns. His legacy is viewed by many as the foundation upon which India's modern economy was built. Beyond his role in shaping economic policy, Dr. Singh is remembered for his personal qualities—his integrity, humility, and commitment to public service. Dr. Singh's tenure also marks a period of intense political change in India. As a leader, he operated in a complex political environment, where coalition politics often dictated the pace and scope of policy reforms. His approach to governance was often described as technocratic, focusing on data-driven decisions and long-term solutions rather than populist measures.

While this made him less charismatic compared to some of his contemporaries, it earned him respect as a leader who put the nation's interests above party politics. His role in stabilizing India's economy, securing foreign investment, and improving India's international standing is widely acknowledged as one of the most significant contributions to the country's modern development narrative. Moreover, the tributes to Dr. Singh also come from those who have studied his economic philosophy and the broader impact of his reforms. Scholars, both in India and abroad, have praised his approach to economic liberalization, which was cautious yet bold, strategic yet inclusive. His economic reforms, particularly in the areas of trade, investment, and industrial policy, created the foundations for India's remarkable rise as a global economic power.

His vision extended beyond merely opening the economy to external markets—he envisioned an India that could compete globally while also ensuring that the fruits of economic progress reached the marginalized sections of society. Beyond economics, Dr. Singh's leadership was also about social and political integration. His tenure saw the introduction of several social welfare programmes aimed at alleviating poverty, improving education, and ensuring better health care for the poor. His government's policies in the areas of rural development, employment, and social justice were designed to bridge the gap between India's rural and urban areas, and to ensure that the benefits of economic growth were not limited to just a small elite.

In conclusion, the reflections on Dr. Manmohan Singh's life and the tributes paid to him from all corners of the world offer a comprehensive view of his immense contributions to India's development and his legacy as an economic leader. While his policies were not without their critics, the general consensus remains that his leadership transformed India's economy and placed the country firmly on the path of sustained growth and development. His legacy is not just one of economic reforms, but also of the values of integrity, foresight, and a commitment to the welfare of the Indian people. The tributes paid to him by national and international figures attest to his enduring influence on global economic thought and India's place in the world order. His contributions will continue to be a benchmark for future policymakers, who will look to his legacy as a guide in navigating the complex and ever-evolving landscape of global economics.

▪ Reflections From Economists and Leaders

Dr. Manmohan Singh, India's thirteenth prime minister, stands as one of the most influential and respected leaders in contemporary history. His career was marked not only by the profound economic reforms he championed but also by his diplomatic acumen and intellectual prowess. Through his leadership, India experienced an economic transformation that propelled it onto the global stage, and his contributions to multilateral diplomacy, inclusive development, and economic governance are widely acknowledged. The tributes he has received from economists, world leaders, and international institutions underscore the profound impact of his policies, vision, and leadership style on both India and the world.

Legacy of Economic Reform

One of the most significant aspects of Dr. Singh's tenure was his role in steering India through a period of unprecedented economic change. In 1991, when India faced a severe balance of payments crisis, Dr. Singh, as the finance minister, took the bold decision to initiate a series of economic reforms aimed at liberalizing the Indian economy. These reforms, which included trade liberalization, industrial deregulation, and financial sector reform, were initially met with scepticism but later came to be seen as the driving forces behind India's remarkable economic growth in the subsequent decades.

Global economists have widely praised Dr. Singh for his role in implementing these market-driven reforms. Institutions such as the International Monetary Fund (IMF) and the World Bank have commended Dr. Singh for his pragmatic approach to economic policy. His policies of opening up the economy, encouraging foreign investment, and dismantling bureaucratic hurdles allowed India to become one of the fastest-growing economies in the world. Economists like Arvind Subramanian, who later became India's Chief Economic Advisor, have often pointed to Dr. Singh's ability to combine academic theories with practical policies, making his leadership a case study in effective economic governance.

Diplomatic and Geopolitical Acumen

Dr. Singh's legacy as a statesman extends far beyond economic reform. His diplomatic acumen in navigating India's complex international relations also earned him tributes from world leaders. His tenure as prime minister saw India engage in significant partnerships with countries across the world, from the United States to the European Union, and from Asia to Africa.

Dr. Singh's ability to balance India's national interests with global cooperation was seen as a hallmark of his diplomatic leadership. Former US President Barack Obama often spoke of Dr. Singh's crucial role in strengthening Indo-US relations. Dr. Singh's leadership during the 2008 global financial crisis, as well as his involvement in multilateral forums like the G20 and BRICS, showcased his ability to represent India's interests while contributing to the global conversation on economic governance. Dr. Singh's strategic focus on multilateralism also earned him respect from leaders across the Global South. His advocacy for developing economies in forums like the WTO was seen as a critical contribution to reshaping global trade dynamics in a way that benefited emerging economies. His leadership was also instrumental in positioning India as a leader within regional organizations, such as the South Asian Association for Regional Cooperation (SAARC), and in strengthening its ties with the countries of Africa and Latin America. The economic partnerships fostered during his tenure, coupled with India's increasing political influence on the global stage, laid the foundation for India's emergence as a key player in global geopolitics.

Thoughtful Governance and Political Stability

Dr. Singh's legacy as a thoughtful and steady leader is another key aspect of the tributes paid to him. His leadership style was often characterized by calm deliberation, intellectual depth, and a long-term vision. While India's political landscape during his tenure was marked by coalition politics, Dr. Singh managed to maintain a stable government, despite significant challenges. His ability to navigate the complex dynamics of coalition politics and keep the government functioning effectively was widely appreciated by political analysts both in India and abroad.

Politicians across party lines have acknowledged Dr. Singh's statesmanship and his ability to prioritize national interests over political gain. His focus on economic growth, poverty alleviation, and inclusive development earned him admiration from political leaders in India. His coalition partners, despite their ideological differences, respected his ability to build consensus and implement policies that benefited the country as a whole. Dr. Singh's commitment to governance and policymaking was rooted in a strong ethical framework. His humble demeanour, intellectual integrity, and avoidance of populist policies endeared him to a wide range of people, both in India and internationally. Critics of his leadership, while they may have disagreed with certain policy choices, often acknowledged his dedication to serving the people and his genuine commitment to making India a better place.

Contributions to Global Economic Leadership

Dr. Singh's influence in global economic leadership cannot be overstated. His advocacy for a more inclusive global economic system, particularly one that benefits developing countries, earned him admiration from leaders around the world. His role in the establishment of BRICS (Brazil, Russia, India, China, and South Africa) and his promotion of multilateralism in trade negotiations have had lasting impacts on the global economic order. As India's representative in the G20, Dr. Singh pushed for reforms in global financial governance, emphasizing the need for better representation of developing economies in international institutions. Dr. Singh's vision for global economic integration, balanced with national interests, was particularly influential during his tenure as prime minister.

His approach to globalization sought to align India's development goals with the benefits of global economic integration, emphasizing the need for fair trade and equitable growth. He was a strong advocate for creating a global economic environment that supported the needs of developing countries, arguing that the global system should be more reflective of the challenges and opportunities faced by emerging economies. In the years following his tenure, global economic experts continue to refer to Dr. Singh's leadership as a model for how emerging economies can navigate the challenges of globalization while preserving their own development agendas. His work in reshaping India's economic policies has set a global precedent for how developing nations can approach market reforms without sacrificing social welfare or inclusivity.

Reflections from Global Economists and Political Leaders

Global economists, scholars, and political leaders have consistently highlighted Dr. Singh's contributions to both India's economic development and global economic discourse. In the academic world, Dr. Singh is often cited as one of the foremost economists of his generation. His role in shaping India's economic transformation is frequently discussed in economics textbooks and case studies, with particular emphasis on his ability to design policies that balanced both market reforms and social equity. In the political sphere, leaders from across the world have expressed their admiration for Dr. Singh's vision and diplomatic skill. Former UK prime minister Gordon Brown, for example, praised Dr. Singh's leadership during the 2008 financial crisis and his efforts to steer India through a period of global economic turmoil. Brown commended Dr. Singh for his ability to advocate for the interests of emerging economies while maintaining close cooperation with advanced economies.

Tributes also came from leaders within India's political spectrum, including President Pranab Mukherjee, who worked closely with Dr. Singh during his tenure. Mukherjee often referred to Dr. Singh as a "man of great vision and profound knowledge" whose economic policies were rooted in the principle of inclusive growth. Despite the challenges and controversies Dr. Singh faced, his political colleagues have repeatedly pointed to his unshakeable integrity and commitment to India's long-term development. In conclusion, the tributes to Dr. Manmohan Singh reflect the immense impact he had on both India and the world. His economic reforms, diplomatic leadership, and ethical governance have left a legacy that will continue to shape India's trajectory for years to come. Through his efforts, India emerged as an economic power, a voice for developing nations, and a key player in global economic governance. His legacy is a testament to the power of vision, intellect, and integrity in leadership.

▪ Personal Leadership Style

Dr. Manmohan Singh's leadership style was marked by humility, integrity, and a commitment to long-term thinking, distinguishing him from many of his contemporaries. These traits earned him respect not only within India but also on the global stage, where he was viewed as a statesman of remarkable character. His approach to leadership was less about populist gestures and more focused on careful planning, steady progress, and ensuring that his actions were always in the best interest of the country. This understated yet effective leadership style allowed him to navigate the complexities of both domestic politics and international diplomacy with finesse. Dr. Singh's humility was one of his most defining qualities. He was a man of few words, preferring action over rhetoric.

Unlike many politicians, he rarely sought the limelight or indulged in grandstanding. Instead, his focus remained on achieving practical outcomes. Even in moments of political pressure or during times of crisis, Dr. Singh maintained a calm demeanour and prioritized the collective good over personal gain or recognition. His modest nature was reflected in his leadership, where decisions were often made based on data, expert advice, and a clear understanding of the long-term implications for the nation. Integrity was another cornerstone of Dr. Singh's leadership. Throughout his career, he maintained an unblemished record of honesty, transparency, and ethical conduct. In an era where corruption scandals and political opportunism were common place, Dr. Singh stood out as a beacon of probity.

He was known for his ability to make decisions based on what was right, rather than what was politically expedient. His approach to governance was characterized by a strong commitment to accountability and transparency, which helped to earn the trust of both the Indian public and the international community. His integrity also allowed him to maintain political stability during times of coalition politics, as his colleagues and political partners respected his personal ethics and trustworthiness. Dr. Singh's long-term vision was another defining feature of his leadership. While many leaders often focused on short-term gains or populist measures to secure electoral victories, Dr. Singh's approach was centred on laying the foundation for India's future growth and development. He understood the importance of reforms that could lead to sustainable progress, even if they were politically challenging in the short-term. His decision to liberalize the Indian economy in the early 1990s, though controversial at the time, was a clear example of his long-term thinking.

Dr. Singh's ability to make tough decisions with foresight and an understanding of future global trends allowed India to become one of the world's fastest-growing economies in the decades that followed. Dr. Singh's leadership was also characterized by a deep sense of responsibility. He understood the weight of the office he held and took it upon himself to ensure that his actions were in the best interests of the Indian people. This sense of duty was evident in his policy decisions, which were often focused on improving the lives of the marginalized, strengthening the economy, and enhancing India's global standing. Despite facing criticism and challenges, Dr. Singh never wavered from his path of steady, inclusive growth. Dr. Manmohan Singh's leadership is often defined by three key qualities: humility, integrity, and long-term thinking. These traits shaped not only his political career but also the trajectory of India's growth and global position in the twenty-first century. Through these qualities, he navigated the complex political landscape of India, earning respect both domestically and internationally. His leadership style was distinguished by an ability to remain focused on India's long-term interests, rather than opting for immediate, short-term gains.

Humility

Humility was perhaps Dr. Singh's most defining trait as a leader. Despite being at the helm of one of the world's largest and fastest-growing economies, he remained remarkably modest, rarely seeking the spotlight or indulging in the rhetoric commonly associated with political leaders. Dr. Singh's humility was reflected in his approach to both governance and public life.

He understood that leadership was not about personal glory or recognition, but about service to the people. This was evident in his demeanour during major international summits or at home, where his quiet, composed presence often overshadowed the more flambuoyant figures in Indian politics. His humility allowed him to focus on substance rather than showmanship, which endeared him to a broad range of constituencies. In an era of media-driven politics, where leaders often compete for attention, Dr. Singh's understated approach allowed him to chart a course of stability, pragmatism, and reasoned decision making. His unwillingness to get caught up in the theatrics of political life made him a respected figure across party lines. Moreover, Dr. Singh's humility facilitated cooperation with a wide variety of political and business leaders, allowing him to achieve consensus on issues that could have otherwise sparked conflict. Dr. Singh's humility was not merely personal but was reflected in his approach to policymaking. He always prioritized the needs of the nation over political expediency, often making difficult decisions with the understanding that the long-term benefits for the country would outweigh short-term political costs. His quiet yet resolute approach was a stark contrast to many of his contemporaries, whose leadership was defined by media appearances and populist rhetoric.

Integrity

Dr. Singh's integrity was one of his most admired qualities and a key element of his leadership. In an era when corruption scandals were rampant, Dr. Singh maintained a reputation for honesty and ethical governance. His leadership was grounded in transparency, accountability, and a steadfast commitment to doing what was right, even when it was not politically popular. Throughout his tenure as India's finance minister and later as prime minister, Dr. Singh adhered to the highest standards of probity, which earned him the trust of the people, the global community, and even his political rivals. One of the most striking aspects of Dr. Singh's integrity was his ability to resist the pressures that often come with power. In a country where political corruption and cronyism can sometimes dominate the discourse, Dr. Singh's leadership provided a refreshing example of ethical decision making. His personal integrity helped him navigate complex situations, such as coalition politics, which often required him to work with parties of diverse ideologies. Even in times of political adversity, when his government was embroiled in controversies such as the 2G spectrum scam and coal allocation issues, Dr. Singh was able to distance himself from the charges of corruption and maintain his integrity.

Dr. Singh's integrity was also seen in his commitment to transparency and accountability in economic policy. His approach to liberalization in the 1990s, for instance, was driven by a clear understanding of the long-term benefits of opening up the economy, rather than any personal or political gain. Even when faced with intense opposition to reforms, Dr. Singh stayed true to his principles, explaining the rationale behind his policies to both the public and his critics. His ability to make decisions based on principle, rather than convenience, helped India chart a path toward becoming one of the largest economies in the world.

Long-term Thinking

Dr. Singh's long-term thinking was perhaps the most crucial element of his leadership style. While many political leaders focus on achieving short-term gains, Dr. Singh understood the importance of strategic planning for the future. His vision for India was not based on immediate returns or quick fixes, but on sustainable growth and inclusive development that would position India as a global power in the long run. One of the most notable examples of Dr. Singh's long-term thinking was his decision to liberalize India's economy in the early 1990s. At the time, India was facing a severe economic crisis, and there was significant opposition to the idea of opening up the economy to foreign investment and competition. However, Dr. Singh, as finance minister, recognized that economic liberalization was crucial for India's growth and development. Despite the risks and challenges, he pursued a series of reforms that would eventually transform India into one of the world's fastest-growing economies.

Dr. Singh's long-term vision extended beyond economic policy to other areas, such as education, health care, and infrastructure. He was deeply committed to creating an inclusive economy that would provide opportunities for all Indians, not just the urban elite. His policies, such as the Mahatma Gandhi National Rural Employment Guarantee Act (MGNREGA), were designed with the aim of improving the living standards of the rural population and reducing poverty in the long run. Dr. Singh believed that inclusive growth was the key to a prosperous India, and he worked tirelessly to ensure that the benefits of economic growth reached all sections of society. In his role as prime minister, Dr. Singh also placed a strong emphasis on India's global positioning. He understood that India's success on the world stage depended on long-term diplomatic relationships and economic partnerships. Dr. Singh's leadership was instrumental in strengthening India's ties with countries in the global south, as well as with major powers like the US and China.

His policies were aimed at ensuring that India would not only be a regional power but would also have a significant influence on global affairs in the twenty-first century. Dr. Manmohan Singh's leadership style—defined by humility, integrity, and long-term thinking—has left an indelible mark on India's political and economic landscape. His leadership was grounded in a deep sense of duty and a commitment to making decisions that were in the long-term interests of the country. Through his quiet and steadfast approach, he was able to achieve monumental reforms, steer India through times of crisis, and position the country as a global player. His leadership provides a powerful lesson in the importance of character, vision, and a focus on the future in shaping the destiny of a nation.

▪ Insights from Close Associates

Dr. Manmohan Singh's leadership was shaped by the insights and experiences of those who worked closely with him, offering a window into his decision making process, work ethic, and personal qualities. Many of his associates and colleagues have shared personal anecdotes that highlight the essence of his leadership, showcasing his calm demeanour, meticulous approach to policy, and unwavering commitment to India's growth and development.

Collabourative Decision-Making Process

One of the most notable aspects of Dr. Singh's leadership was his commitment to a collaborative decision making process. His close associates often recount how he preferred to consult extensively with experts, stakeholders, and colleagues before making any significant decisions. This approach was particularly evident during the economic reforms of the 1990s, when India faced a balance of payments crisis, and the country was on the brink of economic collapse. In the face of this crisis, Dr. Singh was instrumental in driving India's liberalization agenda, but he did so with a collaborative mindset. His associates often mention that, while he was the ultimate decision-maker, Dr. Singh took the time to engage with his team, seeking their input on crucial matters such as fiscal policy, trade liberalization, and industrial deregulation. One of his colleagues described how, during the crucial discussions surrounding the opening up of the economy, Dr. Singh would patiently listen to diverse viewpoints and ensure that every concern was addressed before moving forward. This inclusive approach not only resulted in well-informed decisions but also helped build a consensus around policies that were initially met with resistance. Dr. Singh's leadership was rooted in his belief that collective wisdom could lead to better outcomes for the country.

Composure under Pressure

Dr. Singh's close associates often highlight his remarkable composure, particularly during moments of intense political and economic pressure. One of the most vivid anecdotes shared by those who worked with him revolves around the 1991 economic crisis when India was facing an impending default on its international debt obligations. As finance minister, Dr. Singh played a central role in navigating the crisis, but the decisions were not easy, and they came at a time when the political landscape was highly charged. Despite the pressure, Dr. Singh remained calm and focused, never losing his equanimity. His colleagues recall how, during late-night meetings and intense discussions, he would maintain a level-headed approach, ensuring that his team did not succumb to panic. One of his associates recalled a particularly tense meeting where the decision to devalue the rupee was on the table. The move was seen as highly controversial, and many feared the backlash.

Dr. Singh, however, calmly explained the rationale behind the decision, focusing on the long-term benefits for the country. His ability to remain composed under pressure instilled confidence in his colleagues, and his decision ultimately proved to be one of the cornerstones of India's economic recovery.

Commitment to the Country's Long-term Interests

Another recurring theme in anecdotes from Dr. Singh's associates is his unwavering commitment to the country's long-term interests. He was not driven by short-term political gains or public opinion; instead, his decisions were always guided by a vision for India's future. One of his close associates recalls how, even when faced with intense political opposition to economic reforms, Dr. Singh never wavered from his principles. During the early 1990s, when the idea of economic liberalization was still controversial in India, Dr. Singh's commitment to reform remained steadfast. Many of his colleagues were apprehensive about the backlash from both the political opposition and the public, but Dr. Singh's deep conviction in the need for liberalization led him to press ahead with the reforms. He often said that the decision was difficult but necessary for India's future, and he took solace in the belief that future generations would benefit from the changes he was implementing. This long-term perspective became one of the hallmarks of his leadership style.

Empathy and Understanding of People's Needs

While Dr. Singh was known for his intellectual rigour and technocratic approach to governance, his close associates also point to his deep empathy for the people of India.

He understood that economic reforms had to be inclusive, benefiting all sections of society. One of his former colleagues recalls an instance when Dr. Singh was deeply concerned about the impact of economic policies on the poor and marginalized communities. During a critical phase of liberalization, when industrial deregulation was taking place, Dr. Singh personally took time to address concerns about the adverse effects of these reforms on rural populations and those in the informal sector. In response to these concerns, he advocated for social safety nets and support systems to mitigate the negative effects of economic transitions. Dr. Singh's ability to balance the needs of economic growth with a deep concern for social equity was one of the reasons his leadership was viewed as both pragmatic and compassionate. His associates recall how, during the preparation of key policies such as the Mahatma Gandhi National Rural Employment Guarantee Act (MGNREGA), Dr. Singh was always at the forefront of discussions on how to provide equitable growth opportunities, particularly for the rural poor. His personal commitment to reducing poverty and ensuring that growth reached all corners of India was a reflection of his leadership ethos.

Consensus-building and Patience

Dr. Singh's ability to build consensus, even in highly polarized political environments, is another key aspect of his leadership that is frequently mentioned by those who worked closely with him. In a country like India, where political parties are often deeply divided, achieving consensus on complex issues can be a monumental challenge. Yet, Dr. Singh's associates recall how he managed to forge agreements on contentious policies without ever resorting to coercion or divisiveness. During his tenure as prime minister, particularly during his second term, Dr. Singh worked with a coalition government that included a wide range of political parties with divergent ideologies. His leadership in navigating the intricacies of coalition politics was exemplary. One of his colleagues recalled how Dr. Singh was always willing to listen to the concerns of coalition partners and work patiently to address their issues, even when it meant making compromises. Dr. Singh's ability to build and maintain strong relationships with key political figures, even those from opposing parties, was a testament to his diplomatic skills and his understanding of the importance of collaboration in governance.

Conclusion

The anecdotes shared by Dr. Singh's close associates offer a comprehensive view of his leadership style, highlighting his calm and composed demeanour, commitment to long-term goals, empathy for the people, and ability to build consensus. His decision making was rooted in a deep understanding of India's needs, and his leadership was guided by principles of integrity, humility, and a long-term vision for the country. These personal insights into Dr. Singh's leadership not only illuminate his approach to governance but also offer valuable lessons for current and future leaders who seek to serve their nations with wisdom, patience, and a focus on the greater good.

▪ A Nation's Gratitude: Tributes to Dr. Singh's Legacy

Dr. Manmohan Singh's name is synonymous with the transformation of India's economy, and his legacy is marked by an era of profound change. Often regarded as the architect of India's economic liberalization, Dr. Singh's policies helped transition India from a state-controlled, closed economy to an open, market-driven one. However, his contributions go far beyond economic reforms. His leadership style, personal integrity, and unwavering commitment to the nation's welfare have left an indelible impact on the country's political and economic landscape. Dr. Singh's tenure as the prime minister of India, from 2004 to 2014, was an era marked by significant economic growth, social progress, and India's rise on the global stage.

However, it was during his time as the finance minister in the early 1990s, under Prime Minister Narasimha Rao, that his economic acumen truly came to the fore. When Dr. Singh took office in 1991, India was facing a dire balance of payments crisis, with foreign exchange reserves barely enough to cover three weeks of imports. The country was on the verge of defaulting on its external debts. At that moment, Dr. Singh, along with Prime Minister Rao, made the historic decision to embark on economic liberalization, which included reducing trade barriers, devaluing the rupee, and introducing market-friendly reforms. This bold approach was met with both scepticism and resistance, but over time, it proved to be the foundation of India's modern economic success.

The liberalization policies initiated during the early 1990s helped spur rapid growth, setting the stage for the India of today—an economy with a burgeoning middle class, a growing IT sector, and increasing foreign investment. Dr. Singh's economic vision was grounded in the belief that a more open economy would create opportunities for the Indian people, providing them with access to better goods, services, and employment opportunities. He believed in the power of markets, innovation, and globalization to unlock India's potential and improve the living standards of its people. Dr. Singh's reforms enabled India to embrace globalization and engage with the world on its terms, leading to rapid economic growth that lifted millions out of poverty and put the country on a trajectory of economic prosperity.

In terms of international recognition, Dr. Singh's legacy is equally significant. Under his leadership, India saw its global stature rise significantly. He worked tirelessly to strengthen India's relationships with other nations, particularly with the US, Russia, and the European Union. He also played an instrumental role in securing India's civil nuclear deal with the US in 2008, which marked a new chapter in India's relations with the world's most powerful country. The deal allowed India to access civilian nuclear technology, which was critical for the country's energy needs and marked a significant diplomatic victory for India. His deft handling of foreign policy and ability to position India as a respected player in global affairs remains one of the defining achievements of his tenure. Dr. Singh's leadership, however, was not just defined by economic and foreign policy achievements.

His personal values and principles were integral to his role as a public servant. Throughout his career, Dr. Singh has been known for his humility, sincerity, and integrity. Unlike many of his contemporaries, Dr. Singh avoided the trappings of power and celebrity, preferring a quiet and reflective approach to leadership. He never sought the limelight or engaged in political theatrics, instead opting for steady, deliberate decision making. His modesty and scholarly approach to governance earned him respect from colleagues, rivals, and the general public alike. In an age where politicians often engage in partisan rhetoric and populist measures, Dr. Singh's emphasis on rationality, intellectual honesty, and governance based on principles of equity set him apart as a leader of uncommon vision and moral authority. One of the key areas where Dr. Singh's legacy continues to be felt is in the field of economic policy.

Under his leadership, India adopted a series of structural reforms that transformed the economy, making it one of the fastest-growing in the world. These reforms encompassed areas such as labour laws, taxation, industrial policy, and financial sector reform. Dr. Singh's economic policies were not just about growth for growth's sake; they were about creating an inclusive economy, where the benefits of growth were shared by all sections of society, particularly the marginalized and disadvantaged groups. His commitment to poverty alleviation and inclusive growth was reflected in the launch of several important social welfare programmes, including the National Rural Employment Guarantee Act (NREGA), which aimed to provide employment to rural poor and reduce poverty in rural areas. These initiatives were designed to ensure that India's rapid economic growth was accompanied by efforts to reduce inequality and promote social welfare. However, Dr. Singh's legacy is not without its challenges and controversies.

While his tenure was marked by significant achievements, it was also a period during which India faced several challenges, including rising inflation, corruption scandals, and the slow pace of some reforms. The global financial crisis of 2008 also posed significant economic challenges, as the Indian economy, like the rest of the world, was hit hard by the downturn. Despite these challenges, Dr. Singh's handling of the economy during such turbulent times was widely regarded as pragmatic and measured. His ability to steer the country through the crisis without a major recession demonstrated his leadership and economic wisdom. The legacy of Dr. Singh is also deeply intertwined with the idea of institutional reform. He consistently advocated for a strong, independent institutional framework for the country's economy, believing that the growth of the Indian economy depended on strong regulatory frameworks and institutions.

His government introduced measures to improve the functioning of key institutions such as the Reserve Bank of India (RBI), the Securities and Exchange Board of India (SEBI), and various other financial regulators, which helped build greater trust in India's economic system. His commitment to institutional integrity was a key factor in ensuring that India's economic liberalization was sustainable in the long run. Dr. Singh's influence also extended to the political arena, particularly in shaping the Indian National Congress (INC) party and its approach to governance. As a leader of the Congress, Dr. Singh was seen as a stabilizing force, particularly during the politically turbulent years of his tenure. His stewardship helped the Congress navigate the complexities of coalition politics and allowed the party to stay relevant in a changing political landscape.

His ability to build consensus and negotiate with different factions, while keeping his political principles intact, was a testament to his political acumen and his commitment to democratic governance. The tributes to Dr. Singh's legacy have come from various quarters. Economists, industry leaders, and political figures have lauded his vision, leadership, and accomplishments. His role in transforming India into a global economic powerhouse is often highlighted as one of his most significant achievements. At the same time, his commitment to social welfare and inclusive growth has earned him respect as a leader who not only focused on economic growth but also on improving the lives of India's most vulnerable citizens. Leaders across the world have acknowledged Dr. Singh's contributions to the global economic discourse, particularly in terms of his advocacy for multilateralism and international cooperation. In India, his legacy is particularly celebrated by those who benefited from the reforms he championed.

The rise of India's middle class, the growth of the IT and services sector, and the overall improvement in the quality of life for millions of Indians are direct outcomes of his policies. Dr. Singh's legacy is also honoured by those who admire his personal character and leadership style. His quiet, cerebral approach to politics, his integrity, and his focus on governance based on sound principles have inspired generations of public servants and policymakers. In an era when political leaders are often judged by their charisma or populism, Dr. Singh's legacy stands out as a reminder that true leadership is about vision, principles, and commitment to the nation. As India continues to evolve and face new challenges in the twenty-first century, the lessons from Dr. Singh's tenure remain relevant.

His legacy serves as a guiding light for future generations of leaders, policymakers, and citizens who seek to build a better, more prosperous India. While the country has made tremendous progress, there is still much work to be done to ensure that the benefits of growth are shared equitably and that the foundations of sustainable development are laid for future generations. In this regard, the tributes to Dr. Singh's legacy are not just about celebrating past achievements but also about recognizing the continuing relevance of his vision for India's future. Dr. Singh's leadership and legacy will remain a source of inspiration for years to come. He was not only a leader who transformed India economically but also one who demonstrated that governance, when based on wisdom, integrity, and foresight, can change the course of a nation's history. His contributions will continue to shape India's path to prosperity and global recognition, and his legacy will remain an integral part of the narrative of India's twenty-first century journey.

• Economic Transformation under Dr. Singh: Reflections from Industry Leaders

Dr. Manmohan Singh's tenure as India's prime minister, particularly in the period from 2004 to 2014, witnessed an extraordinary economic transformation that reshaped the country's economic landscape and positioned it as a key player in the global economy. His economic policies, largely rooted in the liberalization framework that he had earlier championed as finance minister in the early 1990s, have been widely credited for steering India through a period of robust growth, even in the face of multiple global challenges. Reflections from industry leaders and entrepreneurs who were active during this time provide invaluable insights into how Dr. Singh's leadership, combined with his economic reforms, not only transformed the Indian economy but also helped elevate India's standing in the world.

One of the central aspects that industry leaders consistently highlight when reflecting on Dr. Singh's economic policies is his visionary approach to India's economic development. Dr. Singh's tenure marked a significant shift in India's economic strategy from protectionism to a more liberalized, market-driven economy. His commitment to liberalizing key sectors such as telecommunications, retail, banking, and aviation, among others, led to significant growth in these industries. Industry leaders frequently acknowledge that it was Dr. Singh's belief in the power of markets and global integration that helped unlock India's potential, making it an attractive destination for both FDI and global businesses looking to expand in emerging markets. During his time as finance minister in the 1990s, Dr. Singh laid the foundation for the economic liberalization that would define India's trajectory in the decades to follow.

Under his stewardship, the government began dismantling the 'Licence Raj', a system that restricted private enterprise through heavy regulation and control. By significantly reducing trade barriers, lowering import tariffs, and attracting international capital, India was able to grow its economy at an average rate of 6-7 per cent annually. This laid the groundwork for India's emergence as a major global economic player. Industry leaders today often credit Dr. Singh's vision for India's continued growth, noting that his focus on ensuring macroeconomic stability and fostering an environment conducive to private sector growth was crucial in attracting investments and encouraging entrepreneurship across various sectors. One of the most significant outcomes of Dr. Singh's economic policies was the growth of India's IT and services sector, which became a cornerstone of the country's economic transformation.

The liberalization of the economy allowed Indian firms to tap into global markets, and the telecommunications reforms introduced by Dr. Singh's government helped to create a thriving digital ecosystem. This transformation laid the groundwork for India to become a global leader in IT services, and industry leaders in the sector often reflect on how this shift was accelerated under his leadership. Infosys co-founder N.R. Narayana Murthy, for instance, has frequently highlighted Dr. Singh's role in the liberalization of the economy as a critical factor in the rise of the Indian IT industry. Murthy has credited Dr. Singh's government for recognizing the potential of the IT sector and creating an enabling environment for its rapid growth. The relaxation of restrictive foreign exchange regulations, the establishment of software technology parks, and the encouragement of global partnerships all played a key role in making India the preferred destination for IT outsourcing.

As a result, India's IT exports grew from a mere $150 million in 1991 to over $150 billion by 2014, cementing India's place as one of the world's largest IT hubs. For many entrepreneurs in the IT and software industries, Dr. Singh's economic policies provided the foundation for their success and contributed to the rise of the country's digital economy. Another key area of economic transformation under Dr. Singh was his government's approach to foreign investment. While the economic reforms of the 1990s focused on liberalizing trade and industry, Dr. Singh's government further built on this momentum by opening up sectors such as retail, insurance, aviation, and banking to FDI. This policy shift had a profound impact on the Indian economy, as it helped infuse much-needed capital, technology, and expertise into various industries.

In particular, the retail sector saw significant growth after the government permitted foreign investments in multi-brand retail, which allowed large global retail chains like Walmart, Tesco, and Carrefour to enter the Indian market. Industry leaders in retail, both domestic and international, have often reflected on how this liberalization helped streamline supply chains, modernize the retail infrastructure, and make consumer goods more accessible to India's growing middle class. Many retail executives and entrepreneurs who were active during this period praise Dr. Singh for his pragmatic approach to foreign investment, which allowed India to gain from the expertise of global players while also providing opportunities for local businesses to grow. Dr. Singh's push for opening up the banking and aviation sectors also played a crucial role in strengthening India's economy.

In the banking sector, his policies helped establish India as an emerging market hub for international banks, with several global banking giants expanding their presence in India during his tenure. In aviation, the liberalization of air travel made it more accessible to middle-class Indians, spurring a boom in both domestic and international air travel, which in turn bolstered the tourism and hospitality industries. From the perspective of industry leaders in these sectors, Dr. Singh's economic reforms created a level playing field for domestic and foreign companies alike, driving innovation and competition. Dr. Singh's leadership was also instrumental in driving the growth of India's infrastructure and manufacturing sectors. The government's focus on infrastructure development, particularly in areas such as roads, ports, and power, was a key factor in the country's economic expansion during this period. Industry leaders in construction, engineering, and infrastructure development often cite the significant increase in public-private partnerships (PPPs) and government investment in infrastructure projects as a game-changer for the Indian economy.

In particular, the growth of India's road and transportation infrastructure helped to reduce logistics costs and improved the movement of goods across the country, benefiting a wide range of industries from manufacturing to retail. The rise of India as a manufacturing hub can also be attributed to the policies of economic liberalization introduced under Dr. Singh's leadership. He recognized the importance of manufacturing in driving employment and reducing poverty, and thus his government took steps to make the manufacturing sector more competitive through reforms aimed at improving labour market flexibility and reducing the regulatory burden on businesses. Industry leaders in manufacturing sectors often reflect on how these reforms created an enabling environment for growth. The introduction of initiatives such as the Special Economic Zones (SEZs) helped to attract foreign investment in manufacturing, particularly in industries such as textiles, electronics, and automobiles.

India became a preferred destination for global manufacturers looking to tap into the country's vast labour pool and growing consumer market. The development of key industrial hubs in regions like Gujarat, Maharashtra, and Tamil Nadu can be directly attributed to the economic reforms initiated during Dr. Singh's tenure. Dr. Singh's economic transformation of India was also marked by his pragmatic and consensus-driven approach to policymaking. Throughout his tenure, he demonstrated a rare ability to navigate the complexities of coalition politics and maintain stability, even in a highly fragmented political environment. Industry leaders often speak about his calm demeanour, his ability to make difficult decisions, and his commitment to maintaining a balanced and inclusive approach to economic growth. While his policies were market-friendly, he also emphasized the importance of ensuring that the benefits of growth were distributed equitably across society.

This was evident in his commitment to social welfare programmes such as the MGNREGA, which aimed to provide employment and income security to rural populations. As India continues to grow and develop, the economic transformation set in motion by Dr. Singh continues to have a lasting impact. Industry leaders across various sectors reflect on how his policies created the conditions for India to become one of the fastest-growing economies in the world. His emphasis on economic liberalization, foreign investment, and infrastructure development laid the foundation for the India we know today: a country with a rapidly expanding middle class, a booming services sector, and increasing integration into the global economy. Dr. Singh's economic legacy is also seen in India's increased global influence.

His policies positioned India as an attractive destination for global businesses and investors, and his emphasis on maintaining macroeconomic stability helped India weather the global financial crisis of 2008 relatively unscathed. Today, industry leaders often cite Dr. Singh's leadership as a key factor in India's rise as a global economic power. In conclusion, Dr. Manmohan Singh's economic transformation of India is a testament to his vision, leadership, and commitment to making India a global economic powerhouse. Reflections from industry leaders underscore the significant role he played in shaping the country's economic policies, fostering growth, and creating opportunities for millions of Indians. His legacy will continue to guide policymakers and business leaders as they strive to build on the foundations he laid and ensure India's continued progress on the global stage.

▪ Commemorating Dr. Singh's Role in Shaping India's Global Image

Dr. Manmohan Singh's role in shaping India's global image is a profound and critical part of his legacy as the prime minister of India. His tenure from 2004 to 2014 saw India's emergence as a significant player on the global stage, not just in terms of economic influence but also in its strategic and diplomatic relationships. Dr.

Singh's diplomatic efforts, particularly his handling of complex international issues, his engagement with global institutions, and his emphasis on strengthening India's bilateral relationships with key nations, contributed to India's transformation from a regional power to a more assertive global force. At the core of Dr. Singh's foreign policy was his pragmatic, thoughtful, and strategic approach to diplomacy.

His government sought to balance India's traditional non-alignment policy with a more proactive engagement with the world, embracing the economic opportunities that globalization offered while preserving India's sovereignty and strategic interests. One of the most significant milestones of Dr. Singh's foreign policy was his leadership in the Indo-US Civil Nuclear Deal, which dramatically shifted India's global standing. The deal, finalized in 2008, allowed India to engage in civilian nuclear commerce with countries that had been previously restricted under international non-proliferation norms. This deal was a reflection of Dr. Singh's vision for India as a key player in global security and economic dynamics. It not only strengthened Indo-US ties but also led to greater cooperation in other critical areas, such as defence, counterterrorism, and technology. The Indo-US Nuclear Deal marked a significant turning point in India's foreign policy trajectory, signalling to the world that India was ready to assume a more influential role on the global stage. The deal was controversial both domestically and internationally, with critics arguing that it would undermine India's strategic autonomy.

However, Dr. Singh's diplomacy turned these challenges into an opportunity to engage with the global community and elevate India's stature as a rising global power. By pursuing this deal, Dr. Singh demonstrated his ability to make bold decisions that would benefit India in the long run, securing greater political and economic leverage for India on the world stage. Dr. Singh's diplomatic acumen was also evident in his handling of India's relationship with China. While the two nations shared a complex history of territorial disputes, Dr. Singh pursued a balanced approach in his engagement with China. He sought to deepen economic ties, recognizing that a stable and prosperous relationship with China was crucial to India's economic growth and regional influence. Under Dr. Singh's leadership, India-China relations saw significant growth, especially in trade.

By the end of his tenure, China had become one of India's largest trading partners, and both nations had begun to cooperate in multilateral organizations such as the BRICS and the Shanghai Cooperation Organization (SCO). At the same time, Dr. Singh was careful to safeguard India's national interests, particularly in relation to border security and regional dominance. He worked to maintain a constructive dialogue on sensitive issues such as the border dispute while also cooperating with China on issues such as climate change and economic development. His diplomacy towards China reflected his belief that economic cooperation, when coupled with strong political dialogue, could mitigate the tensions that had historically defined Indo-China relations. In addition to strengthening ties with the US and China, Dr. Singh's foreign policy also emphasized deepening India's relationships with its immediate neighbours, especially those in South Asia.

While India has long been a dominant force in the region, Dr. Singh sought to promote greater regional integration and cooperation. His government focused on building stronger ties with countries such as Bangladesh, Sri Lanka, Nepal, and Bhutan, with a particular emphasis on regional trade and connectivity. Dr. Singh's government also worked towards resolving long-standing issues with Pakistan, including the Kashmir dispute, through dialogue and diplomatic engagement. Dr. Singh's commitment to regional peace and stability was reflected in his government's efforts to foster greater cooperation within the SAARC. Under his leadership, India played an active role in promoting economic integration in South Asia, despite the challenges posed by tensions with some neighbouring countries. His diplomatic efforts aimed to position India as a leader in regional economic cooperation, helping to create the conditions for increased trade, infrastructure development, and people-to-people connectivity within the region.

Dr. Singh's foreign policy was also characterized by his engagement with global institutions and multilateral organizations. Under his leadership, India took an active role in key global forums such as the United Nations (UN), the WTO, and the G20. His government was particularly active in the G20, where India played a pivotal role in shaping the global economic response to the financial crisis of 2008. Dr. Singh's government advocated for a more inclusive global economic order, one that took into account the needs and aspirations of developing countries. India's leadership in the G20 not only demonstrated its economic strength but also highlighted its growing influence in global economic governance. Dr. Singh's focus on multilateral diplomacy also led to significant advancements in India's engagement with the European Union (EU), Japan, and other key global powers. He prioritized India's strategic interests while advocating for a fairer global trade system and greater representation of developing countries in global institutions.

Dr. Singh's foreign policy was built on the idea that India's voice needed to be heard in global forums, and he worked to ensure that India's interests were represented in discussions on issues such as climate change, economic reform, and peacekeeping. Perhaps one of Dr. Singh's most enduring contributions to India's global image was his calm, composed, and intellectual demeanour, which set him apart as a statesman. His ability to engage with global leaders and navigate complex international issues with finesse earned him respect and admiration on the global stage. Unlike many contemporary leaders, Dr. Singh was not prone to making impulsive or reactionary decisions. Instead, he built a reputation as a leader who was both thoughtful and deliberate in his actions.

This earned him the trust of world leaders and international institutions, reinforcing India's image as a stable and reliable partner in global affairs. Dr. Singh's foreign policy legacy also extended to his handling of global security challenges. He was a staunch advocate for a multipolar world order and sought to ensure that India's security interests were protected while contributing to global peace. Under his leadership, India took a strong stance on combating terrorism, both domestically and internationally. His government worked closely with other countries to combat global terrorism, particularly after the 2008 Mumbai attacks, which were widely seen as an assault on India's sovereignty and security. Dr. Singh's leadership during this period demonstrated India's commitment to global counterterrorism efforts and its readiness to collaborate with other nations in promoting international security.

In conclusion, Dr. Manmohan Singh's contributions to shaping India's global image are a testament to his diplomatic acumen, intellectual foresight, and ability to navigate complex geopolitical dynamics. Through his leadership, India emerged as a major global power with a stronger voice in global economic governance, a more robust diplomatic presence, and a growing role in regional and global security. His foreign policy, characterized by strategic engagement, pragmatism, and a commitment to peace, has left an indelible mark on India's global image and will continue to guide its foreign policy trajectory for years to come. Dr. Singh's legacy as a global statesman is a source of inspiration for future generations of policymakers and leaders, as they work to position India as a powerful, responsible, and respected player in the international community.

▪ Honouring Dr. Manmohan Singh's Vision for India

Dr. Manmohan Singh, India's prime minister from 2004 to 2014, is widely regarded as one of the most influential leaders in shaping modern India's trajectory. His tenure, marked by economic reforms, visionary leadership, and a deep commitment to India's progress, left an indelible impact on the nation. Dr. Singh's vision for India was centred on economic modernization, social justice, sustainable development, and India's rightful place in the global order. Honouring his vision means acknowledging the policies he introduced, the reforms he championed, and the enduring legacy of his leadership in the shaping of India's future. Dr. Singh's tenure began at a critical juncture in India's development, a time when the country was grappling with a host of economic challenges and social disparities. As an economist by training, he was keenly aware of the importance of economic reforms, both in terms of liberalization and strengthening the country's infrastructure.

Under his leadership, India moved forward with a new set of policies aimed at integrating the country into the global economy, fostering sustainable economic growth, and addressing the needs of its vast population. His vision was rooted in the idea of transforming India into a thriving economy that could stand on its own in the twenty-first century. One of Dr. Singh's most significant contributions was his role in championing the liberalization of India's economy in the early 1990s, which laid the foundation for the nation's growth in the following decades. Though he served as finance minister in the 1990s and not as prime minister at that time, his economic reforms—privatization, trade liberalization, and opening up the Indian economy to foreign investments—set the stage for India's rapid growth in the years to come.

This foundation of economic liberalization continued under Dr. Singh's leadership as prime minister, as he pursued policies that encouraged both domestic and foreign investments, improved infrastructure, and boosted India's manufacturing and service sectors. Dr. Singh's vision was not just about economic growth in isolation, but also about inclusive development. He understood that India's vast diversity required policies that were not only economically effective but also socially just. His administration emphasized the importance of improving the lives of India's poorest citizens, ensuring that the benefits of India's economic growth reached every section of society. Dr. Singh focused on eradicating poverty, improving health care, enhancing education, and ensuring that the growth story did not leave behind marginalized communities.

The policies he pursued, including the MGNREGA and initiatives focused on rural development, were designed to create a more equitable society. In his approach to economic growth, Dr. Singh emphasized the importance of sustainable development. His vision for India included a clear understanding of the country's environmental challenges, particularly the issue of climate change. India's rapid economic growth had raised concerns about the environmental impact of industrialization, and Dr. Singh took steps to ensure that the country's development would be balanced with environmental responsibility. India became a participant in international climate agreements, and Dr. Singh's government initiated policies aimed at reducing carbon emissions, investing in renewable energy sources, and promoting energy efficiency. His recognition that economic growth should not come at the cost of environmental degradation placed sustainability at the heart of his vision for India's future.

Education and skill development were also key elements of Dr. Singh's vision for India. He believed that for India to truly achieve its potential, it needed to invest in its most valuable resource—its people. His policies focused on improving the education system, particularly in rural areas, and increasing access to quality education for all citizens. Recognizing that education is the key to economic empowerment, Dr. Singh's government introduced policies aimed at improving literacy rates, expanding vocational training programmes, and fostering innovation in higher education. His efforts helped lay the foundation for India's burgeoning knowledge economy, with a highly-skilled workforce ready to meet the demands of a globalized world. Dr. Singh also placed significant importance on strengthening India's democratic institutions and promoting good governance.

He viewed India's democracy as its greatest strength and worked tirelessly to ensure that the country's political and legal systems remained robust and transparent. He understood that economic progress and social justice could only be realized in a stable democratic framework, and his administration worked to address issues such as corruption, inefficiency, and bureaucratic red tape. His commitment to democratic values was evident in his emphasis on transparency, accountability, and the decentralization of power, which he believed would empower local communities and enable them to take charge of their own development. On the global stage, Dr. Singh's vision for India was that of a peaceful, cooperative, and active participant in the international community. His diplomatic efforts, particularly in strengthening India's ties with global powers such as the US, China, and the EU, were central to his broader vision of elevating India's status as a global player.

Dr. Singh was instrumental in positioning India as a strong advocate for multilateralism and a member of key global organizations such as the UN, the WTO, and the G20. He firmly believed that India's growing economic influence would give it the leverage to shape global policy on issues ranging from trade and security to climate change and nuclear disarmament. Dr. Singh's legacy is also defined by his emphasis on social cohesion and nation-building. He sought to create a unified India, where diversity was celebrated and every citizen, regardless of caste, creed, or religion, could access the opportunities afforded by the country's economic progress. In his vision, India was a nation that embraced its multicultural identity while fostering a sense of shared national purpose.

His administration made significant strides in addressing social inequalities, including gender disparities, with policies aimed at empowering women, promoting their education, and encouraging their participation in the workforce. Perhaps most importantly, Dr. Singh's vision for India was anchored in the belief that the country's future lay in its youth. He viewed the youth as the driving force behind India's progress, and his policies aimed at creating a society where young people could thrive, innovate, and lead. Through investments in education, entrepreneurship, and skill development, Dr. Singh sought to ensure that India's youth would be equipped to tackle the challenges of the twenty-first century. His government's focus on expanding access to higher education, promoting digital literacy, and fostering a culture of innovation helped to create an ecosystem that nurtured the entrepreneurial spirit of young Indians. In conclusion, Dr. Manmohan Singh's vision for India was one of comprehensive development, which integrated economic growth, social justice, environmental sustainability, and global cooperation.

His leadership and policies have played a transformative role in shaping modern India, making it one of the world's fastest-growing economies and a prominent global player. While challenges remain, his vision continues to guide India's development trajectory. By honouring Dr. Singh's vision, India acknowledges the importance of his contributions to the country's growth and global stature and reaffirms its commitment to the principles of inclusive and sustainable development, democratic governance, and global cooperation that he championed throughout his career.

REFERENCES

Gordon, S. (1995). *India's Rise to Power in the Twentieth Century and Beyond.* Macmillan Press Ltd.

Harvey, D. (2005). *A Brief History of Neoliberalism.* Oxford University Press.

Jaffrelot, C. (2003). "India's Look East Policy: An Asianist Strategy in Perspective." *India Review, 2*(2): 35-68.

Malik, J.M. (1991). "India's Response to the Gulf Crisis: Implications for Indian Foreign Policy." *Asian Survey, 31*(9): 847-61. https://doi.org/10.1525/as.1991.31.9.00p0092d

Mohapatra, B. (2014). "India's Look East Policy and Development of North Eastern India: Priorities and Prospects." *Search, 3*(1): 65-70.

Munro, R.H. (1993). "The Loser: India in the Nineties". *The National Interest, 33*: 62-63.

Naidu, G.V.C. (1996). "India and Southeast Asia". *World Focus, 17*(10-12): 82-84.

Nayar, B.R. (1998). "Political Structure and India's Economic Reforms of the 1990s." *Pacific Affairs, 71*(3): 337-60. https://doi.org/10.2307/2761414

Saikia, H. (2010). "Look East Policy: Southeast Asian Economic Integration of India". *Applied Economic Journal, 17*(2): 1-11.

Sreedhar. (1994). "Security Situation in Southern Asia". *Strategic Analysis, 16*(11): 1431-42.

15

Lessons for Policymakers

■ Key Takeaways from His Leadership

Dr. Manmohan Singh's leadership offers numerous lessons for policymakers, particularly in developing nations. His approach to governance, economic reforms, and international diplomacy provides valuable insights into how countries with emerging economies can navigate the challenges of growth, stability, and sustainable development. Drawing on his tenure as the finance minister and prime minister of India, the following key takeaways provide a framework for developing nations seeking to chart their own paths to prosperity.

Importance of Economic Reforms and Liberalization

Dr. Singh's leadership demonstrated the critical role of economic reforms in transforming developing economies. His bold decision to usher in liberalization during the 1991 economic crisis was a game-changer for India. By embracing free market policies, deregulating industries, and opening up the economy to global trade, Dr. Singh initiated a process of structural reforms that helped India overcome stagnation and set the country on a growth trajectory that continues to this day. For developing nations, Dr. Singh's example underscores the importance of carefully managed economic liberalization. While the transition to a market-oriented economy can be challenging, particularly for those accustomed to a state-controlled model, strategic reforms can provide the foundation for long-term growth. Developing countries should focus on deregulation, reducing barriers to trade, and encouraging foreign direct investment (FDI), all while ensuring that reforms are gradual and mindful of social impacts.

Balancing Growth with Social Equity

One of Dr. Singh's key contributions to economic policy was his ability to balance growth with social equity. While liberalization and market-driven policies were essential for India's economic transformation, Dr. Singh never lost sight of the need to address the concerns of marginalized groups. His commitment to poverty reduction, rural development, and inclusive growth was evident in policies such as the Mahatma Gandhi National Rural Employment Guarantee Act (MGNREGA), which provided employment opportunities to the rural poor, and the push for social safety nets to protect vulnerable populations during times of transition.

For developing countries, the takeaway here is that growth should not be pursued at the expense of social equity. While economic liberalization can stimulate growth, policymakers must also prioritize inclusive development to ensure that the benefits of growth are equitably distributed. Investment in education, health care, and social welfare programmes is crucial to ensuring that all segments of society benefit from the country's economic success.

The Value of Technocratic Leadership

Dr. Singh's tenure as finance minister and prime minister highlighted the value of technocratic leadership—leaders who prioritize expertise, data-driven decision making, and evidence-based policies. Unlike populist leaders who often make decisions based on short-term political gains, Dr. Singh focused on long-term solutions rooted in economic theory and empirical evidence. For developing nations, this approach underscores the importance of having leaders who understand the complexities of economic management and who can make decisions based on sound knowledge. Building and maintaining a cadre of skilled technocrats in key sectors such as finance, trade, and infrastructure can help ensure that economic policies are both effective and sustainable in the long run.

Commitment to International Cooperation

Dr. Singh's leadership was not only marked by his focus on domestic reforms but also by his commitment to fostering India's position in the global economy. His active participation in multilateral organizations like the World Trade Organization (WTO), the G20, and BRICS was crucial in advancing India's economic interests on the global stage. He recognized the importance of India's integration into the global economy, advocating for multilateralism and

Fig. 15.1: India's Engagement with IMF to Tackle Global Recession.

international cooperation, particularly for the Global South. For developing nations, the key lesson is the importance of engaging with the global economy through international partnerships and cooperation. Participating in global trade agreements, aligning with regional economic initiatives, and being part of international organizations allows countries to benefit from global markets, access technology, and secure foreign investment. In today's interconnected world, no country can thrive in isolation.

Fostering Infrastructure Development

During his tenure, Dr. Singh recognized that infrastructure development was crucial for India's economic growth. He pushed for improvements in the country's physical infrastructure, including roads, electricity, and telecommunications, as well as in its social infrastructure, such as education and health care. This focus on infrastructure not only supported economic growth but also helped enhance the quality of life for millions of people. For developing nations, infrastructure is often the key to unlocking economic potential. Building and upgrading infrastructure in sectors like transportation, energy, and communications is essential for attracting investment, improving productivity, and ensuring the efficient movement of goods and services. Prioritizing infrastructure projects, while also balancing the needs of environmental sustainability, can have long-lasting positive effects on economic growth and national development.

Navigating Political Challenges

Dr. Singh's leadership was also marked by his ability to navigate complex political dynamics, particularly during his tenure as prime minister. Leading a coalition government with diverse political interests, he displayed remarkable diplomatic skills, working with coalition partners to implement important reforms. His leadership in passing critical legislation, such as the Goods and Services Tax

(GST) and the Nuclear Deal with the United States (US), was a testament to his ability to build consensus in a politically charged environment.

For developing nations with complex political landscapes, Dr. Singh's leadership offers valuable insights into the importance of coalition-building, compromise, and consensus. In countries with fragmented political systems, leaders must be adept at negotiating with multiple parties, managing political opposition, and maintaining stability while pushing forward with necessary reforms.

Resilience in the Face of Crisis

Dr. Singh's leadership during the 2008 global financial crisis provided a textbook example of resilience and strategic thinking in the face of economic turmoil. While many countries struggled to cope with the crisis, India weathered the storm relatively well, thanks in large part to the economic reforms that had been implemented earlier in the decade. Dr. Singh's quick response with fiscal stimulus measures and his focus on infrastructure spending

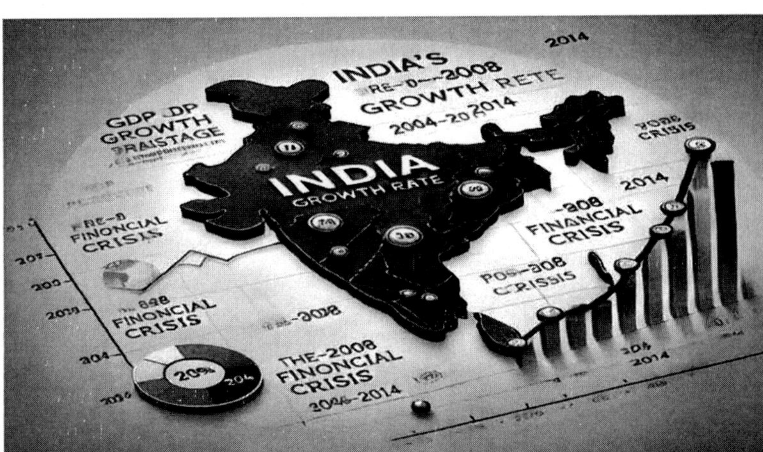

Fig. 15.2: Timeline of Major Global Events and Policy Responses During the 2008 Financial Crisis.

helped cushion the economy from the worst effects of the global downturn. For developing nations, Dr. Singh's response to the financial crisis highlights the importance of building resilience through sound economic policies and a diversified economy. Countries should ensure that their economies are not overly reliant on a single sector or market, and that they have contingency plans in place to deal with external shocks. Furthermore, developing nations should focus on building strong financial institutions that can withstand global financial crises.

Emphasizing Education and Human Capital Development

Dr. Singh was a strong advocate for education and human capital development. He recognized that for any economy to be truly competitive in the global market, it needed a skilled and educated workforce. His tenure saw an emphasis on higher education reforms, including the establishment of new institutions of excellence and the promotion of skill development. For developing nations, investing in education and skill development is crucial. A highly-skilled and educated population is essential for fostering innovation, increasing productivity, and ensuring that the workforce can compete in a rapidly changing global economy. Developing countries should prioritize educational reforms that focus on quality and accessibility, particularly in science, technology, engineering, and mathematics (STEM) fields, to drive economic growth in the future.

Leadership Beyond Economics

Dr. Singh's leadership was not solely focused on economics; it also involved fostering social cohesion, political stability, and national unity. He was known for his quiet demeanour, humility, and integrity, and he was respected for his ability to remain above the fray of political mudslinging. His leadership style emphasized long-term goals and national interests over short-term political victories. For developing countries, the lesson here is that effective leadership requires a holistic approach. Leaders must not only be skilled in managing economic issues but also in navigating political, social, and cultural dynamics. A focus on ethical leadership, humility, and national unity can help build trust in government institutions and create an environment conducive to sustainable development. Dr. Manmohan Singh's leadership offers valuable lessons for developing nations navigating the complex terrain of economic growth and development. His emphasis on economic reforms, inclusive growth, political consensus, global integration, infrastructure development, and education provides a blueprint for countries seeking to advance on the global stage. At the same time, his focus on resilience in the face of crises and his commitment to long-term goals offer enduring insights into how developing nations can build strong, sustainable economies that benefit all citizens.

Table 15.1: Sectoral Growth During the Recession

Sector	2008 Growth Rate (%)	2009 Growth Rate (%)
Agriculture	1.6	0.1
Industry	4.1	8.2
Services	9.8	10.1

• Balancing Growth with Social Equity

Balancing growth with social equity is one of the most significant challenges in developing economies, and Dr. Manmohan Singh's leadership underscores the importance of ensuring that economic progress is both broad-based and inclusive. While economic growth is crucial for raising living standards, creating employment opportunities, and reducing poverty, it must be accompanied by policies that ensure the benefits of growth reach all segments of society, especially marginalized and vulnerable populations. For Dr. Singh, inclusive development was not just an economic objective but also a moral and social imperative.

Importance of Inclusive Development

Inclusive development refers to a development process that ensures all individuals and communities, regardless of their background, have the opportunity to contribute to and benefit from economic growth. It is grounded in the principle that development should not just increase the overall wealth of a country but should also reduce disparities in income, access to resources, and opportunities. Dr. Singh recognized that without addressing these inequalities, growth could lead to social tensions and political instability, undermining long-term economic progress. Dr. Singh's policies aimed at creating a development framework where growth was sustainable and equitable.

He understood that economic liberalization, if not managed carefully, could exacerbate disparities by disproportionately benefiting wealthier groups or regions. His emphasis on inclusive development was grounded in the belief that economic policies must not only focus on macroeconomic stability and growth but also ensure that the poor, rural communities, and other disadvantaged groups benefit from the country's progress. Inclusive development entails both reducing absolute poverty and addressing relative poverty—ensuring that no group is left behind in a growing economy. For Dr. Singh, this meant focusing on sectors such as agriculture, education, health care, and rural infrastructure to provide opportunities for marginalized communities to improve their socio-economic conditions. Furthermore, his approach sought to empower women, Dalits, Adivasis, and other socially excluded groups, ensuring that they were not left behind in the rush to modernize and globalize the economy.

Policies for Inclusive Growth

Dr. Singh's vision of inclusive development was reflected in several key policy initiatives during his tenure as prime minister and finance minister. Among the most prominent were his efforts to create social safety nets and direct support programmes that would empower the disadvantaged. One of the landmark policies was the Mahatma Gandhi National Rural Employment Guarantee Act (MGNREGA), which guaranteed a minimum number of days of employment in rural areas. This was aimed at providing income support to the rural poor, especially during the agricultural off-season when work was scarce. It also helped build essential rural infrastructure, which contributed to long-term improvements in rural productivity and living standards. The Act's success showed that growth could be more equitable when it was coupled with programmes that directly targeted poverty alleviation and employment creation in disadvantaged areas. Another critical area of focus was health care and education.

Dr. Singh pushed for increasing government spending in these sectors, with a particular emphasis on improving access to education and health care in rural and remote areas. The government implemented the Right to Education Act, which made education a fundamental right for children between the ages of 6 and 14. This initiative sought to address educational inequalities and ensure that every child had access to quality schooling, regardless of their socio-economic background. Dr. Singh also supported policies to improve public health infrastructure, particularly in rural and underserved areas. The National Health Mission was designed to increase access to affordable health care services, which was particularly important in a country like India, where large disparities existed between urban and rural health care outcomes.

Table 15.2: Employment Statistics in India (2005–2010)

Year	Unemployment Rate (%)
2005	7.5
2007	7.3
2009	10.2
2010	9.8

Fostering Rural-Urban Linkages

In Dr. Singh's view, inclusive development could not be achieved without addressing the disparities between rural and urban areas. Rural areas, where the majority of India's population resided, had long been neglected in terms of economic infrastructure, education, health care, and employment opportunities. While urban centres attracted foreign investment and became engines of growth, rural areas continued to face significant challenges in terms of poverty, underdevelopment, and lack of access to basic services. To bridge this gap, Dr. Singh's government focused on improving rural infrastructure, which included the development of roads, electricity, irrigation, and access to clean water.

The government's initiatives such as the Pradhan Mantri Gram Sadak Yojana (PMGSY), aimed at connecting rural areas with better road networks, helped to integrate these areas into the national economy. The improvement of rural roads and transportation networks allowed rural communities to better access markets, health care facilities, and educational institutions, thereby improving their overall quality of life. In addition, policies were designed to promote rural entrepreneurship and support local industries, including agriculture-based industries, handicrafts, and small-scale manufacturing. These initiatives helped create jobs in rural areas, providing alternatives to traditional agricultural employment and reducing migration to cities.

Sustainable Growth and Environmental Considerations

Dr. Singh was also committed to ensuring that inclusive development did not come at the expense of environmental sustainability. He believed that economic growth and environmental conservation must go hand in hand. Sustainable development meant fostering growth that would improve people's lives while protecting natural resources for future generations. His government supported programmes that promoted clean energy, sustainable agriculture, and forest conservation. In particular, Dr. Singh championed India's position at international climate change negotiations, advocating for development that was environmentally sound but still supported economic growth. In addition, his policies on water management and natural resource utilization sought to strike a balance between development needs and environmental protection. He recognized that climate change and environmental degradation disproportionately affected the poorest communities, particularly those dependent on agriculture and natural resources for their livelihoods.

Addressing Regional Disparities

Dr. Singh's commitment to inclusive development was also reflected in his approach to addressing regional disparities within India. While liberalization and globalization led to rapid economic growth in some regions, other areas remained economically stagnant or lagged behind. For example, the eastern and northern parts of India, including states like Bihar, Odisha, and Uttar Pradesh, remained among the poorest in the country, while southern and western states like Tamil Nadu, Karnataka, and Gujarat experienced faster growth. To reduce these regional disparities, Dr. Singh advocated for special development programmes for backward regions, including enhanced central assistance for infrastructure development, capacity-building, and industrial growth. His government introduced measures to attract investment to less-developed states by offering tax incentives, financial subsidies, and infrastructure development programmes tailored to regional needs. His focus on inclusive regional growth was aimed at ensuring that the benefits of India's rise as an economic powerhouse were shared across the country.

Challenges in Achieving Inclusive Development

Despite these efforts, inclusive development remained a challenging goal throughout Dr. Singh's tenure. Several obstacles, including bureaucratic inefficiencies, corruption, and policy implementation gaps, limited the full realization of his vision. Additionally, while India's growth trajectory accelerated during his leadership, inequality remained high, and poverty levels, though reduced, remained significant in some areas. The benefits of liberalization were not always distributed equally, and some sections of society, especially in rural areas, were left out of the growth story.

While the middle class grew, the economic empowerment of marginalized groups—especially those from historically disadvantaged communities––was slower. This disparity was exacerbated by the challenges posed by India's diverse socio-economic landscape, where issues such as caste, religion, and gender added layers of complexity to policymaking. Balancing growth with social equity is an ongoing challenge for developing nations, and Dr. Manmohan Singh's leadership in this regard provides important lessons. His emphasis on inclusive development—ensuring that the benefits of growth are equitably distributed across society—was a cornerstone of his economic policies. While there were challenges in fully achieving this goal, Dr. Singh's vision set the stage for future efforts to reduce poverty, improve living standards, and create more equitable opportunities for all.

Developing nations can learn from his approach by prioritizing both economic growth and social justice, ensuring that their development strategies are inclusive, sustainable, and responsive to the needs of all citizens, particularly the most marginalized.

■ The Role of Humility in Leadership

Dr. Manmohan Singh's leadership, defined by humility, integrity, and long-term thinking, was a defining characteristic that set him apart from his peers. In a political environment where leaders often thrive on rhetoric and assertiveness, Singh's leadership was a stark contrast—reserved, principled, and centred on substance rather than style. His political journey and tenure as prime minister of India brought a unique blend of economic reforms and a governance model that focused on the greater good over personal gains or showmanship. His quiet, yet effective leadership remains one of his greatest legacies, shaping India's growth and international position during some of its most turbulent times.

The Quiet Leadership Approach

The hallmark of Dr. Singh's leadership was his quiet demeanour, which often left critics questioning his assertiveness. However, those who worked closely with him knew that his leadership style was not about seeking the limelight but about delivering tangible results for the nation. His humility did not stem from a lack of confidence but from an intrinsic understanding that leadership is not about ego or personal accolades. It was about making decisions that would best serve the nation, even if they did not earn immediate praise or recognition. Dr. Singh's calm and reasoned approach to leadership allowed him to effectively manage India's affairs during times of economic crisis and political turbulence.

For instance, during the 1991 economic balance of payments crisis, when India was facing an acute financial emergency, his leadership was crucial in guiding the country through a transformation. The reforms he implemented in that period were not just bold but also required him to take positions that were not widely popular, particularly in a politically volatile environment. His ability to focus on the larger picture and long-term outcomes, rather than short-term populism or personal political gain, showcased the depth of his leadership. One of the most notable features of his leadership during this period was his ability to maintain a steady hand even in times of extreme pressure. Unlike many politicians, who might have resorted to drastic or theatrical measures, Dr. Singh navigated India through the crisis with a level-headed, careful strategy.

The result was a set of economic reforms that laid the foundation for the country's rapid economic growth in the subsequent decades, even as they were initially met with resistance.

Leading with Integrity

Humility in Dr. Singh's case also meant integrity in leadership. Integrity is often seen as a fundamental trait of great leadership, but in practice, it requires immense self-discipline and the ability to resist personal temptation for the greater good. Dr. Singh's track record in this regard is exemplary. His decision making process was always guided by a sense of duty to the people of India, rather than by considerations of personal advantage or political expediency. His integrity was particularly visible in his approach to governance, which was free from the corruption that has often plagued Indian politics.

While the political landscape around him was rife with controversies, Dr. Singh was always viewed as an honest and incorruptible figure. He was known for his focus on ensuring that the policies and reforms he championed were aimed at uplifting the country and its people, not at serving the interests of any specific group or individual. This integrity also manifested in his approach to international relations. As India's economic landscape was transformed, Dr. Singh worked tirelessly to position the country as a key player on the global stage. His policies, both domestic and foreign, were aimed at ensuring that India would not only grow economically but would also do so with dignity and respect on the world stage. His unwavering commitment to India's sovereignty and interests, even in the face of global pressure, was one of the cornerstones of his leadership.

Humility as a Strength

While many political leaders project forceful, charismatic personalities, Dr. Singh's humility became his strength. In a world where political leaders often rely on public personas to garner support, Dr. Singh's low-key approach allowed him to avoid the pitfalls of self-promotion. His leadership was not about grandstanding but about carefully crafting policies that would ensure India's long-term economic prosperity. His humility made him approachable, even to his political opponents, and this characteristic played a crucial role in building the trust needed to implement his policy initiatives. By avoiding the ego-driven battles that characterize much of politics, Dr. Singh focused on creating a space for collaboration, where consensus-building took precedence over conflict. This was particularly crucial in the context of India's coalition politics, where Dr. Singh's ability to balance the diverse interests of various political factions was essential for implementing reform and maintaining political stability.

His willingness to listen and learn from others, whether in government, business, or civil society, enabled Dr. Singh to make well-informed decisions that reflected a variety of viewpoints. This approach allowed him to foster a sense of collective responsibility in governance, where success was not just attributed to one leader but to the collective efforts of the team.

An Example of Resilience

Dr. Singh's leadership was not only marked by humility but also by resilience. Leading a country as diverse and complex as India demands more than just economic expertise; it requires the ability to face criticism, opposition, and political intrigue without compromising one's principles. Throughout his tenure, Dr. Singh faced immense pressure, both from within his party and from the opposition, but he remained unwavering in his commitment to his vision for India's growth. Even when confronted with personal and political attacks, Dr. Singh never allowed them to sway his policy decisions or his leadership approach. This resilience was key to his ability to push through reforms such as the 1991 economic liberalization, which were met with fierce opposition but ultimately transformed India into one of the world's fastest-growing economies. Dr. Singh's resilience was also evident in his handling of the 2008 global financial crisis, where many of the world's leading economies faltered. In the face of an unprecedented global economic downturn, Dr. Singh used his economic expertise and steady leadership to safeguard India's economy from the worst effects of the crisis. His ability to manage this crisis with humility and without resorting to extreme measures demonstrated the strength of his leadership.

Humility in the Face of Adversity

Dr. Singh's ability to remain humble, even when faced with intense scrutiny and political attacks, is a testament to his character. His approach to leadership was never about asserting personal dominance but about serving the country with quiet determination. He believed that his role as a leader was to work for the betterment of the nation, and he did so with patience and grace, even in the face of adversity. This humility allowed Dr. Singh to maintain a sense of dignity, which made him a beloved figure not just in India but internationally as well. His quiet strength, based on his integrity and focus on the country's long-term interests, earned him the respect of both his peers and the international community. Leaders like Dr. Singh remind us that leadership is not about seeking power or personal fame but about serving others with humility, integrity, and vision.

In conclusion, Dr. Singh's leadership was a lesson in the power of humility. It was his quiet, thoughtful approach to leadership that enabled him to navigate India through some of its most critical moments in modern history. His leadership serves as a reminder that humility, integrity, and long-term thinking are not just values for personal growth but essential qualities for effective governance and nation-building. In a world where political leadership is often equated with boldness and bravado, Dr. Singh's example stands as a powerful testament to the strength of quiet, principled leadership.

▪ Embracing Economic Liberalization with Caution

Dr. Manmohan Singh's economic reforms, which began in

1991, marked a turning point for India's economy. The process of liberalization, characterized by reducing tariffs, promoting foreign investment, opening markets to global competition, and modernizing industrial policy, aimed to integrate India more deeply into the global economy and position the country for future growth. These reforms resulted in rapid economic expansion, with India's GDP growth surging to over 7 per cent annually for much of the 2000s. Foreign investment poured in, particularly in sectors like information technology, telecommunications, and manufacturing, while industries like software services, pharmaceuticals, and retail were significantly boosted by global demand. The liberalization policies helped India establish itself as a prominent player in the global market and ushered in an era of enhanced growth, prosperity, and consumer choice.

However, alongside these successes, India's experience with liberalization reveals important lessons about the need for caution and the gradual approach to policy changes. While the reforms undoubtedly led to an increase in wealth and improved living standards for many, they also exposed vulnerabilities and inequities that could have been mitigated with a more cautious and inclusive approach. The benefits of liberalization were clear: foreign direct investment (FDI) surged, economic growth accelerated, and India's global economic stature was enhanced. These reforms unlocked new opportunities for businesses, particularly in urban centres. The services sector, especially information technology, received a significant boost, and India became a global hub for outsourced services, leading to job creation and a growing middle class. However, these benefits were not uniformly distributed across the country. The sharp focus on sectors like services and manufacturing often neglected agriculture and rural industries, which continued to face challenges in the post-liberalization era.

Agricultural growth stagnated as the sector struggled with the competition posed by global markets. Small-scale industries, which were a significant part of India's economic fabric, were unable to compete with larger multinational companies that flooded the domestic market with cheaper goods. As a result, millions of farmers and workers in small-scale industries experienced economic distress, and inequality between urban and rural areas deepened. Furthermore, the process of liberalization was not just about opening the markets but also about dismantling a vast range of regulatory controls and protections that had long governed the economy. This sudden shift led to significant disruptions in certain sectors. While the business climate became more favourable for large corporations, many small and medium-sized enterprises (SMEs) struggled to adapt. SMEs, which had flourished in a protected environment, were now exposed to intense competition from both domestic and international firms.

The result was job losses, factory closures, and a growing sense of economic insecurity for many workers who felt the brunt of the changes. This highlights one of the most critical lessons for future policymakers: economic liberalization should be implemented gradually and carefully, ensuring that the structural changes in the economy do not result in massive job displacement or sectoral collapse. Rather than implementing sweeping reforms all at once, a gradual, phased approach to liberalization would have allowed industries to adjust over time, providing them with the breathing room to modernize and become globally competitive. Protecting vulnerable sectors through temporary tariffs, subsidies, or financial assistance programmes would help mitigate the shock of liberalization, preventing massive disruption to livelihoods and ensuring that the benefits of growth are more broadly shared.

Another important aspect of liberalization was the impact it had on income inequality. While liberalization generated significant wealth, it also exacerbated the gap between the rich and poor. The most visible manifestations of this inequality were the differences in wealth and opportunity between urban and rural areas. The services sector boomed in metropolitan cities, and the middle class expanded as new opportunities emerged in industries like IT, finance, and retail. However, rural areas, which were still heavily reliant on agriculture, saw fewer benefits from the liberalization process. The rural-urban divide deepened, and poverty remained a persistent problem for millions of rural Indians. The economic policies under Dr. Singh's government, while successful in stimulating growth in certain sectors, did not adequately address these regional disparities, and the benefits of growth were not sufficiently inclusive. To remedy this, future policymakers must focus on creating inclusive growth strategies that prioritize equitable distribution of wealth and opportunities.

Policies must be designed to address regional disparities, ensure that rural areas receive the benefits of development, and bridge the gap between urban and rural incomes. Investing in rural infrastructure, health care, and education, alongside providing financial support for agricultural modernization, can help ensure that the fruits of liberalization are shared more widely across the population. One of the most critical lessons that India's experience with liberalization teaches is the importance of a strong safety net for vulnerable groups. The government must ensure that policies are in place to protect those who may be left behind by rapid changes in the economy. Programmes like the MGNREGA, which guarantees a minimum level of employment to rural workers, are a step in the right direction.

Similarly, investments in health care, education, and skill development programmes are vital to ensuring that all sections of society can benefit from the economic opportunities created by liberalization. Additionally, environmental degradation is another concern that was not fully addressed during the early years of liberalization. Rapid industrialization, urbanization, and increased consumerism came at a cost to India's natural resources. Air and water pollution, deforestation, and over-extraction of water resources became major issues as India embraced more industrial growth. The government's focus on increasing production, exports, and industrial output sometimes took precedence over environmental protection. Policymakers must recognize that economic growth cannot be sustained if environmental concerns are ignored.

It is crucial to implement policies that promote sustainable development by ensuring that industrial growth is accompanied by robust environmental protections. Investing in renewable energy, promoting energy efficiency, and encouraging green technologies should be central to any future development plan. Additionally, strengthening environmental regulations and ensuring compliance with international standards can help mitigate the long-term environmental consequences of rapid industrialization. Another critical lesson from India's experience with liberalization is the need for strong institutions and regulatory frameworks to support the growth of the economy. The success of economic reforms depends not only on market liberalization but also on the strength and efficiency of institutions that oversee economic activity. India's economic liberalization created opportunities for growth, but without strong institutions to enforce regulations, ensure transparency, and protect public interests, these opportunities could be undermined.

The lack of transparency in some sectors, coupled with corruption and inefficiency in government institutions, hindered the potential benefits of liberalization. Future policymakers must focus on strengthening institutions, improving governance, and creating a more transparent regulatory environment to ensure that liberalization leads to inclusive, long-term growth. Building institutions that promote fair competition, protect consumers, and enforce environmental and labour laws will be key to ensuring that the benefits of liberalization are sustainable and broadly shared. In conclusion, while Dr. Singh's economic liberalization policies were crucial in transforming India's economy and opening it up to the global market, the lessons learned from this period are equally important. The key takeaway for policymakers is the need to embrace liberalization cautiously, with careful planning, gradual implementation, and strong social and institutional safeguards. Ensuring that the benefits of liberalization are shared equitably, addressing regional disparities, investing in human capital, and protecting the environment should be central to any future policy agenda. By learning from the successes and challenges of the 1991 reforms, India can chart a more inclusive, sustainable, and balanced path toward future growth.

▪ Balancing Growth with Inclusivity

Balancing growth with inclusivity remains one of the most profound challenges faced by policymakers, especially in a country like India, which has witnessed rapid economic growth over the past few decades. Dr. Manmohan Singh's economic reforms, particularly those in the early 1990s, facilitated a remarkable period of economic expansion. However, this growth was not without its contradictions. While India's GDP grew at an impressive rate, significant sections of the population remained untouched by this economic prosperity. The challenge for policymakers is not merely achieving high growth but ensuring that the benefits of growth are widely distributed across all sections of society—especially marginalized communities, the rural population, and lower-income groups. Dr. Singh's reforms brought India closer to global markets, but they also highlighted deep-rooted inequalities that required attention. A focus on balancing economic growth with inclusivity involves addressing these disparities, ensuring that growth is not only achieved but also shared by all Indians, regardless of their socio-economic background. When India opened up its economy in the 1990s, the services sector, particularly information technology (IT), saw explosive growth. The burgeoning middle class in urban centres thrived, and foreign investments poured into sectors like telecommunications, manufacturing, and retail.

The liberalization process enabled India to become a global player in industries such as IT and pharmaceuticals. However, while urban areas were booming, the rural economy continued to lag behind. Rural India, which accounts for a significant portion of the population, did not immediately benefit from the liberalization process. Agriculture, which remains the backbone of the rural economy, faced challenges related to globalization, with farmers struggling to compete against cheaper, imported goods. Additionally, the shift from an agrarian economy to an industrial and service-based economy left rural communities increasingly marginalized, widening the income gap between urban and rural areas. The key to addressing this imbalance lies in understanding that economic growth, in its most sustainable form, cannot be achieved without ensuring that the benefits are broadly distributed. Growth should not simply be a statistical measure of GDP expansion but must be seen through the lens of human development education, health care, access to jobs, and social mobility.

For policymakers, this means that the design of economic policies must include provisions for the poorest segments of society, ensuring they are not left behind as the country moves forward. To achieve this balance, a significant focus needs to be placed on rural development. While urban centres have witnessed rapid infrastructure growth, rural areas have often remained underdeveloped, with inadequate access to basic services such as education, health care, and clean drinking water. It is crucial for policymakers to create a more inclusive development strategy, one that promotes rural development alongside urban growth. This could involve investing in rural infrastructure—such as roads, electricity, irrigation systems, and digital connectivity—that would facilitate agricultural productivity and create opportunities for small and SMEs to thrive.

A stronger rural infrastructure would also help improve access to education and health care, which are essential for social mobility and improving living standards. Agricultural reforms are another important aspect of balancing growth with inclusivity. While the Green Revolution in the 1960s and 1970s boosted agricultural productivity in India, subsequent years have seen stagnation in rural agricultural growth. The introduction of more modern farming practices, better access to technology, and improved credit facilities for farmers can help revive the sector. Additionally, policies focused on agricultural sustainability and organic farming would not only address the environmental concerns associated with intensive farming practices but would also create a more resilient agricultural sector in the long run. This is crucial for ensuring that rural communities remain integrated into the broader economic growth process.

Another area where inclusivity can be achieved is through social policies that promote education, health, and skill development. Education is often touted as the most powerful tool for poverty alleviation, and it remains true that equitable access to education can break the cycle of poverty. Policymakers must focus on improving access to quality education for all, particularly in rural and underprivileged urban areas. This includes both primary education and vocational training. A well-educated population is not only more likely to contribute meaningfully to the economy but also more likely to benefit from the economic opportunities available in the labour market. Skill development programmes are equally important in ensuring that workers especially those in rural areas or low-income urban areas—can adapt to the changing demands of the job market.

In particular, as the global economy increasingly relies on technological innovation, ensuring that workers possess the necessary digital and technical skills will be critical in ensuring inclusivity. Moreover, promoting social safety nets is essential for fostering inclusivity in times of economic transition. As India's economy has liberalized, certain segments of society—especially unskilled labourers and those working in informal sectors—have found themselves vulnerable to job losses, income inequality, and the erosion of traditional livelihoods. Strengthening social welfare programmes, such as unemployment benefits, pensions, and health care subsidies, can ensure that no one is left behind during periods of economic restructuring. The government's implementation of the MGNREGA is a positive example of such an initiative, as it provides guaranteed employment to rural households and ensures that workers have a safety net.

Such programmes can also stimulate local economies by providing income and purchasing power to rural communities, which in turn boosts demand for goods and services, creating a virtuous cycle of growth. To make the growth process more inclusive, Dr. Singh's government, and future policymakers, must also address income inequality, which has risen in many parts of the country. Economic growth, if left unchecked, can lead to greater wealth concentration among the elite, while leaving vast sections of the population struggling to make ends meet. While the Indian economy grew substantially during the years of liberalization, the benefits of this growth were unevenly distributed. The challenge lies in implementing progressive taxation, where wealthier individuals and corporations contribute a fair share to the public coffers, which can then be reinvested into programmes that benefit the wider population. Strengthening the tax base, increasing financial transparency, and addressing tax evasion are essential steps in this direction.

Policymakers should also consider implementing policies that directly address inequality, such as increasing wages for low-income workers and improving the minimum wage, which would help narrow the gap between the rich and poor. Financial inclusion plays an integral role in achieving a more inclusive economy. The financial sector is a critical enabler of economic participation. However, a large portion of India's population, particularly in rural and semi-urban areas, lacks access to formal banking services, which limits their ability to save, invest, and benefit from economic opportunities. Expanding financial services to rural and marginalized communities through digital banking, microfinance, and credit schemes can help promote economic participation and foster inclusivity. With the rise of digital financial tools, there is also an opportunity to reach previously underserved populations, providing them with access to financial resources and the ability to engage in entrepreneurial activities. India's future growth needs to be aligned with social justice.

While the government should aim for rapid economic growth, it should also prioritize policies that create equal opportunities for all. By ensuring that growth is inclusive, India will be able to address both economic and social inequalities, which is critical for long-term stability. Inclusion must be the guiding principle of every policy—whether economic, social, or environmental—to ensure that economic prosperity benefits all segments of society, from urban elites to rural labourers. In conclusion, balancing growth with inclusivity is one of the most critical aspects of ensuring that India's rapid economic expansion is sustainable and equitable. Dr. Manmohan Singh's economic liberalization policies set the stage for significant growth, but future policymakers must recognize that growth must be accompanied by measures that ensure equal access to opportunities, social welfare, and economic mobility. To achieve this balance, India must prioritize rural development, improve access to education and health care, address regional disparities, and create a robust social safety net to protect the most vulnerable. Inclusivity should be the cornerstone of India's growth strategy, ensuring that the benefits of a booming economy reach every corner of society.

▪ Investing in Human Capital: Education and Skill Development

Investing in human capital is crucial for sustainable economic growth, social mobility, and reducing poverty in a rapidly developing country like India. As the nation strives to achieve higher levels of prosperity and economic development, one of the most significant areas of focus is education and skill development.

These two pillars form the foundation of human capital investment, empowering individuals with the necessary knowledge and skills to actively participate in and contribute to the economy. Dr. Manmohan Singh's tenure as the prime minister of India saw significant strides in economic liberalization, but alongside these developments, there was also an emphasis on the importance of education and skill development in shaping India's workforce to meet the challenges of a globalized world. While India's services sector saw rapid growth due to its highly-skilled workforce, many other sectors lagged behind, and millions of young Indians continued to face barriers in accessing quality education and training. To address this, investing in human capital through education reform, skill development programmes, and vocational training is essential for not only reducing poverty but also ensuring India's long-term competitiveness on the global stage.

The importance of education as a driver of social and economic development cannot be overstated. Education empowers individuals to improve their lives by providing them with knowledge, skills, and the ability to make informed decisions. It is a cornerstone of human capital development, and for a country like India, where the youth population constitutes a significant portion of the total population, education plays an especially critical role. However, despite the progress made in expanding access to primary and secondary education, significant challenges remain in terms of quality and access. India has made notable strides in increasing literacy rates, but the quality of education in many rural and underserved areas remains sub-par. This is especially true in remote and economically disadvantaged regions, where access to quality teachers, infrastructure, and learning materials is limited.

Dr. Singh's government initiated several programmes aimed at improving the education system, such as the Right to Education Act (RTE) in 2009, which made education a fundamental right for children aged 6 to 14. While the RTE marked a significant step forward, challenges in implementation remain, including overcrowded classrooms, a shortage of qualified teachers, and a lack of basic infrastructure in many schools. To ensure that all children receive quality education, especially in rural and underprivileged areas, the government must focus on addressing these structural challenges. Investing in building more schools, providing teacher training programmes, and improving the overall quality of education in schools are vital steps to ensure equitable access to education. Additionally, digital education and e-learning can be powerful tools for reaching underserved populations, especially in the context of the COVID-19 pandemic, which highlighted the importance of online education in ensuring continuity of learning.

Moreover, as India's economy has shifted from an agrarian to an industrial and service-oriented one, the demand for skilled workers has grown exponentially. However, the education system has been slow to adapt to this shift, with many graduates lacking the practical skills required by employers. This skills gap is one of the most pressing challenges facing India today. Dr. Singh's government recognized the need for skill development and launched several initiatives aimed at bridging this gap, such as the National Skill Development Mission and the Skill Development and Entrepreneurship Ministry. However, the success of these programmes has been mixed, and there remains a need for more targeted efforts to address the diverse needs of the Indian workforce. Skill development is an essential aspect of preparing India's youth for the workforce.

A strong focus on vocational training, technical education, and lifelong learning is necessary to equip individuals with the skills needed to thrive in a rapidly changing job market. The government must invest in training programmes that provide practical, hands-on experience in areas like manufacturing, construction, IT, and health care. These sectors are critical to India's economic development, and ensuring that workers have the appropriate skills to meet the demands of these industries is essential for both individual empowerment and national prosperity. One of the key challenges in skill development is the lack of coordination between the education system and the needs of the labour market. While India has a large pool of educated youth, many of them are not adequately prepared for employment. To address this, the government should collaborate with the private sector, industries, and educational institutions to create a more integrated approach to education and skill development.

Industry-specific training programmes, apprenticeships, and internships can provide students with the real-world experience they need to succeed in the job market. Moreover, partnerships between educational institutions and industries can help ensure that curricula are aligned with current and future job market demands. Another critical area for human capital investment is the need for continuous skill upgrading and lifelong learning. In a fast-paced, globalized economy, job requirements are constantly changing, and workers must be equipped with the ability to adapt to new technologies, processes, and markets. This is particularly important for sectors such as information technology, where rapid innovation and the emergence of new technologies require workers to stay up to date with the latest developments. Policymakers must create an ecosystem that encourages lifelong learning by providing access to affordable, flexible, and high-quality training opportunities for workers at all stages of their careers.

This can be achieved through online learning platforms, professional development programmes, and industry-recognized certifications that allow individuals to enhance their skills and remain competitive in the labour market. In addition to technical and vocational training, soft skills—such as communication, problem-solving, and teamwork—are increasingly in demand by employers. Soft skills are essential for workers to succeed in the modern workplace, where collaboration, leadership, and interpersonal abilities are highly valued. These skills are not always adequately addressed in the formal education system, and as such, there is a need to place greater emphasis on developing soft skills alongside technical knowledge. Policymakers must work with educational institutions to integrate soft skills training into the curriculum and promote the development of these skills through extracurricular activities and community engagement.

Moreover, the issue of gender inequality in education and skill development must be addressed to ensure that women have equal access to opportunities. Despite progress in gender equality in education, women, particularly in rural areas, continue to face barriers to accessing quality education and skill development programmes. Empowering women through education and skills training is essential for breaking the cycle of poverty and promoting economic growth. The government must focus on promoting gender-sensitive policies that ensure equal access to education and training programmes, as well as provide support for women's entrepreneurship and employment opportunities. Dr. Singh's vision for human capital development was not limited to the formal education system alone but extended to other areas such as health and social welfare.

A healthy workforce is critical for economic productivity, and investments in health care can have significant returns in terms of human capital development. Ensuring access to health-care services, particularly in rural and underserved areas, can help improve overall productivity, reduce absenteeism, and enhance the quality of life for workers. Furthermore, nutrition and well-being are integral to human capital development, as malnutrition and poor health can hinder educational attainment and productivity. In conclusion, investing in human capital through education and skill development is essential for India's continued economic growth and social development. Dr. Manmohan Singh's government recognized the importance of this investment, but challenges remain in terms of ensuring quality education, addressing the skills gap, and promoting inclusivity.

Policymakers must prioritize education and skill development as a central part of India's development strategy by focusing on equitable access to quality education, investing in vocational training, fostering partnerships with industries, and promoting lifelong learning. By doing so, India can harness the potential of its youth population and ensure that economic growth is inclusive, sustainable, and beneficial for all.

▪ Harnessing Technological Innovation for Sustainable Development

Harnessing technological innovation for sustainable development is an essential aspect of achieving long-term economic growth, social progress, and environmental protection. In the modern world, technological advancements have become the driving force behind almost every aspect of development, from agriculture and health care to education, energy, and manufacturing. The adoption and integration of technology not only help countries improve efficiency, productivity, and competitiveness, but they also provide opportunities for addressing some of the most pressing challenges faced by society today, including poverty, inequality, and climate change.

India, with its large and growing population, is uniquely positioned to benefit from technological innovations that can help accelerate its progress towards sustainable development. Dr. Manmohan Singh's leadership in economic reforms during the 1990s set the stage for India's integration into the global knowledge economy, and technology has played a central role in driving this transformation. However, for technological innovation to contribute to sustainable development, it must be effectively harnessed and aligned with India's developmental goals, including environmental sustainability, social equity, and economic inclusion. In India, the role of technology in sustainable development can be viewed through several lenses, such as the digital economy, renewable energy, agriculture, health care, and education.

Over the years, India has made significant strides in various technological domains, especially in information technology (IT), telecommunications, and space exploration. The country's IT sector, in particular, has become a global leader, with millions of skilled workers and a thriving tech ecosystem that contributes significantly to India's GDP. However, despite these successes, there remains much work to be done to ensure that technological innovations benefit all segments of society, including the rural poor, marginalized communities, and underdeveloped regions. One of the most important areas where technology can play a crucial role in sustainable development is in addressing the challenges of environmental sustainability.

As India continues to grow economically, the environmental costs of this growth, particularly in terms of air pollution, water scarcity, and deforestation, have become increasingly evident. Technological innovations in renewable energy, such as solar, wind, and hydropower, offer a promising solution to these challenges. India is already one of the world's largest producers of solar energy, with significant investments in solar power infrastructure, and the government has set ambitious targets for expanding renewable energy capacity. By leveraging advances in energy storage, smart grids, and energy efficiency, India can reduce its reliance on fossil fuels, mitigate the impact of climate change, and promote sustainable energy solutions for its growing population.

The integration of clean energy technologies is not only crucial for reducing greenhouse gas emissions but also for ensuring energy security and access to electricity for rural and remote areas. In addition to renewable energy, technology can also contribute to sustainable development in agriculture, which remains a key sector of the Indian economy. Despite the growth of the services and manufacturing sectors, agriculture continues to employ a significant portion of the population, particularly in rural areas. However, the sector faces numerous challenges, including low productivity, water scarcity, soil degradation, and the effects of climate change. Technological innovations in agriculture, such as precision farming, remote sensing, and biotechnology, offer solutions to these challenges by improving crop yields, optimizing resource use, and reducing environmental degradation.

Precision farming, for example, uses data from sensors, satellite imagery, and drones to monitor soil conditions, weather patterns, and crop health, enabling farmers to make data-driven decisions about irrigation, fertilization, and pest control. By adopting such technologies, farmers can increase productivity while minimizing the use of water, pesticides, and fertilizers, leading to more sustainable farming practices. The application of biotechnology in agriculture, particularly in the development of genetically modified (GM) crops, has also garnered attention as a means of increasing food production and ensuring food security. GM crops that are resistant to pests, diseases, and extreme weather conditions can help reduce crop losses and increase yields, which is particularly important given the growing global population and changing climatic conditions. However, the adoption of biotechnology in India has been a subject of debate, with concerns over the potential environmental and health risks of GM crops.

Therefore, it is crucial for policymakers to strike a balance between harnessing the potential of biotechnology and ensuring strict regulations and safety measures to protect human health and the environment. In the health-care sector, technological innovations have the potential to transform the way health care is delivered and accessed. India faces a dual challenge of improving health care access in rural and underserved areas while also addressing the rising burden of non-communicable diseases (NCDs) in urban populations. Digital health technologies, such as telemedicine, electronic health records (EHR), and mobile health applications, can play a critical role in bridging the health-care gap. Telemedicine allows health-care providers to offer consultations, diagnostics, and treatments remotely, overcoming geographical barriers and reducing the burden on already overstretched health-care infrastructure.

Mobile health applications, on the other hand, enable individuals to monitor their health, access medical information, and seek medical advice from the comfort of their homes. In rural India, where access to health-care facilities is often limited, such technologies can improve health outcomes by providing timely medical intervention and preventive care. Furthermore, advances in biotechnology and medical devices have enabled the development of more effective treatments and diagnostic tools for a wide range of diseases. For example, the development of affordable diagnostic kits and portable medical devices can help detect diseases such as tuberculosis, diabetes, and cancer at early stages, leading to better treatment outcomes. Moreover, the integration of artificial intelligence (AI) and machine learning (ML) into health-care systems can enhance the accuracy of diagnoses, improve treatment plans, and predict disease outbreaks.

AI algorithms can analyse vast amounts of medical data, including images, test results, and patient histories, to identify patterns and provide personalized treatment recommendations. These technologies cannot only improve the quality of health care but also reduce costs by streamlining operations, reducing the need for unnecessary tests and procedures, and optimizing resource allocation. In the education sector, technological innovation is transforming the way students learn and interact with educational content. The advent of digital platforms, online courses, and e-learning tools has expanded access to education, particularly for those in remote or underserved areas. For example, platforms like SWAYAM, which offer free online courses, and various e-learning apps are providing opportunities for millions of students to acquire knowledge and skills outside traditional classroom settings.

Digital education can also bridge the gap between urban and rural students, allowing children in remote areas to access the same quality of education as those in cities. Moreover, technology can enable personalized learning, where students can progress at their own pace and receive tailored content based on their learning needs. This shift towards digital learning is not only important for improving educational outcomes but also for preparing students for the demands of the modern workforce, where digital literacy and technological skills are increasingly required. However, the successful harnessing of technological innovation for sustainable development requires addressing several key challenges. One of the primary challenges is ensuring equitable access to technology, particularly for disadvantaged groups such as those in rural areas, women, and marginalized communities.

The digital divide, which refers to the gap between those who have access to technology and those who do not, remains a significant barrier to achieving inclusive development. To overcome this, policymakers must invest in expanding digital infrastructure, improving Internet connectivity, and providing affordable access to devices and technology. Additionally, digital literacy programmes should be implemented to ensure that individuals have the skills and knowledge to effectively use technology for personal and professional development. Another challenge is ensuring that technological innovations are aligned with the principles of sustainable development. While technology has the potential to address environmental and social challenges, it can also have unintended consequences, such as increased e-waste, resource depletion, and job displacement due to automation. To mitigate these risks, policymakers must adopt a holistic approach to technological innovation that considers its social, economic, and environmental impacts.

This includes promoting green technologies, supporting industries that focus on recycling and waste management, and ensuring that workers are retrained and upskilled to adapt to new technologies and automation. In conclusion, harnessing technological innovation for sustainable development is key to addressing the complex challenges faced by India in the twenty-first century. Technology can drive progress in sectors such as energy, agriculture, health care, and education, helping to improve the quality of life for millions of people while also promoting environmental sustainability. However, for technology to truly contribute to sustainable development, it must be inclusive, equitable, and aligned with the principles of social justice and environmental protection. By investing in technology, expanding access to digital tools, and ensuring that technological innovations are applied in ways that benefit all segments of society, India can create a more sustainable and prosperous future for its people.

REFERENCES

Gordon, S. (1995). *India's Rise to Power in the Twentieth Century and Beyond.* Macmillan Press Ltd.

Harvey, D. (2005). *A Brief History of Neoliberalism.* Oxford University Press.

Jaffrelot, C. (2003). "India's Look East Policy: An Asianist Strategy in Perspective." *India Review, 2*(2): 35-68.

Malik, J.M. (1991). "India's Response to the Gulf Crisis: Implications for Indian Foreign Policy." *Asian Survey, 31*(9): 847-61. https://doi.org/10.1525/as.1991.31.9.00p0092d

Mohapatra, B. (2014). "India's Look East Policy and Development of North Eastern India: Priorities and Prospects". *Search, 3*(1): 65-70.

Munro, R.H. (1993). "The Loser: India in the Nineties." *The National Interest, 33*: 62-63.

Naidu, G.V.C. (1996). "India and Southeast Asia." *World Focus, 17*(10-12): 82-84.

Nayar, B.R. (1998). "Political Structure and India's Economic Reforms of the 1990s." *Pacific Affairs, 71*(3): 337-60. https://doi.org/10.2307/2761414

Saikia, H. (2010). "Look East Policy: Southeast Asian Economic Integration of India." *Applied Economic Journal, 17*(2): 1-11.

Sreedhar (1994). "Security Situation in Southern Asia." *Strategic Analysis, 16*(11): 1431-42.

16

The Future of Manmohanomics

Dr. Manmohan Singh's tenure as finance minister in 1991 and later as prime minister from 2004 to 2014 fundamentally reshaped India's economic trajectory. His leadership brought about significant changes, particularly with the introduction of policies focused on economic liberalization, privatization, and globalization—elements that have collectively come to be known as Manmohanomics. These reforms were pivotal in transforming India's economy from a closed, protectionist model to one that embraced market-driven growth and global integration. However, as the global economic landscape continues to evolve, the future of Manmohanomics raises important questions.

Will the principles that led to India's economic success continue to be relevant in the face of challenges such as technological disruption, rising inequality, climate change, and geopolitical tensions? The initial reforms introduced by Dr. Singh in 1991 were aimed at addressing the severe economic crisis India was facing. The country's foreign exchange reserves were dangerously low, and inflation was high. In response, Dr. Singh spearheaded a series of bold economic measures. These included the devaluation of the rupee to boost exports, a reduction in import tariffs, and the opening up of key sectors to foreign investment. The government also focused on privatizing state-owned enterprises and reducing bureaucratic controls. These reforms were not without controversy, especially among those who believed in India's socialist economic framework.

Yet, they laid the foundation for India's future growth, helping to create a dynamic economy that could compete in the global market. Over the next few decades, India's economy began to transform. The liberalization policies initiated by Dr. Singh's government catalyzed rapid growth, particularly in sectors such as information technology, telecommunications, and services. The country saw an expansion of its middle class, a surge in foreign investment, and an increase in global trade. The GDP growth rate averaged around 6-7 per cent during the early 2000s, and India emerged as one of the world's fastest-growing economies. The success of these reforms was particularly evident in the urban centres, where rapid infrastructure development and job creation were visible. However, the benefits of this growth were not equally distributed across all sections of society. While urban areas flourished, rural areas, particularly in northern and eastern India, continued to lag behind.

Inequality widened as economic growth concentrated in cities, while the rural poor remained mired in poverty. Addressing these disparities became a key challenge for Manmohanomics. Dr. Singh recognized the need for inclusive growth—policies that would ensure that economic progress reached all segments of society, particularly marginalized communities. In his second term as prime minister, Dr. Singh's government introduced several important social welfare initiatives aimed at promoting inclusive development. One of the most significant of these was the Mahatma Gandhi National Rural Employment Guarantee Act (MGNREGA), which guaranteed employment for rural households and sought to provide a safety net for the poorest segments of the population.

Additionally, the Right to Education (RTE) Act, passed in 2009, ensured free and compulsory education for children, making it a fundamental right. These policies were designed to address the social and economic inequalities that had emerged during the liberalization period. They reflected Dr. Singh's belief that growth should not only be about increasing GDP but also about improving the quality of life for India's most disadvantaged populations. Despite these efforts, India's economic transformation has not been without its challenges. The gap between the rich and the poor has continued to widen, and unemployment remains a persistent issue. Additionally, while urban areas have thrived, rural areas have seen less benefit from India's economic boom. In the future, Manmohanomics will need to address these issues more effectively.

The focus will have to be on not just economic growth, but also on creating opportunities for those left behind. This may involve expanding social safety nets, increasing access to quality education and health care, and investing in infrastructure that benefits to rural and underserved regions. At the same time, India must focus on fostering technological innovation and digital transformation. Under Dr. Singh's leadership, India made strides in information technology, particularly in software services and outsourcing. This was a key component of India's growth strategy during the 1990s and 2000s. The country became a global hub for IT services, with companies like Infosys and Wipro leading the charge. The digital economy continues to be a significant driver of India's growth today. Digital India, launched in 2015, aimed to expand digital infrastructure and make government services more accessible to citizens. India's growing number of Internet users, along with the rise of digital payments and e-commerce, has further accelerated the country's transition into the digital age.

The future of Manmohanomics lies in fully harnessing the potential of emerging technologies like Artificial Intelligence (AI), Machine Learning (ML), and Big Data. These technologies have the potential to revolutionize industries such as health care, agriculture, and manufacturing. For instance, AI can help optimize agricultural yields, ML can improve the delivery of health-care services, and big data can transform sectors like transportation and logistics. India's ability to innovate in these fields will be crucial to its economic future. However, it will also need to focus on the digital divide—ensuring that rural populations and those without access to technology are not left behind. Another key challenge India faces is environmental sustainability. India's rapid industrialization and urbanization have resulted in severe environmental degradation.

The country grapples with issues such as air pollution, water scarcity, and deforestation. As climate change accelerates, India's vulnerability to natural disasters and environmental challenges will increase. Dr. Singh's government was one of the first to recognize the importance of addressing climate change, and his leadership saw the creation of the National Action Plan on Climate Change (NAPCC) in 2008. This laid the groundwork for policies aimed at reducing India's carbon footprint and promoting the use of renewable energy. In the future, Manmohanomics will need to integrate sustainability into its economic framework. India must strike a balance between economic growth and environmental protection. This can be achieved by increasing investment in green technologies, such as solar and wind power, and encouraging more sustainable practices in sectors like agriculture, manufacturing, and construction.

Furthermore, India will need to prioritize climate resilience, especially in regions that are most vulnerable to the impacts of climate change, such as coastal areas and agricultural communities. The global economic environment is also likely to influence the future trajectory of Manmohanomics. As the world becomes more interconnected, India must navigate the complexities of global trade, investment, and international relations. The rise of protectionism in many parts of the world, particularly in developed economies, poses a challenge to India's export-driven growth model. At the same time, India's growing influence in international organizations like the World Trade Organization (WTO), BRICS, and the United Nations (UN) offers opportunities to shape global trade policies in ways that benefit its economy. The future of Manmohanomics will require India to continue its liberalization efforts while adapting to the changing global environment. This may involve strengthening trade relations with new partners, expanding the services sector, and investing in areas such as global supply chains and foreign direct investment (FDI).

Additionally, India will need to ensure that its domestic industries remain competitive by fostering innovation and improving productivity across all sectors of the economy. As India approaches the future, the evolution of Manmohanomics will depend on its ability to adapt to emerging challenges while staying true to the principles that have guided its economic transformation. The integration of technology, sustainability, and inclusivity will be key to ensuring that the benefits of economic growth are felt by all segments of society. India's ability to address the challenges of inequality, environmental degradation, and technological change will determine whether it can sustain the progress made under Manmohanomics. Ultimately, the future of India's economy will be shaped by its ability to innovate, adapt, and build a more inclusive and sustainable growth model for the twenty-first century.

The Evolution of Manmohanomics: Economic Reforms of 1991

Dr. Singh's pivotal role in initiating India's economic reforms in 1991 cannot be overstated. At a time when the country was facing a severe balance of payments crisis, high inflation, and stagnation, the government, under the leadership of Prime Minister P.V. Narasimha Rao and Finance Minister Dr. Singh, took the bold step of liberalizing the economy. The reforms introduced in 1991 were designed to tackle these economic challenges and open India's doors to global markets. The immediate steps included a significant devaluation of the rupee to make exports more competitive, as well as reducing import tariffs and licencing requirements that had previously hampered the growth of industries. These changes were aimed at improving the balance of payments and attracting foreign investment.

Alongside these trade reforms, the government also focused on financial sector reforms, including the privatization of state-owned enterprises, banking sector reforms, and the development of stock markets. While the initial reforms were controversial, especially for those accustomed to India's socialist policies, they laid the foundation for a period of unprecedented economic growth. The opening up of sectors like telecommunications, aviation, and information technology spurred innovation, creating millions of jobs and propelling India's growth rate to around 6-7 per cent annually during the early 2000s. By 2000, India was recognized as one of the world's fastest-growing economies, driven largely by the expansion of its middle class and a burgeoning service sector. However, as the global landscape continues to evolve, the policies introduced by Dr. Singh in the 1990s may need to be revisited. The future of Manmohanomics will depend on whether India continues to embrace liberalization, or if the focus shifts towards protectionist measures in light of global uncertainties.

Will India continue to rely on market-driven reforms, or will it need to find a balance between liberalization and domestic protection?

Inclusive Growth and Poverty Alleviation: A Vision for Equitable Development

Dr. Singh's vision for India was not solely focused on rapid economic growth; he was equally concerned with ensuring that the benefits of growth were shared across society, particularly with those who had been left behind by the earlier growth models. His commitment to inclusive growth became a defining feature of Manmohanomics. Key policies aimed at achieving inclusive growth included the National Rural Employment Guarantee Act (NREGA), which was designed to provide employment to rural households and reduce poverty. The Right to Education Act (RTE) was another landmark policy, aimed at making education accessible to all children, thereby ensuring the development of human capital for future generations. These initiatives were important steps in addressing India's socio-economic challenges, such as rural poverty, illiteracy, and inequality.

Despite these efforts, India still faces significant challenges in achieving true inclusivity. A large portion of the population, particularly in rural areas, remains marginalized. Income inequality has continued to widen, with the benefits of economic growth largely concentrated in urban centres. The future of Manmohanomics will need to focus on finding more effective ways to ensure that the fruits of India's growth are more equally distributed. This may include greater investment in social welfare programmes, job creation in rural areas, and addressing regional disparities. India also faces the challenge of unemployment, particularly among the youth. With millions of young Indians entering the workforce each year, the government will need to focus on creating new jobs and ensuring that young people are equipped with the skills necessary for a modern economy. The National Skill Development Corporation (NSDC), which was launched during Dr. Singh's tenure, has already started addressing some of these issues by providing vocational training. However, the scale of the problem requires greater innovation and cooperation between government, industry, and educational institutions.

Technological Transformation: A New Era of Innovation and Opportunity

In the twenty-first century, technological advancements are fundamentally reshaping economies. India, under Dr. Singh's leadership, made significant strides in harnessing technology for economic development.

The Information Technology (IT) revolution, in which India became a global leader in software services and outsourcing, was one of the most significant outcomes of Manmohanomics. The country's IT sector, led by companies like Infosys and Tata Consultancy Services (TCS), provided millions of jobs and helped boost the country's GDP growth. The digital economy has continued to evolve since then, with India seeing an explosion in digital payments, e-commerce, and fintech. The Digital India initiative, launched in 2015, sought to further promote digital infrastructure and online services, with the aim of making government services more accessible to all citizens. However, as India's digital economy grows, it must also address challenges such as data privacy, cyber security, and bridging the digital divide between urban and rural populations.

Looking ahead, India has the potential to harness the power of emerging technologies such as Artificial Intelligence (AI), Machine Learning (ML), and Big Data. These technologies could provide significant opportunities for growth, particularly in sectors such as health care, agriculture, education, and manufacturing. However, India must also prepare its workforce for this technological transition. There will be a need for large-scale upskilling initiatives, particularly for those in traditional sectors like agriculture and manufacturing who may be displaced by automation. The future of Manmohanomics will need to focus on fostering an innovation-driven economy while ensuring that technology benefits are broadly distributed. This includes supporting digital literacy, encouraging entrepreneurship, and investing in cutting-edge technologies that can drive sustainable growth.

Sustainability and Green Growth: Addressing Environmental Challenges

As India continues to grow economically, it faces significant environmental challenges. The rapid pace of industrialization and urbanization has led to air pollution, deforestation, water scarcity, and increased carbon emissions. Dr. Singh's government was among the first to recognize the need for sustainable development. The National Action Plan on Climate Change (NAPCC), which was introduced during his tenure, laid the foundation for India's response to climate change by focusing on areas like energy efficiency, renewable energy, and sustainable agriculture. However, as the global climate crisis deepens, India will need to do more to ensure that its growth is environmentally sustainable. The future of Manmohanomics must incorporate policies that address the twin challenges of economic development and environmental sustainability.

This includes investing in green technologies, promoting the use of renewable energy sources such as solar and wind, and encouraging sustainable practices in agriculture, manufacturing, and urban planning. India's future economic growth must be aligned with its commitments to international climate agreements, such as the Paris Agreement. This will require both public and private sector cooperation in the development of low-carbon technologies and the reduction of India's carbon footprint. The growing importance of **green growth** will likely play a central role in shaping the economic policies of the future.

• Relevance in Contemporary India

Dr. Manmohan Singh's leadership and policies remain highly relevant in contemporary India, particularly in light of the nation's ongoing economic challenges. As the country grapples with issues such as inequality, unemployment, fiscal deficits, inflation, and global economic volatility, the lessons from Dr. Singh's tenure can offer valuable insights and solutions. His approach to economic reform, balanced growth, and social equity continues to resonate in today's policymaking, especially as India seeks to secure its place as a global economic power while addressing pressing domestic issues. One of the key lessons from Dr. Singh's era is the importance of balancing economic liberalization with social equity. While his reforms, particularly those in the 1990s, helped India transition into a market economy, they were not devoid of a focus on social welfare. This balancing act remains crucial today, as India faces a widening income gap and challenges in providing employment for its growing youth population.

Dr. Singh's commitment to inclusive development, as reflected in policies like the MGNREGA and his focus on improving infrastructure and education, continues to provide a framework for policymakers dealing with similar issues in the present. In the current era, India's economy is experiencing rapid growth, but it also faces significant inequalities and social unrest. Dr. Singh's vision of economic growth that benefits all sections of society is especially pertinent now. His model of governance, which emphasized long-term stability over short-term populism, provides a guiding principle for today's leaders who face immense pressure to deliver quick fixes. Dr. Singh demonstrated that reform, although often controversial and difficult, is necessary for long-term prosperity, and this lesson is more applicable now than ever. Another important lesson is the necessity of a stable, credible financial and fiscal framework.

Dr. Singh's tenure was marked by the successful implementation of structural reforms in the banking, taxation, and foreign investment sectors. These reforms helped stabilize the Indian economy during difficult times and laid the groundwork for sustained growth. Today, as India faces challenges related to fiscal deficits and a highly competitive global economy, his focus on financial discipline and policy predictability remains highly relevant. Dr. Singh's experience also underscores the value of multilateral engagement in global economic forums. His active participation in organizations such as the G20 and BRICS set the stage for India to claim its rightful place in the global economic order. In today's increasingly interconnected world, where issues such as climate change, trade imbalances, and economic security require global cooperation, his approach to diplomacy and multilateralism remains instructive.

In addressing contemporary economic challenges, Dr. Singh's belief in the power of education and human capital development also holds significance. With a young and rapidly growing workforce, India's economic future hinges on the quality of its human resources. Dr. Singh's focus on education, skill development, and job creation is a reminder that sustainable economic growth can only be achieved when investment in human capital is a priority. In conclusion, Dr. Manmohan Singh's economic philosophy and policies provide valuable lessons for India as it navigates its current economic landscape. His commitment to economic reform, inclusive growth, fiscal responsibility, and multilateral engagement offers a roadmap for tackling the challenges of the twenty-first century. As India continues to rise as an economic power, the legacy of Dr. Singh's leadership remains a touchstone for policymakers striving to balance growth with equity, stability, and long-term prosperity.

Relevance in Contemporary India

Dr. Manmohan Singh's leadership and policies continue to hold significant relevance in the current economic and political landscape of India. As the nation faces a variety of complex economic challenges, such as unemployment, inflation, fiscal deficits, and income inequality, the lessons from his tenure offer valuable guidance for contemporary policymakers. The evolving needs of India's economy, including its role in global trade, its demographic shifts, and the rising expectations for social equity, find roots in the principles Dr. Singh laid down during his time in office. His balanced approach to economic growth, governance, and social welfare offers a pathway for addressing today's challenges in a sustainable and equitable manner.

Balancing Growth with Social Equity

One of the key take aways from Dr. Singh's policies is the emphasis on balancing economic growth with social equity. In the 1990s, his reforms marked a paradigm shift from a state-controlled to a market-driven economy, and these changes were instrumental in India's growth trajectory. However, Dr. Singh did not prioritize growth at the cost of social welfare. He understood that economic reforms must be inclusive and ensure that marginalized sections of society are not left behind. This approach is more relevant than ever today, as India faces a widening gap between the rich and poor, and regional disparities continue to persist. The current government is tasked with addressing these inequalities while ensuring the country remains on a path of growth. Dr. Singh's model of inclusive development through policies like the MGNREGA, rural development programmes, and increasing access to education and health care remains pertinent.

The Role of Inclusive Growth in Today's Economy

India's rapid economic growth, especially in the post-reform era, has been accompanied by increasing concerns over inequality. The current economic challenges India faces, such as unemployment, inflation, and the lack of adequate health care and educational facilities in many parts of the country, continue to exacerbate social divides. Dr. Singh's vision of inclusive growth, which sought to bridge the rural-urban divide and bring marginalized communities into the mainstream of economic activity, provides a template for today's policymakers. His focus on creating job opportunities, improving rural infrastructure, and facilitating social security mechanisms should serve as a foundation for current strategies to ensure equitable growth. Moreover, Dr. Singh's economic policies were not just about encouraging private sector participation in growth but also about empowering the government to play a key role in ensuring that the benefits of this growth trickled down to the most vulnerable sections of society. Today, with over a billion people, India's socio-economic challenges are more complex, requiring an approach that integrates both market forces and state intervention in strategic areas to foster long-term equity.

Financial Discipline and Policy Predictability

Another lesson from Dr. Singh's tenure that holds immense relevance today is his commitment to maintaining financial discipline and ensuring policy predictability. India's economic journey, particularly after the liberalization reforms of the 1990s, required steady fiscal management, which Dr. Singh exemplified during his tenure. His role in stabilizing the economy after the 1991 balance of payments crisis through deft economic planning and international negotiations is an important reference point for today's policymakers. In the current economic environment, where India is grappling with fiscal deficits, rising public debt, and inflationary pressures, maintaining financial discipline is essential for long-term economic health. Dr. Singh's focus on fiscal prudence, especially his emphasis on managing inflation and keeping the fiscal deficit within reasonable limits, should guide contemporary strategies in the face of current challenges like the COVID-19 pandemic-induced economic slowdown and global inflationary trends.

Multilateral Engagement and Global Leadership

Dr. Singh's active participation in multilateral organizations like the G20, BRICS, and the World Trade Organization (WTO) set the stage for India's growing role in the global economic landscape. India's rise as a global economic power is not just about its domestic growth but also about its ability to engage with global institutions and shape international economic policies. Dr. Singh's tenure saw India emerge as a key player in these forums, advocating for developing economies and pushing for reforms in global governance. India today, as a member of these international bodies, has the opportunity to assert its economic leadership in global debates, particularly around issues such as climate change, trade policies, and economic security. Dr. Singh's advocacy for multilateralism in these forums should inform India's approach to international relations today. His emphasis on cooperative global solutions to economic and political issues resonates strongly in today's interconnected world, where no nation can thrive in isolation.

Dr. Singh's Vision of Global Integration

Dr. Singh's approach to economic liberalization was not merely about opening up the Indian market to global forces; it was about balancing the forces of globalization with India's national interests. He was keenly aware of the need to preserve India's sovereignty and cultural identity while embracing the benefits of globalization. This vision remains highly relevant in today's context, as India continues to engage with global markets and strives to achieve greater economic integration without compromising on its domestic goals. Today, India faces challenges similar to those Dr. Singh addressed during his time, including managing its external vulnerabilities and securing its place in the global economy while addressing internal challenges such as job creation and social welfare. His strategy of pragmatic engagement with the world economy while safeguarding national priorities provides a valuable blueprint for today's policymakers who are navigating the global economic maze.

The Importance of Education and Human Capital Development

Dr. Singh was deeply committed to the idea that investment in education and human capital was critical to India's economic success. During his time in office, he focused on increasing access to quality education, skills training, and health care. These areas are crucial in today's context, as India has a young and dynamic population, which, if harnessed effectively, could drive the nation's economic growth in the coming decades. At a time when India is facing challenges related to youth unemployment, skill mismatches, and the need for more accessible and affordable education, Dr. Singh's emphasis on human capital development provides a roadmap for addressing these challenges. His policies sought to build a knowledge-driven economy, which is a vision that remains just as critical today in light of the increasing role of technology, innovation, and entrepreneurship in driving global economic progress.

In conclusion, Dr. Manmohan Singh's economic philosophy and governance model offer a wealth of insights for India as it confronts its current and future economic challenges. His emphasis on inclusive development, financial discipline, multilateral engagement, and human capital development are just as relevant today as they were during his time in office. As India navigates its role in the global economy and addresses domestic issues like poverty, inequality, and unemployment, Dr. Singh's legacy continues to guide the nation's policymaking and offers valuable lessons for both current leaders and future generations of policymakers. His balanced, pragmatic approach to governance and development provides a foundation for a sustainable and inclusive economic future for India. As the country continues to grow and evolve in the twenty-first century, the lessons learned from Dr. Singh's tenure will continue to inform decisions that shape India's economic trajectory for years to come.

▪ Evolving His Ideas

Dr. Manmohan Singh's adaptability to modern economic challenges is a testament to his deep understanding of both India's unique position in the world and the dynamic nature of global economies. Throughout his career, he demonstrated a remarkable capacity to reframe his ideas in response to new opportunities and risks. His leadership was defined not only by the success of his policies but also by his continuous refinement of those policies based on evolving circumstances. Whether addressing the global financial crisis or managing the complexities of India's domestic economy, Dr. Singh's intellectual flexibility and pragmatic approach were central to his long-lasting influence on the country's economic trajectory.

A pivotal example of Dr. Singh's evolving principles is his approach to India's economic integration with the global market. In the 1990s, he championed the cause of liberalization, driving policies that opened up the Indian economy, encouraged foreign investment, and embraced global trade. The success of these policies during a period of economic crisis marked a significant shift in India's growth model. However, over time, Dr. Singh's vision began to acknowledge the complexities of a rapidly globalizing world, including the challenges posed by international financial instability and the pressures of global capital flows. In response to these challenges, Dr. Singh's policies began to take on a more cautious and pragmatic tone, particularly in the 2000s. His response to the global financial crisis of 2008 is perhaps one of the clearest reflections of his adaptability. While many countries were forced to retreat into protectionism, Dr. Singh remained committed to economic openness, but with an emphasis on ensuring stability and mitigating risks.

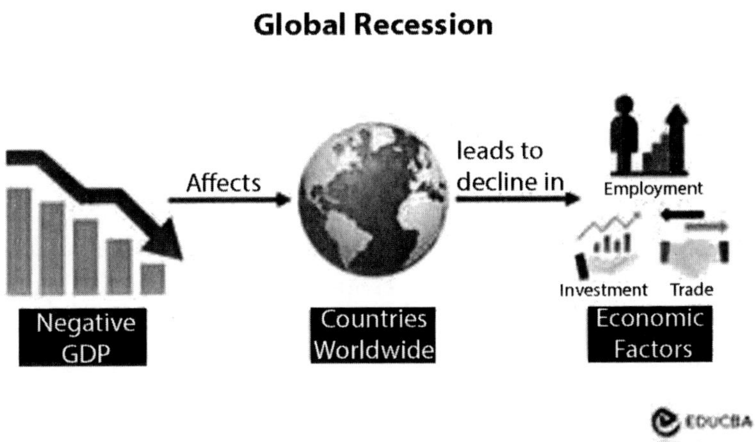

Fig. 16.1: Regional Variations in the Economic Impact of the 2008 Financial Crisis.

He recognized the need to recalibrate India's growth model, and as such, he promoted fiscal stimulus and public sector investments in infrastructure to ensure that the economy would not fall into a deep recession. By balancing market forces with the necessary regulatory oversight, he was able to steer India through one of the most tumultuous periods in global economic history, all while preserving the integrity of his original economic reforms. This ability to adapt and recalibrate his approach reflects a core aspect of Dr. Singh's philosophy: he always viewed policy as a tool to address real-world challenges, rather than as a rigid ideological framework. His focus on achieving sustainable growth by emphasizing human capital, social welfare, and infrastructural development was a clear recognition of the emerging challenges India faced in the twenty-first century.

As technology became a central component of the global economy, Dr. Singh acknowledged the importance of the digital economy and the need for India to not only embrace this change but also actively participate in shaping it. His emphasis on building a knowledge-based economy and strengthening India's position in the global digital marketplace was a natural extension of his earlier work on liberalization. At the same time, Dr. Singh's focus on maintaining social equity in the face of rapid economic growth continued to be a guiding principle. While his early years in office focused on reducing poverty and providing for the basic needs of the population, by the time of his second tenure as prime minister, his focus shifted to ensuring that the benefits of growth reached the most marginalized segments of society. In this context, Dr. Singh became an advocate for more inclusive growth strategies, encouraging policies aimed at reducing income disparities and improving access to education, health care, and housing for underserved populations.

He strongly believed that economic growth and social equity must go hand in hand, and as such, his policies always sought to strike a balance between economic liberalization and social welfare. This balancing act between liberalization and welfare was tested during his tenure, particularly as India's economy grew at an unprecedented rate. As the middle class expanded, so did the demands for better public services, infrastructure, and employment opportunities. Dr. Singh responded to these challenges by advocating for long-term investments in education and skills development, recognizing that a rapidly growing economy would require a highly-skilled workforce. His reforms in the education sector, including the expansion of higher education and vocational training, were aimed at preparing India's workforce for the demands of a modern, knowledge-driven economy.

Furthermore, Dr. Singh's vision of a globalized economy did not merely reflect a desire for integration into global markets; it also emphasized the importance of India asserting itself as a global leader in shaping economic and environmental discourse. His efforts to position India as an emerging economic power were aligned with his focus on multilateralism. While many of his contemporaries focused on bilateral agreements and partnerships, Dr. Singh was a staunch advocate of strengthening multilateral institutions like the WTO and the G20, believing that the future of global governance would lie in collective decision making. As part of this vision, Dr. Singh emphasized India's role in representing the interests of developing countries, and his advocacy for the Global South became a defining feature of his foreign policy.

His leadership in forums like BRICS and the G20 highlighted India's importance not just as an emerging economy, but also as a leader in promoting inclusive global economic policies. His ability to foster diplomatic ties, while simultaneously promoting India's economic interests on the global stage, ensured that the country could maintain an active role in shaping the global economic landscape. In modern times, Dr. Singh's principles have continued to resonate in India's ongoing economic and political evolution. Today, the country is faced with new challenges, such as the rise of automation, the importance of AI, and the growing concerns around climate change. Dr. Singh's core principles—his belief in inclusive development, social equity, and international cooperation—provide a framework for addressing these issues.

His ability to adapt his vision to the changing contours of global economic challenges ensures that his ideas remain relevant and actionable in contemporary India. Dr. Singh's vision for India's economic future has also found resonance in the ongoing debates about economic nationalism and the rise of protectionist policies around the world. His commitment to balancing globalization with national interests offers a valuable lesson for countries navigating the complex waters of global economic integration. His policies serve as a reminder that economic growth should not come at the expense of social equity, and that economic liberalization, when coupled with robust regulatory frameworks, can be a tool for long-term prosperity. In conclusion, Dr. Manmohan Singh's ability to evolve his ideas and adapt his policies over time has ensured that his economic philosophy remains as relevant today as it was when he first championed economic reforms in the 1990s. His enduring influence on India's economic trajectory is a testament to the power of adaptable leadership and the importance of understanding the ever-changing global economic landscape.

Evolving His Ideas

Dr. Manmohan Singh's economic philosophy, shaped by his deep academic roots and pragmatic experiences, has proven adaptable to changing global and domestic circumstances. Over the years, his principles, deeply rooted in the belief in liberalization, economic openness, and social equity, have evolved to reflect new challenges and opportunities. As India's economic landscape continued to shift, so did his views on how to manage growth, social development, and global integration. His ability to evolve his ideas in response to shifting realities—both internal and external—has made his economic vision highly relevant in today's fast-changing world. Dr. Singh's approach to economic governance was inherently flexible, allowing him to adjust his methods while maintaining a core set of values. His initial advocacy for economic liberalization and free markets in the 1990s, during a time of deep economic crisis, gave way to a more nuanced understanding of growth when confronted with issues like inequality, unemployment, and regional imbalances. Similarly, as the global economic order continued to evolve, Dr. Singh's principles were consistently recalibrated to integrate India into a more interconnected world economy while safeguarding national interests.

Adapting His Principles for Modern Times

One of the key strengths of Dr. Singh's leadership was his ability to modify his economic strategies in response to changing times. In the 1990s, his focus was on integrating India into the global economy by dismantling protectionist policies and encouraging foreign investment. However, as the economy grew, new issues emerged that required a different set of tools. The rapid pace of technological innovation, the rise of digital economies, and the need for climate-resilient policies are just some of the challenges that required a shift in focus. In today's context, for instance, the emphasis on sustainable development, green energy, and technological innovation is a natural extension of the ideas Dr. Singh introduced but adapted to the twenty-first century's priorities. He believed in the importance of infrastructure development for long-term economic growth, but modern challenges like climate change, urbanization, and the digital economy have led to a greater focus on environmentally sustainable infrastructure and the expansion of technology-driven industries. Dr. Singh's principles of social welfare and inclusive growth were foundational in guiding these transitions, with an evolving emphasis on digital inclusion, job creation in high-tech sectors, and sustainable growth practices.

Dr. Singh's vision of economic reform also became more sophisticated as the global financial crisis of 2008 exposed vulnerabilities in the international financial system. His policy responses during the crisis reflected an ability to adapt his thinking to contemporary global challenges. While liberalization and market reforms were crucial in the 1990s, by the 2000s, there was a need to balance these principles with regulatory mechanisms that would safeguard against market excesses and ensure more equitable distribution of economic benefits. His approach to fiscal and monetary stability, his cautious but progressive opening to global markets, and his focus on mitigating social risks during times of upheaval exemplify how Dr. Singh continuously adapted his policies to meet the changing needs of the nation and the world. Additionally, Dr. Singh's commitment to multilateralism and India's role on the global stage saw an evolution in his approach to foreign policy and trade.

While he had initially championed liberalization to integrate India into the global economy, by the 2000s, he was also focused on ensuring that India had a voice in global economic forums such as the WTO, the G20, and BRICS. His advocacy for developing countries, and his efforts to bring global attention to the issues facing the Global South, became increasingly relevant as economic and geopolitical dynamics shifted. His vision of an inclusive global economic order and multilateralism remains central to India's current foreign policy. Dr. Singh's evolution as a leader is not just about adjusting to changing economic circumstances but also understanding the shifting global power dynamics. As the twenty-first century progresses, the role of emerging economies like India becomes more pronounced, and Dr. Singh's principles of promoting economic cooperation and reducing global inequalities align with modern challenges. His ability to rethink policies to adapt to these emerging realities ensures that his economic philosophy remains grounded in the needs of the present while drawing from the lessons of the past.

Table 16.1: Timeline of Policy Responses in India

Date	Policy Measure
Oct. 08	Repo rate cut by 100 basis points
Dec. 08	First fiscal stimulus package announced
Jan. 09	Second fiscal stimulus package announced
Jul. 09	Union Budget focuses on infrastructure spending

▪ Ongoing Transformation

Dr. Manmohan Singh's legacy has had a lasting impact on India's transformation, and it continues to shape the country's future trajectory. His pioneering role in opening up India's economy in the 1990s and his steadfast commitment to liberalization laid the foundation for the country's subsequent economic growth. Even though his tenure as prime minister was marked by significant political challenges, his economic reforms ushered in a new era for India. Today, as the world navigates a rapidly changing geopolitical and economic landscape, India finds itself at a crossroads, and much of its modern economic identity owes itself to the groundwork laid by Dr. Singh. One of the most significant ways his legacy continues to influence India's future is through the ongoing economic reforms that were initiated during his time in office.

Dr. Singh's focus on transforming India's economy through liberalization, market-oriented policies, and increased foreign direct investment (FDI) set the stage for the country's rise as a global economic power. His emphasis on human capital, technological innovation, and infrastructure development continues to resonate in India's current economic policies, as the government focuses on enhancing its manufacturing capabilities and embracing the digital economy. Dr. Singh's approach to economic governance was pragmatic, and his ability to make long-term policy decisions has been a guiding principle in shaping the future direction of the economy.

His belief in inclusive growth continues to be central to India's development agenda. India's current government has built upon the foundations of his policies by pushing for greater financial inclusion, rural development, and initiatives aimed at reducing poverty. Programmes such as Make in India and Digital India reflect Dr. Singh's enduring vision of leveraging India's strengths to secure its place on the global economic map. The growing emphasis on innovation and the knowledge economy is another way in which Dr. Singh's legacy shapes India's future. His early recognition of the IT sector's potential and his role in establishing a favourable regulatory environment for its growth laid the groundwork for India to become a global leader in information technology and services.

As India moves forward, technology and innovation continue to be key pillars of its growth strategy, and much of the country's rise in the global digital economy is a direct result of the policies Dr. Singh championed. Dr. Singh's role in global economic leadership also remains a vital part of India's future. His work in strengthening multilateral institutions such as the WTO and G20 helped position India as a key player in global economic governance. This international outlook has only grown in importance as India continues to expand its influence on the world stage. Today, India's economic leadership is crucial in addressing global challenges, from climate change and trade imbalances to the ongoing debates on digital sovereignty and the future of work. India's success in maintaining a strong voice in these discussions is built on the foundations of the multilateralism Dr. Singh championed.

Moreover, Dr. Singh's focus on long-term, sustainable growth continues to resonate in India's policy formulation. His emphasis on infrastructure development, rural-urban integration, and poverty alleviation remains a guiding principle in the country's quest to address its current challenges. India's rapidly expanding infrastructure sector, its push for renewable energy, and its efforts to improve social indicators such as health care and education can all be seen as extensions of Dr. Singh's vision of equitable, inclusive development. His belief that economic growth should benefit all sections of society has paved the way for the government's focus on social welfare programmes and initiatives aimed at reducing inequality. As India faces new global challenges, such as the rise of protectionism, climate change, and the growing demand for clean energy, Dr. Singh's legacy will remain influential in shaping the country's response.

His ability to navigate economic crises and his consistent belief in a balanced approach to growth and development provide a solid foundation for India's future economic strategy. Today, as India seeks to become a global economic leader, Dr. Singh's policies serve as a reminder of the importance of sound economic governance, long-term vision, and an unwavering commitment to inclusive growth. In conclusion, Dr. Manmohan Singh's legacy continues to shape India's future by providing a roadmap for growth, development, and global engagement. His visionary policies in the 1990s opened up new avenues for economic growth and positioned India as a global player. His emphasis on human capital, technology, and inclusive development laid the groundwork for India's transformation into a modern, knowledge-driven economy. As India faces new challenges in the global economic and political landscape, Dr. Singh's principles of liberalization, multilateralism, and sustainable growth remain as relevant as ever, guiding the country's path forward.

His contributions will continue to resonate in India's policies for years to come, ensuring that his legacy remains integral to the ongoing transformation of the nation.

Ongoing Transformation: How Dr. Singh's Legacy Shapes India's Future

Dr. Manmohan Singh's impact on India's trajectory is far-reaching, as the reforms he set in motion decades ago continue to guide the nation toward a more prosperous future. His policies of economic liberalization, fiscal responsibility, and global engagement set the foundation for India's rise on the global stage. These reforms were essential to turning the country's economy from a stagnating, highly-regulated system into one more integrated into the global market. However, the scope of his legacy is not limited to the economic reforms of the 1990s, but extends into India's broader developmental and foreign policy strategies. Today, India continues to benefit from the groundwork laid by Dr. Singh, and the ongoing transformation of the nation is a testament to his enduring influence.

Economic Reforms: A Legacy of Liberalization

Dr. Singh's most significant contribution to India's future remains his leadership in implementing economic reforms that opened up the country's economy. The liberalization policies that Dr. Singh championed in 1991 laid the foundation for the economic prosperity India enjoys today. His belief in creating a market-driven economy, reducing the state's role in business, and encouraging foreign investment played a critical role in transforming India from a largely agrarian economy into a burgeoning industrial and services powerhouse. The ongoing transformation of India's economic landscape continues to reflect these reforms. The emphasis on opening sectors such as telecommunications, banking, and infrastructure has driven growth in these critical areas. Today, India is home to one of the world's largest consumer markets, and FDI continues to flood in, reinforcing Dr. Singh's vision of a more globally connected India.

The Role of Human Capital and Technology

One of the cornerstones of Dr. Singh's vision for India was the development of human capital and technological innovation. His recognition of India's potential in the information technology sector was visionary, and the policies implemented during his tenure helped India emerge as a global IT powerhouse. The software industry, driven by the growth of companies like Infosys, TCS, and Wipro, owes much of its success to the regulatory reforms put in place during his time as finance minister and prime minister.

Today, India continues to expand its technological and digital footprint. With programmes such as Digital India and the push for a cashless economy, Dr. Singh's early initiatives in fostering a robust IT ecosystem remain pivotal. Furthermore, India's rise as a leader in the global outsourcing industry, with significant growth in sectors such as software development, engineering services, and IT consulting, is a direct result of the groundwork laid during Dr. Singh's leadership.

Sustaining Economic Growth: Infrastructure and Innovation

Dr. Singh's commitment to infrastructure development has played an important role in India's ongoing economic transformation. During his tenure, major reforms were undertaken in key infrastructure sectors like roads, railways, and energy, which enabled faster growth. The expansion of infrastructure remains a central policy priority in India, and Dr. Singh's vision of modernizing the nation's infrastructure continues to shape current policies aimed at supporting urbanization, improving connectivity, and driving economic growth. The Smart Cities Mission, Make in India, and initiatives aimed at enhancing the ease of doing business all reflect the ongoing commitment to improving the physical and economic infrastructure that drives growth. Furthermore, these initiatives show how Dr. Singh's legacy has influenced the government's approach to fostering a favourable environment for industrial growth, domestic manufacturing, and foreign investment.

Global Leadership: India's Role on the World Stage

Dr. Singh's influence on India's foreign policy and global engagement remains significant. As a proponent of multilateralism and a strong advocate for India's place in the international community, his tenure as prime minister saw India assume an increasingly important role in global economic governance. His participation in international forums such as the G20 and the WTO ensured that India's voice was heard in shaping global economic policies. Dr. Singh's diplomatic leadership helped position India as an emerging power with a global economic outlook. Today, India continues to assert its economic leadership on the global stage, building on Dr. Singh's vision of a more integrated global economy. The country's participation in global initiatives such as the Paris Agreement on climate change, the promotion of sustainable development goals (SDGs), and its strategic alliances within the BRICS and G20 groups reflect Dr. Singh's legacy of promoting India's interests through multilateral diplomacy.

Social Equity and Inclusive Growth: A Commitment to Development

In addition to driving economic reforms, Dr. Singh was committed to ensuring that growth benefited all sections of Indian society. His policies focused on poverty alleviation, rural development, and expanding access to education and health care. These social welfare initiatives have been carried forward by successive governments, ensuring that India's growth is not just limited to the urban elite, but reaches the rural poor and marginalized communities. Programmes like the Mahatma Gandhi National Rural Employment Guarantee Act (MGNREGA) and the push for financial inclusion through the Jan Dhan Yojana, which provides access to banking services for the underprivileged, echoes Dr. Singh's vision of inclusive growth. As India continues to grapple with its challenges of poverty, inequality, and rural-urban disparities, these initiatives remain central to the country's long-term developmental strategy.

The Rise of India as a Global Power: India's Strategic Interests

Dr. Singh's approach to foreign policy was shaped by his vision of India as a rising global power. His leadership in advocating for multilateralism and strengthening India's strategic partnerships paved the way for the country's growing influence in global politics. India's engagement with countries in the Global South, its leadership role in forums like BRICS, and its advocacy for the interests of developing economies continue to be central to India's global strategy. As India faces emerging challenges such as trade wars, global health crises, and the shifting dynamics of geopolitics, Dr. Singh's commitment to a strong, independent foreign policy remains relevant. His emphasis on strategic autonomy and non-alignment, combined with his focus on economic diplomacy, has shaped India's current global positioning.

Sustainability and Green Growth: A Vision for Future Generations

Dr. Singh's legacy also extends to India's commitment to sustainability and environmental protection. While his tenure as prime minister did not see a major shift toward green growth, his recognition of the importance of sustainable development has informed subsequent policies aimed at combating climate change. India's commitment to renewable energy, particularly solar energy, as well as its push for clean energy technology, echoes Dr. Singh's broader vision of balancing economic growth with environmental sustainability. Today, India is working to become a leader in green energy, with ambitious goals set for renewable energy generation. These policies not only reflect Dr. Singh's foresight but also reinforce his commitment to leaving a sustainable economic model for future generations.

As India grapples with the effects of climate change, Dr. Singh's legacy continues to inspire policies that prioritize environmental sustainability alongside economic growth.

Long-term Economic Vision: India's Path to Future Prosperity

Dr. Manmohan Singh's legacy is one of foresight, strategic thinking, and economic pragmatism. His policies reshaped India's economy and global standing, positioning the country for success in the twenty-first century. As India moves forward, it continues to draw upon the principles Dr. Singh set forth in the 1990s—economic liberalization, inclusive growth, technological innovation, and a strong global presence. The ongoing transformation of India is a direct result of Dr. Singh's vision, and his legacy will continue to guide the country as it faces new challenges and opportunities. From infrastructure development to technological leadership, from social equity to global diplomacy, Dr. Singh's contributions have set the stage for India's continued success. His influence will remain felt in the decades to come as India seeks to emerge as a leading global economic power, while ensuring that its growth benefits all of its people. In conclusion, Dr. Manmohan Singh's vision and leadership have shaped India's ongoing transformation into a global economic powerhouse. His policies, grounded in liberalization, human capital development, and inclusive growth, continue to guide India's economic and social policies today. As India faces the future, Dr. Singh's legacy serves as a reminder of the importance of thoughtful, long-term policymaking and global engagement, and it will remain integral to the nation's ongoing success.

REFERENCES

Held, D. (1999). *Global Transformations.* Stanford University Press.

Kapur, A. (2006). *India: From Regional to World Power.* Routledge.

Mansingh, L. (1997). *Indian Foreign Policy.* Foreign Service Institute in association with Konark Publishers.

Ministry of Defence, India. (1990). *Annual Report 1989-90.* Ministry of Defence, Government of India.

Nanda, P. (2003). *Rediscovering Asia: Evolution of India's Look East Policy.* Lancer Publishers & Distributors.

Nye, J.S. (1968). *International Regionalism.* Little Brown.

Smith, A. (1909–1914). *Wealth of Nations* (C.J. Bullock, Ed.). The Harvard Classics. P.F. Collier & Son.

Taneja, N. (2005). "Informal Trade in SAARC Region: Implication for Free Trade Agreement". In S. Soz, S.K. Sahni & R.N. Srivastara (Eds.), *Towards South Asian Economic Integration and Unity* (pp. 13-21). Foundation for Peace and Sustainable Development.

World Bank. (1994). *India: Macroeconomics and Political Economy 1964–1991.* World Bank.

Yuan, J.D. (2006). *China-ASEAN Relations: Perspective, Prospects and Implications for U.S. Interests.* Strategic Studies Institute, U.S. Army War College.

17

Conclusion

Dr. Manmohan Singh's tenure as the finance minister and later as the prime minister of India marks one of the most transformative periods in the country's economic history. Under his leadership, India transitioned from a heavily regulated, protectionist economy to one that embraced globalization, market reforms, and integration with the world economy. His intellectual brilliance, combined with a steady hand in governance, laid the groundwork for India's emergence as a global economic power. Dr. Singh's legacy, particularly in economic policy, is far-reaching. The reforms that he ushered in during the early 1990s in response to a looming balance of payments crisis not only saved India from economic disaster but also set the stage for decades of high growth and structural transformation.

At the core of his approach was a belief in liberalization an unwavering commitment to freeing the Indian economy from the shackles of excessive government control and fostering a market-driven approach to development. His belief that economic freedom was essential for poverty alleviation and wealth creation found expression in the policies of industrial de-licencing, foreign direct investment (FDI) liberalization, and trade liberalization, which transformed sectors such as manufacturing, services, and agriculture. His commitment to inclusive growth was equally critical in shaping his policy approach. While the overarching focus of the economic reforms was on accelerating growth, Dr. Singh ensured that policies were aimed at reducing poverty and inequality, addressing rural-urban disparities, and fostering a more equitable distribution of the benefits of economic development.

Programmes such as the Mahatma Gandhi National Rural Employment Guarantee Act (MGNREGA) are a testament to his vision of creating opportunities for marginalized sections of society. By focusing on rural development and providing employment opportunities, he ensured that India's economic growth was inclusive, not just concentrated in urban centres or large industrial hubs. The banking and financial sector reforms during his tenure were crucial in modernizing India's economy. The introduction of market-based systems, deregulation, and the modernization of India's financial infrastructure allowed the Indian economy to better withstand external shocks and cater to the growing needs of a modernizing economy. Dr. Singh's policies attracted foreign investment, especially in the IT and telecommunications sectors, which became engines of growth in the early twenty-first century.

His economic diplomacy was also a cornerstone of his leadership. Through strategic engagement with international organizations like the World Trade Organization (WTO), the International Monetary Fund (IMF), and the G20, Dr. Singh played an instrumental role in strengthening India's position on the global stage. His vision for multilateralism and a global economy that was inclusive of developing countries helped position India as a prominent player in shaping global economic governance. His leadership in the G20 and BRICS, two of the world's most influential economic groupings, cemented India's role as a leader in the Global South, advocating for the interests of emerging economies and championing reforms to the global financial architecture. Moreover, his leadership in ensuring India's preparedness for external shocks, such as the global financial crisis of 2008, showcased his foresight and crisis management capabilities.

The stimulus packages he introduced, focusing on infrastructure spending and domestic demand creation, ensured that India weathered the storm of the global recession much better than many of its counterparts. His emphasis on economic resilience, self-reliance, and fiscal prudence helped India maintain stability and high growth even during global economic turbulence. While Dr. Singh's contributions to India's economic growth and stability are unquestionable, his tenure was not without controversy. His leadership style, often seen as technocratic and understated, was at times criticized for being too cautious or lacking in political assertiveness. The political opposition to his policies, particularly from those sceptical of liberalization, as well as the challenges of managing coalition politics, were persistent themes throughout his career.

Nonetheless, his resilience in defending his economic vision, despite political challenges and external criticism, speaks to his deep conviction and commitment to India's long-term growth. The controversies surrounding the 2G spectrum scam and the coal allocation issues during his tenure as prime minister, however, have had a significant impact on his public image. Critics have argued that the perceived inaction on these matters under his leadership has tarnished the image of his government. Yet, those who worked closely with him continue to highlight his integrity, calm demeanour, and methodical approach to decision making. His ability to remain focused on long-term goals, even in the face of political and public pressure, showcases a leadership style that prioritized the greater good over political expediency. Dr. Singh's legacy is not just confined to his tenure in office; it has shaped India's economic trajectory in the long run.

Under his guidance, India moved towards becoming a global economic powerhouse, not just in terms of GDP growth but also in terms of strategic positioning in the world. The reforms that began under his leadership have continued under successive governments, with the core principles of economic liberalization, market-driven development, and inclusive growth still guiding Indian economic policy today. Dr. Singh's economic philosophy, often referred to as 'Manmohanomics', remains relevant even in the present context. His focus on economic liberalization, infrastructure development, financial inclusion, and human capital development laid the foundation for the new India we see today.

His legacy continues to influence the country's policymakers, many of whom continue to draw inspiration from his ability to navigate complex economic challenges with a steady, pragmatic approach. The lessons from his leadership humility, integrity, and a commitment to long-term vision—are critical not just for India but for other developing nations grappling with the challenges of economic development in a rapidly changing global order. As India continues to rise as an economic power, Dr. Singh's contributions to the nation's economic growth and international stature will remain a guiding light. His leadership set in motion a process of transformation that has fundamentally altered the trajectory of India's economic development. His work remains a cornerstone for future economic policymakers who will look back at his tenure as a model for navigating the complexities of modern economic governance.

Summary of Contributions

Dr. Manmohan Singh's legacy is an enduring testament to his transformative role in shaping modern India. His contributions spanned various dimensions, from economic reforms to international diplomacy, leaving a profound imprint on the country's trajectory. Dr. Singh is widely recognized for his pivotal role in the liberalization of India's economy, which laid the groundwork for the country's rapid growth and integration into the global economy. At the heart of Dr. Singh's legacy is the economic liberalization of the 1990s, which he spearheaded as finance minister during a period of deep economic crisis.

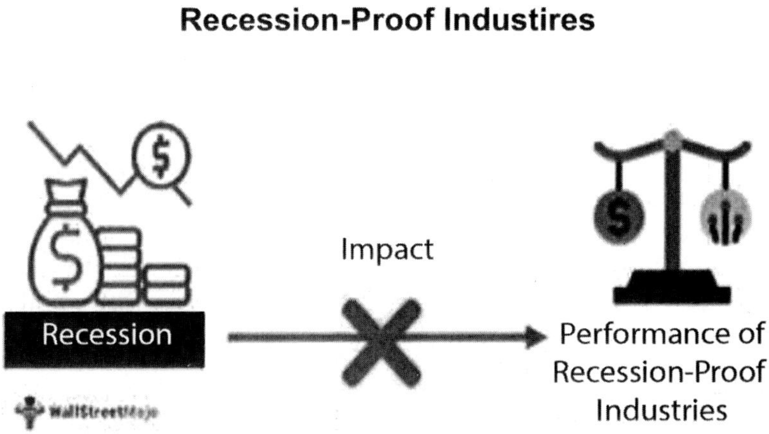

Fig. 17.1: Indian Industries Adapting and Recovering after the Global Recession.

The balance of payments crisis in 1991, coupled with a skyrocketing fiscal deficit, forced India to rethink its economic policies. Dr. Singh, a seasoned economist, crafted a series of bold reforms that included reducing import tariffs, privatizing state-owned enterprises, and encouraging foreign direct investment (FDI). These measures, along with others aimed at industrial de-licencing and financial sector reforms, marked the beginning of India's transition from a protectionist, state-controlled economy to a more market-oriented one. His strategic vision turned India into one of the world's fastest-growing economies, fostering a dynamic private sector and increasing the country's competitiveness on the global stage. Beyond domestic reforms, Dr. Singh's leadership extended into the realm of international diplomacy.

As a proponent of multilateralism, he played a critical role in strengthening India's position in global forums such as the G20, BRICS, and the WTO. His diplomatic initiatives ensured that India's voice was heard in the global economic dialogue, advocating for the interests of the global south and fostering stronger economic cooperation among developing nations. Dr. Singh's leadership in these forums cemented India's role as an emerging economic power with a growing influence on global trade and finance. A core tenet of Dr. Singh's economic philosophy was balancing growth with social equity. While he prioritized rapid economic growth, his government also introduced policies aimed at reducing poverty and addressing regional disparities. Programmes like the MGNREGA were launched to provide employment opportunities to millions of rural Indians, alleviating poverty and improving infrastructure in the country's most underdeveloped areas.

His commitment to inclusive development also extended to education, health, and rural development, demonstrating his belief in a holistic approach to economic progress. Under Dr. Singh's leadership, India also saw significant advances in the financial sector. The banking reforms initiated during his tenure, including the modernization of the financial system and greater liberalization of the banking sector, helped to create a more resilient economy that was better equipped to withstand global financial shocks. His policies laid the foundation for the rise of India's services sector, particularly in information technology (IT) and telecommunications, which have become key drivers of economic growth and job creation in the twenty-first century. However, Dr. Singh's tenure was not without its challenges. His government faced criticism, particularly regarding allegations of corruption, such as the 2G spectrum scam and coal allocation controversies.

Critics questioned his leadership style, accusing him of being too passive and failing to assert political control over his cabinet. Despite these criticisms, Dr. Singh's supporters continue to praise his integrity, professionalism, and focus on long-term policy goals, which allowed him to navigate complex political landscapes without compromising on his commitment to economic reforms. In conclusion, Dr. Manmohan Singh's legacy is defined by his unwavering commitment to economic reform, social equity, and global cooperation. His visionary policies transformed India's economy, making it one of the most dynamic in the world today. His approach to governance—balancing pragmatism with idealism, and growth with social welfare—offers valuable lessons for policymakers in India and around the world. Dr. Singh's legacy continues to shape the trajectory of India's development, serving as a model for future generations of leaders seeking to navigate the complex intersection of economic growth, social equity, and global leadership.

■ Implications for the Future

As India continues its trajectory as an emerging global economic power, the implications of Dr. Manmohan Singh's contributions to the nation's growth and reform policies are becoming increasingly significant. The reforms initiated during his tenure laid the foundation for an economy that is now one of the largest in the world. Looking ahead, India's continued rise is poised to be shaped by the groundwork he set, even as new challenges and opportunities present themselves. The key to India's sustained growth and its evolution into an economic powerhouse lies in building on the legacy of his policies while addressing the emerging demands of the twenty-first century.

Key Contributions to India's Growth

India's position as an economic leader has been solidified over the past few decades, and much of this success can be traced back to the economic liberalization initiated under Dr. Singh's leadership. The liberalization policies of the 1990s not only spurred a rapid expansion of industries such as IT and pharmaceuticals but also led to a more competitive manufacturing sector and a booming services industry. These sectors, in turn, contributed significantly to India's GDP growth and helped to lift millions out of poverty.

Demographic Advantage and the Future Workforce

As India enters the next phase of its economic evolution, several areas will be critical for sustaining this momentum. First, India's demographic advantage—its young and growing population—

presents both opportunities and challenges. Dr. Singh's policies, particularly in areas like education, health, and rural development, were aimed at creating a more skilled and capable workforce. Moving forward, there is a need to continue investing in education, skills development, and job creation, particularly in the context of rapid technological advancements. India's ability to harness its demographic dividend will depend on its ability to equip its workforce with the necessary skills to thrive in an increasingly automated and digital economy.

Importance of Infrastructure Development

Second, the continued emphasis on infrastructure development, a core element of Dr. Singh's governance, will remain crucial for supporting long-term growth. India's infrastructure needs, particularly in rural and semi-urban areas, remain vast. While strides have been made in expanding roads, electricity, and connectivity, there is a need to accelerate these efforts to facilitate growth in India's manufacturing and services sectors. The ongoing push for smart cities and enhanced urban-rural connectivity will be pivotal in driving inclusive economic growth and ensuring that the benefits of development reach every corner of the country.

Financial Inclusion and Digital Finance

Third, Dr. Singh's emphasis on financial inclusion, through initiatives like expanding access to banking services and promoting digital finance, is more relevant than ever. India's fintech sector has seen explosive growth in recent years, and this trend will continue to shape the future of India's economy. Ensuring that underserved populations in rural and remote areas have access to financial services will remain an essential part of India's economic strategy.

Moreover, strengthening the resilience of the financial system, building trust, and addressing challenges such as non-performing assets (NPAs) will be critical for ensuring sustained economic stability.

India's Role in Global Trade and Economic Leadership

In terms of global influence, India's rising economic power provides it with a greater opportunity to assert its position on the global stage. Dr. Singh's diplomatic efforts in multilateral forums like the G20, BRICS, and the WTO laid the groundwork for India's emerging leadership role in global trade and economics. Moving forward, India is well-positioned to champion the cause of developing countries, advocating for reforms in international trade and finance, and promoting greater inclusivity in global economic decision making. As the world becomes increasingly interconnected, India's voice in shaping the global economic order will continue to grow, and the country will need to leverage its influence to secure access to new markets, technology, and investment.

Balancing Growth with Environmental Sustainability

At the same time, India must confront several emerging challenges in its quest for sustained growth and global leadership. One of the biggest hurdles is the need to address climate change and environmental sustainability. India's rapid industrialization and urbanization have led to increased pollution and environmental degradation. Moving forward, balancing economic growth with environmental protection will require the adoption of green technologies, renewable energy, and sustainable development practices. Dr. Singh's approach to balancing growth with social equity can be extended to include ecological equity, ensuring that economic development is sustainable and does not come at the cost of the environment or future generations.

Addressing Social Inequality

India must also continue to work towards improving social equity, especially in the context of rising inequality. Although millions of people have been lifted out of poverty, income disparity remains a significant issue. Ensuring that the benefits of growth are broadly shared will be crucial for maintaining social stability and preventing political polarization. Initiatives aimed at improving health care, education, and social welfare will remain key to India's long-term success.

Fostering Innovation and Technological Growth

Finally, fostering a climate of innovation will be central to India's continued rise as an economic power. The global economy is undergoing a digital transformation, and countries that lead in technology and innovation will reap the benefits of this shift. Dr. Singh's policies in the 1990s laid the foundation for India's IT revolution, but to remain competitive, India will need to continue investing in research and development, fostering entrepreneurship, and building an innovation-driven economy.

In conclusion, India's continued rise as an economic power is inextricably linked to the policies and reforms initiated under Dr. Manmohan Singh. His vision of an open, market-driven economy laid the foundation for India's growth and positioned the country as a key player in the global economic arena. Moving forward, India's success will depend on its ability to adapt to changing global dynamics, address emerging challenges such as climate change and inequality, and foster an environment that supports innovation and inclusive growth. By building on Dr. Singh's legacy, India can continue to evolve into a global economic leader and ensure that the benefits of its growth are shared by all its citizens.

▪ Final Reflections

Dr. Manmohan Singh's legacy as a policymaker remains one of the most significant in contemporary India's history. His tenure as the finance minister in the early 1990s, followed by his leadership as the prime minister, transformed India from an economy characterized by sluggish growth and dependency to one that is today recognized as one of the fastest-growing economies in the world. The enduring impact of his work on Indian policymaking can be seen in several key aspects of the nation's economic and political evolution. His policies of economic liberalization, financial reforms, and commitment to social equity have had lasting effects on the country's economic structure, its global position, and its future growth trajectory. At the core of Dr. Singh's influence was his understanding that India's economic challenges required bold, far-reaching reforms. The 1991 economic crisis presented India with a stark choice—either to continue with the status quo of economic stagnation or to embrace fundamental changes. Dr. Singh chose the latter, steering the country toward economic liberalization. His belief in the power of markets, combined with a strong state role in providing a stable policy environment, has created a balance that continues to drive India's development.

This approach remains a cornerstone of India's economic policymaking, influencing successive governments, even as political dynamics and global conditions have evolved. Dr. Singh's contributions were not limited to economic reforms alone. His tenure also reshaped India's social and political landscape. While focused on building a robust economic foundation, he also prioritized inclusive growth, seeking to ensure that the benefits of liberalization were shared across all segments of society. His policies aimed at reducing poverty, improving education, and providing health care laid the groundwork for the country's transformation into a more prosperous society. Despite facing numerous challenges, such as political opposition and governance issues, his vision remained steadfast: economic growth should lead to social justice and better living standards for all Indians.

One of the most remarkable aspects of Dr. Singh's policymaking was his quiet yet resolute leadership style. Unlike many politicians of his time, he did not rely on rhetoric or populism to win political favour. Instead, he demonstrated a calm and methodical approach to governance. His decisions were often based on rationality and long-term vision rather than short-term political expediency. This approach has left an indelible mark on Indian politics, establishing a precedent for future leaders to focus on substantial, sustained change over immediate gains. Furthermore, Dr. Singh's legacy is also seen in the context of India's integration into the global economy. He championed multilateralism and strengthened India's role in key international forums such as the G20, BRICS, and the WTO. His efforts in these areas were aimed at promoting a more balanced global economic order that was sensitive to the concerns of developing countries.

This commitment to global cooperation and the pursuit of national interests in a world that is increasingly interconnected was crucial in establishing India's position as an economic leader in the global south. Another significant aspect of Dr. Singh's policymaking was his role in shaping India's financial and banking systems. The banking reforms he spearheaded in the 1990s not only modernized the financial infrastructure but also laid the groundwork for India's resilience during global financial crises. His emphasis on financial inclusion ensured that India's underserved populations had access to banking services, and his policies continue to influence the country's approach to digital finance and financial services. Dr. Singh's commitment to balancing economic growth with social equity is one of the defining features of his legacy. He firmly believed that economic liberalization should not come at the expense of social welfare and that the fruits of economic growth must reach all sectors of society, especially the poor and marginalized.

This belief in inclusive development was reflected in key initiatives such as the Mahatma Gandhi National Rural Employment Guarantee Act (MGNREGA), which aimed to provide employment to millions of rural households, and his focus on improving the quality of education and health care. In the contemporary context, Dr. Singh's legacy is still relevant, especially as India faces new challenges. The country is grappling with issues such as rising inequality, environmental degradation, and the need for innovation-driven growth. The principles that guided Dr. Singh's policymaking—openness to global markets, a commitment to social justice, and a focus on long-term growth—remain crucial in addressing these challenges. Policymakers today can draw lessons from his ability to navigate the complexities of global economic systems while ensuring that India's growth benefits its citizens. As India continues to grow and develop, Dr. Singh's influence will continue to be felt in the nation's economic and political frameworks. His legacy has shown that policies grounded in economic liberalization, social equity, and global cooperation can propel a country forward, even in the face of significant challenges. The future of India's economy, and the future of policymaking in India, will undoubtedly bear the imprint of Dr. Singh's vision and leadership. His impact on Indian policymaking is, therefore, enduring, as his reforms and ideas continue to shape the direction of the country's development for years to come.

Index